Seduced by Grace

A potent collection of thoughtful writings by Kelly, the noted Australian Catholic dissident, *Seduced by Grace* gathers essays, articles, letters and talks he has produced over almost a decade, from late 1998 to May 2004, that are at once an acutely accurate critique of the shortcomings of the Church and a poignant testimonial to the heroic spirit that has, at times, invigorated it.

Victor Marsh – *White Crane Journal*

These are the passionate dispatches of a reporter from one of the most hostile – for gay men and women – regimes on earth: the Catholic church. Michael Kelly has come out but stayed in. His indictment of the church is stark but his vision of what it might become has the power to move even hardened atheists.

David Marr – author of *The High Price of Heaven,* and *Patrick White: A Life*

Michael Kelly writes with great precision and poignancy of a yearning which everyone shares. A yearning for love, both physical and spiritual. A yearning for completion. In this wonderful collection of essays, Kelly seduces the reader with his insights into those fleeting moment in which we encounter the greatest mystery of all.

Fiona Capp

Every chapter in this book is an invitation. It's thoughts and stories carry you over and over again into a deeper place where you can reflect on your own life and, indeed, universal life. At one point, its author observes 'religious talk is about religious talk. Life becomes a footnote.' Life is never a footnote for Michael Kelly. His close experience of the engaging of religion with life is both challenging and inspiring.

Rev Dorothy McRae-McMahon

Michael Bernard Kelly was born in Melbourne in 1954. He held professional qualifications in theology, spirituality, education and creative media. For seventeen years he was employed as a Religious Education specialist in the Catholic education system. In 1993 he came out as an openly gay man, and his career in Catholic education ended. Michael then committed himself to living contemplatively and to shaping new forms of ministry with gay and lesbian people. He was a freelance writer, speaker, activist, counsellor and educator, specialising in spirituality, sexuality and human integration. His ministry included creating rituals, speaking at conferences, leading retreats, offering spiritual direction, and writing for journals, newspapers and books in Australia, the US and the UK. Michael died in November 2020.

Michael was an Adjunct Research Associate at Monash University's Centre for Religious Studies, Australia. He is the author/presenter of *The Erotic Contemplative* video-lecture series (Erospirit Institute, 1995) and accompanying *Study Guide* released to coincide with the relaunch of the videos (Clouds of Magellan Press, 2020); author of *Seduced by Grace: Contemporary Spirituality, Gay Experience and Christian Faith* (Clouds of Magellan Press, 2007); and, based on his 2015 PhD, *Christian Mysticism's Queer Flame: Spirituality in the Lives of Contemporary Gay Men* (Routledge Studies in Religion, 2020).

Seduced by Grace

Contemporary spirituality, Gay experience,
and Christian faith

updated edition

MICHAEL BERNARD KELLY

Foreword by The Honourable Michael Kirby AC CMG

Clouds of Magellan Press | Melbourne

ISBN: 978-0-6451935-2-7

Original edition first published 2007 Clouds of Magellan Press.

www.cloudsofmagellanpress.net

Publication and distribution, Lightning Source, through eBook Alchemy.
ebookalchemy.com

Acknowledgements

Articles and essays in this collection have appeared in *The Age*, *The Australian*, *Sydney Morning Herald*, *Campaign Magazine*, *Eureka Street*, *Sydney Star Observer*, and Online Catholics, and in publications from Haworth Press and Yale Divinity School.

Publisher's Note

This edition of *Seduced by Grace* includes modifications to the original biographical note, and some notes have been added through the text for clarification, for instance, where given website addresses are no longer active. This edition now includes a new letter from Michael, originally published in *Bent Street* journal (Issue 1 - 2017), which carries us ten years on from the original collection, showing Michael's interests following the completion of his PhD. We have also added to the dedication page the opening lines from Michael's *The Erotic Contemplative* lecture series. Otherwise, all of the original articles from the first edition are retained.

To all the gay contemplatives, known and unknown, who have kept alive, on the margins of society and church, the flame of radical love.

*

I'm aware that as I begin to talk, although we're separated by time and space, we truly are not separate. Because in spirit, there's no separation, there's no time and space, there's no division. As Thomas Merton said, in the last talk he gave before he died, 'Brothers, we are already one, we only imagine that we are not.' So, let's take a moment to be silent and to be still, so that we may really be in our hearts, that what I speak may be from my heart, and perhaps in some sense from the heart of God. And that it may also speak to your heart where you are in your place, in your time, in your life's journey.

Michael Bernard Kelly

Contents

Foreword

The Honourable Michael Kirby AC CMG

Readers will have different reactions to this book. I know what my long-suffering partner of four decades, Johan, would say about it: 'Why doesn't he get over it? If the institution of the Church hurts him so much, why not give it away? Why not explore some other avenue of spirituality? Like Buddhism? Or Theosophy? Or perhaps just become an old-fashioned humanist and rejoice in common human goodness? Why does he torture himself with the perceived cruelty of his Church in its dealings with him?'

The author of this book, a son of Melbourne, worked for many years for the Roman Catholic education system that nurtures a large and growing proportion of Australia's schoolchildren. But when he openly revealed that he was homosexual, he had to go. Priest or teacher, sister or gardener, there is, it seems, no space in the Church or its institutions for open people like him. True, if they remain silent, they do not confront Church leaders with the 'inconvenient truth' of their sexuality. It is the 'intrinsic tendency to evil', that is bound up in their sexual orientation that supposedly requires this modern vow of silence. Of course, it is a 'vow' that promotes hypocrisy, deceit, bitterness and self-loathing. For many, the 'vow' ends up being a greater burden than the knowledge that, in this particular, the individual is a little different from the majority of humanity.

'No. No. You must understand', I would say. 'He stays with his Church because it is part of his being. It is a link with his most beloved family members and friends. It brings comforting memories of his safe and secure days of childhood. It contains people who are good and noble and do wonderful things for many. Above all, the Church is the ultimate guardian of the most precious message of a divine guide to us on Earth – Jesus'. So I would tell Johan. 'He cannot let it go because of love. He refuses to let a few powerful old men in frocks divorce him from the Faith that he learned as a boy and that is part of his very essence. He truly believes that Faith. And he knows that it is a religion of love and equality, with respect for the dignity of each and every one of us. He knows (or at least hopes) that we are going through a bad patch of unkindness, power-play, hypocrisy. When the central message of the religion is lost, drowned out by angry voices and a few selected passages of Scripture, read in isolation from their context and seemingly deliberately misunderstood'.

'How can you believe all this?' Johan will reply. 'How can you, and he, obviously very intelligent men, take seriously the absurdities of your religion. Let's face it. It has always been oppressive. Oppressive to women and unequal in the space it allows them in the Church. Oppressive to people of colour, to slaves, to indigenes under the conquering Europeans. Oppressive to gays. I just scratch my head and cannot understand why you and he persist. Give it away. It will make you feel more at peace. By the way, it will also make those narrow minded bigots feel a whole lot happier. You can meet the 'good and noble' types in other contexts. And anyway, as the author himself found in the Internet chat room which he recounts, with the inquisitive priest 'Bill', some of the harshest oppressors in the Church are gay themselves. They are struggling with demons in their own minds. Cut yourself clear from them. It will be better for all concerned'.

I did not grow up in the Roman Catholic tradition of Christianity. Some things in this book appear alien to my understandings. The holy water. The Marian prayers. The seeming fear of the Vatican. The close attention to Papal encyclicals. The 'sacred gift' of celibacy these last 1700 years. For me, the Church of my childhood was the Church of England, now called Anglican. It is, as the author describes it, a church that daily 'has our fights for us'. There were always flags near the altar of my church. God, King and country were intimately associated in those boyhood days of the British Empire. Yet it seemed a pretty tolerant space. Inclusive even. There always had to be room for the catholics and protestants in the post-Reformation English Church.

I watched with expectation the outreach of my denomination in the ordination of women priests and the consecration of women bishops. I saw its growth in Africa and other lands of people formerly oppressed. Yet, lately, those who were oppressed seem to have turned their new-found power on the sexual minorities within Anglicanism. Like some of the leaders of the Roman tradition, described in this book, a few Anglican leaders have attempted to snuff out the ever-so-tentative moves to welcome and accept gay people to an equal place at the Table of the Lord.

In Australian Anglicanism, there are Church leaders who oppress and trouble my spirit, just as the author's spirit is troubled. They deny the pulpit to voices they see as discordant. They refuse engagement with new ideas. They turn their backs on the rational tradition of the Christian Reformation. Little wonder that Bishop John Shelby Spong calls for a new Reformation in Christianity. One that will reach out to the alienated and restore the true universality of the Christian Communion.

Michael Bernard Kelly is a powerful writer. Notice how, in many of the short and painful essays in this collection, he uses the rhetorical device of repetition. Words and phrases are repeated, like the chants of the monks of old and the beautiful collects of Cranmer's *Common Prayer*. I understand and share his pain, without necessarily agreeing with all of his tactics. I am not, of course, competent to assess the response of his Church. Doubtless it would have its own viewpoints. However, I am thankful that great churchmen of our age, like Bishop Desmond Tutu, are now lifting their voices to demand an end to the oppression of sexual minorities. In Nairobi, in January 2007, the South African Nobel Laureate Tutu told a conference:

> I am deeply disturbed that in the face of some of the most horrendous problems facing Africa, we concentrate on 'what do I do in bed with whom'. For one to penalise someone for their sexual orientation is the same as penalising someone for something they can do nothing about, like ethnicity or race. I cannot imagine persecuting a minority group which is also being persecuted.

Sad that it took apartheid to teach a Christian Bishop that lesson. Happy that he learned the lesson and now teaches it to millions.

The answer that Michael Bernard Kelly and I give to Johan is a simple one. We love and accept the universal message of Jesus. We refuse to let it go. We deny anyone the right to take it from us. We do not for a moment accept that we are beyond the pale. We know that, in the end, the universality of love and belief will be restored. Nothing else would be rational or just. Nothing else would be true to the central message of our Faith that so many good people accept and live by.

Everything else is peripheral. In the words of the Talmudic scholar, although we may not see our conviction fulfilled, neither are we free of the moral obligation to tell its message.

Michael Kirby
1 October 2007

Introduction

This collection of essays, articles and talks, written over a ten-year period, represents the public expression of one man's inner journey of struggle and contemplation, as he faced the challenge of becoming vulnerable to the seduction of grace.

This seduction is not simply a matter of an inner, 'spiritual' journey; it is also woven into an actual historical situation. It is in the daily challenges and struggles of ordinary living that we must learn to become open to grace, that we must discern the movement of God's seduction.

As expressions of my own flawed process of giving in to grace, the writings in this collection have very particular personal and historical contexts. Many of them emerge from the wrestling and reflection of this man who happens to be both gay and Catholic, and who is living at a time when this experience is just beginning to find a little breathing space and some tentative articulation. I regard it as profound grace to find myself in this historical and personal place, and to be one of those called to speak some words of hope and challenge, where before there was only silence or condemnation.

At the same time, as the quote from Jeremiah suggests, opening oneself to this kind of grace comes at a cost, and there are times when one feels one has gambled everything on the folly of faith, and lost. God, our seducer, is not what we think God is, and if we give in to this seduction we will, sooner or later, lose everything – including any notion we have of God or faith or grace. Mystics like Meister Eckhart may say that the soul grows by a process of subtraction, modern writers like Simone Weil may claim that there is a kind of atheism that is a purification of the notion of God, but in the midst of radical loss all of this can seem bitter and foolish. 'My one companion is darkness', says the Psalmist, and if we follow the lead of the Spirit, we too will find we are walking with just such a companion. This desolate experience comes to everyone who trusts in God, and when it comes perhaps the only comfort we have is the knowledge that we are in the company of people like Jeremiah – and, of course, Jesus. In such company we endure and abide. This book is a record of one gay man's particular version of what it looks like to gradually give in to God, and gamble with losing everything he once valued.

In saying this, I am expressing one of the key principles that has guided the writing in this book: that life as a gay person in the contemporary world, with all of its ordinariness, anguish and beauty, can open us at depth to the journey into the mystery of the Divine. For some people it may seem shocking and even blasphemous to claim that life as a self-affirming, sexually expressive gay man can – indeed, must – become a pathway into maturity and holiness. This type of reaction, which I have faced often enough, is hardly surprising, since the voices of gay people have been silenced for so long that any articulation at all tends to seem both novel and startling. This makes it all the more urgent that we speak.

This speaking is not simply for the sake of ourselves and other gay people. Almost any passing engagement with thoughtful adults in the developed societies of our time quickly reveals the deep disillusionment and even cynicism with which organised religion in general, and Christianity in particular, are regarded.

If Christianity is to be credible – let alone inspirational – to people of our time, its leaders will have to get over their addiction to power and learn to listen to the wisdom and pain of those who speak about embodiment, erotic grace, radical justice and the incarnate love that flourishes beyond the bounds of the officially sanctioned 'sacred'.

One of the blessings and liabilities of a collection such as this, which ranges over a decade of the writer's life, is that it is not the product of a grand thesis. Rather, it shows the evolution of several key ideas, of a certain approach to life and to spirituality, of the ongoing process of shaping a public voice. This public voice has been expressed in newspaper articles, reflective essays, chapters in anthologies, formal lectures and informal talks, and my publisher and I have chosen to retain the different textures and styles of the original pieces, avoiding extensive footnotes and keeping contextual information to a minimum. We have also kept the writings in their original chronological order except in a few cases where, for reasons of balance and variety, it has seemed prudent to make adjustments.

However, both the first essay and the last have their place not because of chronology, but because they represent key movements in my own life. They are like bookends, the first leading us into the collection and the last ending it by pointing to a new chapter that is yet to be written.

The first essay speaks of a movement that pre-dates all of the writing in this collection. It was a movement into a contemplative way of living that emerged strongly in my life in 1988. I have no doubt that this simple, unobtrusive, relentless movement into contemplative spirituality prepared me for the letting go of my career, my dreams, my security, and the affirmation of my ecclesial community – the Catholic Church – which lay some years ahead. The gradual opening of my life to the hidden demands and gentle grace of contemplative life is the first of two foundations on which these writings stand.

The second foundation, my claiming the freedom to speak the truth of my experience as a gay man, took shape as I was losing my career in the Catholic Church, back in 1993. This process unfolded over several months. I had already given an initial 'yes' to the call to come out publicly, just as I was leaving my position as a campus minister in a Catholic college. Some months later, in the midst of personal and financial difficulties, I was offered another position in ministry, in another Catholic college. All that was required was that I sign a document that would have guaranteed that, though I might be privately known to be gay, I would not be a 'troublemaker'. Of course, the actual words used were more elevated than that, but that's what they meant. It was at this point that my practice of 'letting go' not only allowed me but, as I experienced it, called me to refuse the deal being offered, a deal which would have made it impossible for me to speak the deep truths of my body and my soul. To have signed would have been not only to collude in the lie that the Church tells about gay people, it would have been to refuse to trust the God who had been leading me, often in spite of myself, on a path of surrender, simplicity and trust. I feel a certain gratitude towards the person who offered me the document – his action helped make it clear that my life as a closeted Catholic educator was over. I was now free to be who I was, and say what I thought, both for my own sake and the sake of others.

So, being gay and contemplative has been for me a kind of 'double-whammy': through being gay I have faced losing everything I once thought I valued and hoped to be; through being contemplative I have been freed to let the losing happen. This seems to me to be the shape that the seduction of grace has taken in my life. Not coincidentally, it was only at this point that the writings in this collection became possible.

Throughout this same period, including the entire period covered by this collection, I began to face chronic health problems. So, where I might otherwise have just gone out and found a job of some kind, my feet were kept to the fire of loss by the collapse of my health. Though I have faced this with some kicking and screaming, it has also freed me to say what I needed to say, to write what I needed to write, to travel when invited, to walk the empty beaches and sit in the empty silence, to look at life and spirituality from the margins, to become something of a troublemaker.

Many of the essays that follow give expression, in diverse ways, to the kind of 'troublemaking' I have engaged in. Some of that has meant reflecting in my public writing on new ways to explore, embrace and integrate the mystery of incarnation, of embodiment – so long preached, and feared, by the churches. Some of it has meant exposing the flaws, brokenness, hypocrisy and hard-heartedness that have so diseased the church, and calling for honest dialogue and radical change. Some of it has taken the form of public activism with the Rainbow Sash Movement in Australia[1], as, with other friends and companions, we created a voice for gay and lesbian Catholics where before no voice existed.

Through it all lies the story of one man's faltering attempt to discern and respond to the call of Divine Love in his life. It is this movement of the heart and soul that I invite you to listen for as you read this collection. There is a seduction going on here, both in my writing and in your reading, a hidden seduction that will lead us where we thought we would rather not go, a tender but ruthless seduction that will unravel our dreams, expose our tawdry ambitions, unwrap our fingers from the grasp we have on our lives, and teach us how to let go into the mystery of love. Despite all our misunderstandings, stubbornness, vanity and brokenness – yours and mine – God is seducing us into life beyond our imagining.

Surrendering to this seduction, however, can be frightening and bewildering and it is not wise to face it alone. One of the worst features

---

[1] The activities and ethos of the Rainbow Sash Movement are discussed in several articles in this collection. See the Appendix at the end of this volume for a more extensive history and discussion of the Rainbow Sash Movement.

of the spiritual oppression of sexual minorities has been the deep isolation so many of us have suffered, as we have struggled to deal with life and faith with all of their terror and beauty. At the heart of Jesus' message is the promise that where two or three gather in his name, he would be there in the midst of them. Gay people, however, have been denied the chance to gather together – and certainly not in Christ's name – because we have been forbidden to speak the truth of our deep selves in the community of God's people. This is grave oppression.

I regard it as a miracle of grace that, despite everything, gay people have begun to find their voice and find one another. The final essay in this collection, the second 'book-end', is about the longing for community, for brotherhood, for companions on the road into the desert of the Divine. As he lay dying, St Francis said that when he set out on his spiritual journey, 'No-one showed me what to do, but the Lord himself led me', but then he added, 'and the Lord gave me some brothers'. It was with the giving of those brothers that the Franciscan movement came into being. We need loving community as we seek to build a world where no-one will be a spiritual outcast, where everyone will be welcomed as sister and brother, where wise companions will support us as we surrender to the mystery of God.

Around the world there are attempts being made to form new spiritual communities, and these tentative, fragile experiments are bringing a new quality of hope into the lives of many gay people. I wrote the final essay in this book while staying with a very traditional community of Trappist monks, and just two weeks before encountering the Easton Mountain Retreat community in upstate New York, where gay men from a variety of spiritual traditions are forming a new kind of religious brotherhood. There is something symbolic in this movement from traditional religious forms, into solitude and search, then into evolving models of spiritual community. We need to come together, drawing both from traditional sources of wisdom and from our own particular insight and experience, and learn to support one another in ways that conventional religious institutions cannot even imagine. As we do this, we offer inspiration, challenge and witness to other spiritual seekers, from every religious tradition and every sexual orientation, that they can do the same. And so, not for the first time, gay people can become spiritual pioneers for the human family.

To do this, however, we must go deeply into our experience of life and of God, we must face and challenge both the beauty and brutality of our traditional religious institutions and teachings, we must reclaim, re-imagine and re-embody the revelation of Divine Love, the mystery ever ancient, ever new, that is manifesting in every moment, in every being, in every beat of every human heart. If this collection of essays offers some witness to this challenge, this vocation, this hope, then all the struggle and contemplation that lie behind these words will have been simply the play of grace.

A note on language

One of the most contentious issues facing anyone who writes about the experience of people belonging to 'sexual minorities' is the question of which words to use. Gay, queer, gay and lesbian, LGBT (lesbian, gay bisexual, transgender), lesbigay, homosexual, men-who-love-men and women-who-love-women – all of these terms and more have been tried – and each is contentious. Some people, for example, would see 'gay' as referring only to those who are fully out and proud, rather than to 'homosexuals' in general. Other people would question whether the word 'queer' can be used of, say, affluent, conservative men who love men, or whether it should be restricted to folks who are 'alternative', irrespective of who they might sleep with. Then, of course, there are the more academic concerns of the deconstructionists – which are valid and important but beyond the scope of this note. Suffice it to say that any use of language in the area of sexuality and gender must be conscious, clear and somewhat provisional. The best we can hope for, perhaps, is transparency about our particular use of particular words.

To speak personally, then, it was when I came across LGBTQIQ (lesbian, gay, bisexual, transgender, queer, intersex questioning), a seven-letter attempt to cover all the bases, that I finally abandoned my efforts to keep up with the ongoing search for new terms to name and describe 'sexual minorities'. I decided to return to using the shortest word of all: gay. I do not discount the important issues that lie behind each of these terms. I would suggest, however, that the issues are not happily solved by adding new letters, and that someone who aspires to be a writer, especially in public forums, needs to make choices.

For the most part, I have chosen to use the words 'gay' or 'gay people' to refer to those whose primary sexual and emotional attractions are to those of their own sex. I usually refer to 'gay men' when I am writing specifically about the experience of 'men who love men'. I do value and occasionally use some of the other terms, however, and I hope that my writing will be relevant to a variety of people who, for a variety of reasons, may find themselves outside the sexual mainstream. Personally, I identify as a gay man, and it is from this perspective that I write.

Michael Bernard Kelly

On the Peninsula, alone with God

When I am asked these days, 'What do you do?' I am stumped. The monk Thomas Merton wrote: 'What I do is live. How I pray is breathe.' The southern Mornington Peninsula, with its clean winds and endless ocean, is a good place to learn to live and breathe.

In 1988, exhausted after years of teaching and ministry, I moved down here to rest and live alone for a year. I walked the beaches and sat by the fire, and slowly I fell in love with a contemplative way of being. Contemplatives, they say, are not people who have solved the mystery of God. They are those who can no longer keep the mystery at bay.

My life here is quiet and unremarkable, often enough boring and lonely. I have my times of prayer and meditation, but mostly I just 'chop wood and carry water', as Zen puts it. It's all quite ordinary, but somehow the plainness and spaciousness of it keeps calling me home, often in spite of myself. Living simply, attentively, it becomes hard to sustain your illusions and ambitions, and impossible to miss the restless striving of your spirit. You start to live through the different 'shapes' your longing takes, and you enter the longing itself. In the still centre of your soul, you begin to taste deep silence.

The Spanish poet Machado wrote: 'Is my soul asleep? No, my soul neither sleeps nor dreams, but watches, its clear eyes wide open... and listens at the shore of the Great Silence.' I remember walking up the track from Bushrangers Bay on a windy afternoon five years ago. It was a time when the endless letting go asked of me seemed almost overwhelming. I looked across to the old hills sweeping down to the sea and was suddenly struck dumb by the sense that all our religions, sciences and philosophies are just toys and bones tossed on the edges of this Unknown Sea. We sit on the shore and play games with them to keep away our fear. We must face our fear, stop our games and turn our gaze to that sea. Living contemplatively means shaping your life so that you will be led continually to do just that.

For me this has meant learning the tough lessons of silence and solitude, but also coming to terms with chronic health problems. Together these have imposed a discipline and rhythm that have kept me slow-dancing on that empty shore as my old games have been inexorably exposed. For many contemplatives this all happens amid structured rituals, rules, robes and regulated practices, and sometimes I miss them in my dishevelled way of living. They have great value, but if you take them too seriously they can also insulate you against the rawness of life and the shock of the unknown. In time, they too must be let go.

At a deeper level still, all doctrines, concepts and images of God must be lived through and allowed to crumble. Leaving them, at last, on the shore, we enter the dark waters, allowing them to lift and carry us in naked simplicity and trust. Here we come to the heart of the matter. Contemplatives long to experience, unmediated, the Divine Mystery itself, to breathe ocean winds, to become one with the deep. For this they risk everything – like people in love. These words are, I know, cryptic and obscure – but what words will do? Call this a 'ray of darkness', a 'cloud of unknowing', a 'divine wasteland' – it remains more simple, silent and subtle than words can describe.

I often ask myself: 'Who wants this emptiness, this desert?' For this is not just about inner prayer, but also actual, everyday life. 'Nothing, nothing, nothing…' wrote St John of the Cross, and some days that's exactly how it feels. Yet the same John also wrote: 'My Beloved is the mountains, the solitary wooded valleys, the whispering of love-stirring breezes at the rising of tranquil dawn, resounding rivers, silent music.' In the emptying is the embrace. Gradually, gently, you come to know this. I sometimes say that contemplative experience is nothing much – but it's a 'nothing much' I'd give everything for.

Of course, it's important to keep balanced – this is a way of living, not a short retreat or a week at the beach. Merton sometimes used to slip out of his hermitage to drink whisky and listen to jazz in nearby Louisville. I know I often need to get to the city, have a drink at the Portsea pub or catch a film in Rosebud. The company of friends and the warmth of a sensuous embrace are also sweet gifts of God that I delight in when I can.

In the simplicity of this life, you come home to yourself. You slowly become who you truly are, you breathe deeply, open to the wonder of what is. On a wild beach, in the silence after midnight, over a quiet coffee on a sunny afternoon, you trust and let go. 'I cast the anchor of my life down and let its line run deep into the heart of the ocean of God on whose breast I rest.'

In the resting, and from the silence, you may sometimes be asked to speak, and you may then discover a strange freedom that comes, in part, from having little left to lose. Contemplatives, they say, have often been troublemakers.

Published in The Age *as a Faith column in December 1998.*

Christmas, sex, longing and God

towards a spirituality of desire

All my life I have been haunted by longing.

Do you remember Christmas mornings? In our house they used to begin very, very early. After sleeping in fits and starts one of us children would shake the others awake in the still, pre-dawn darkness, wondering if it was 'time' yet. Giggling, with a delicious sense of conspiracy, we would tiptoe breathless and wide-eyed through the slumbering house to peek at the Christmas tree. 'Mum! Dad! Father Christmas has been!' And the door would be flung open and we'd be on our knees before all these brightly wrapped marvels, tumbling in anticipation and delight.

And if you were lucky, there was at least one special present, one that you couldn't guess. You'd hold it and shake it and turn it, and you'd wonder. I would unwrap this present slowly, not looking, not wanting to catch a glimpse of a label on the box and guess the secret before the wondrous moment of unveiling. Savouring the edge of possibility. Tasting the wonder, the miracle of this gift that could be – anything! Could be the very thing I longed for, which I could not name myself, which I had wanted and waited for, without knowing it, all my life. Could this be It?

Here, now, in this moment I was on the threshold, I was touching the hem. Was this how the woman in the Gospel felt when she touched Jesus' garment, hoping to be made well (Luke 8: 43-48)?

Eventually, inevitably, the present was unwrapped. Immediately, something wondrous was lost. This was not It. And yet... there was that moment, that luminous moment when everything was possible. Such a moment! Even today something in me rises to meet it, wide-eyed and open-hearted.

Why do adults so love Christmas time, so often reflecting that 'it's just not the same without children'? I believe that the sweetness of this remembered childhood moment lingers. Something in us all is still waiting, still longing, still hoping. Just to be here again on this threshold is delight, as we see, shining in the eyes of children, our own wonder and hope. Perhaps this year!

We are all children, waiting on the threshold for the Wonder to show itself. We are all haunted by longing.

Do you remember your first orgasm? I remember mine. I didn't really know what it was. I was used to the excitement and pleasure of arousal, but this was completely new and unexpected. I remember very clearly saying to myself that it felt in that moment as if everything I had ever wanted had been given to me. Everything. Not this and that, but the Essence. It. I had tasted that for which I longed. In that brief splinter of time all was ecstatically complete, fulfilled.

Yet, even as it burst into my life it was gone. Of course I soon learned I could taste this delight again and again, and despite the turmoil, chaos and guilt that came to accompany it, the purity and power of that moment of ecstasy remained. It fired my longing and undid both my own plans and the dictates of a repressed and frightened Church. Again and again I would stand on the threshold and, unlike the Christmas present, this did not disappoint. Here, however fleetingly, I crossed the threshold and tasted the wonder. Yet, like Christmas, it too was gone in the very moment of its sweetest delight.

Do you remember your first taste of spiritual joy? As a boy I had been very religious, loving ritual, prayer and 'holy things'. However, when I was about fourteen, something new broke into my life. One day when I was spending a lonely lunchtime in the school chapel trying some simple methods of prayer that I had read about, I had a sudden sense of immediate, mirror-like contact with the One to whom I prayed. It was simple (no visions or lights or anything) and it was intoxicating, like drinking at a fountain of joy. For several months this continued, especially after Holy Communion when I alternately felt as if I were flying as high as the ceiling, or as if I were about to burst from joy. God only knows what my schoolmates, bored by the daily liturgy, must have thought as I closed my eyes and drank from this hidden spring.

Again, I was on the threshold, again tasting It. Yet It withdrew. Soon the spring dried up, went underground and my prayer became plain and dry. However, I had known what it was to have my heart on fire and I would never be satisfied until it consumed me completely.

The liminal moment

These three sacred moments: the gift giving of Christmas, sexual awakening and spiritual awakening, can be called 'liminal' experiences. *Limen* is the Latin word for 'threshold', and it refers in a special way to the threshold of the temple: an entrance, a barrier, a meeting place between the 'sacred' and the 'secular', between the 'divine' and the 'human', between my 'deepest self' and my ordinary 'daily self'. In liminal states we taste a level of awareness beyond the rational, analytical and image-making mind, sometimes even tasting the deepest centre of self that opens into Absolute Mystery, that ground of our being where 'God's Spirit with her own Being is effective'.[1]

These liminal experiences cannot truly be controlled by the individual, by Church or by society. They take us beyond. And that is the point. They are profoundly free and freeing, shaking up all the structures of the self and unmistakably asserting the sovereign freedom of God in the heart and soul of every person. All are called to ecstasy.

The liminal experience comes in many ways and with many textures – I have mentioned only three. In this essay I wish to talk specifically about two: the spiritual and the sexual.

It is especially in these two areas that society and the Church set out to claim, construct, sanction and control the liminal experience. This happens primarily through the structures of marriage and of official religious ritual. Some experiences, some pathways into the Mystery, become hallowed, celebrated, enshrined, even made mandatory, while others are forbidden, condemned, denied and even demonised. Some people and their experiences are 'in', and other people and their experiences are 'out'. However, true liminal experiences cannot be legislated for or legislated against. Indeed, in them a deep freedom and truth is discovered, a touchstone by which to test the preaching and posturing of the institutions themselves, if we have the integrity and the courage.

All the same, it is not simply malice and power that lead society and the Church to try to control and issue caveats around these experiences. That which is tasted in them, whether it comes through

---

[1] Meister Eckhart, quoted in M Fox, *Original blessing*, Bear and Co., New Mexico, 1983, p. 132.

prayer, sex, nature, drugs, dance or ritual is intensely powerful, even overwhelming. Wisdom, prudence and guidance are essential in the drinking of this water, as a little taste of it goes a long way. We all know, I suspect, the seductive tendency to seek the thrill of the liminal moment again and again at the expense of 'ordinary' life, relationships and commitments, ultimately forfeiting the true transformation to which the liminal moment itself points, as we shall see.

But first, if we are to be human, to be free, it is essential that we become profoundly open and deeply attentive to our own liminal experiences, and especially in the areas of our sexuality and in our prayer. There can be no true spirituality or growth without this. The 'Wisdom of the Ages' is vital, but we must live our own lives, live from our own deepest centre, which is sensed and glimpsed in these moments. We must embrace them even as we are embraced in them. Better, we must embrace not the liminal moment itself, nor its context (church, sex, dance, drugs, nature, etc.), but rather we must embrace that which the liminal moment reveals to us: that Mystery, that essence, which we taste and surrender to, inarticulate and inarticulable, utterly free. We must embrace and drink deeply of the Mystery whenever and wherever and however and in whomsoever it reveals itself. Laws must not stop us.

Elsewhere I have referred to this as 'telling the truth', first to ourselves.[2] Let us drink deeply, letting the 'chips' of social, religious and personal structures fall where they may in that moment. We who are ourselves 'on the edge', whose spiritual and sexual experiences are so routinely condemned and denied, can we have the courage to 'drink of the truth' and to proclaim it to others, witnessing to the freedom of the Spirit who will not be articulated, legislated or controlled, who 'blows wherever she wills' (John 3:8)? Here is a truly prophetic, truly revolutionary, truly human vocation!

What then of the wisdom and prudence I spoke of earlier? And what of the inevitable, all too immediate moment when the tasting, the embracing, the showing is gone, and we either tumble deliciously in its wake like dolphins behind a ship, or feel the chaos and emptiness it has stirred up in our stagnant pond of a life? What then?

---

2 See my video course *The erotic contemplative: the spiritual journey of the gay/lesbian Christian*, vol. 1, Erospirit Research Institute, Oakland CA, 1994.

The showing and the withdrawing

This withdrawing, this 'hide-and-seek' is the other essential quality of the liminal experience. It must be faced. All too often we, who are excluded from so much that society and Church hold dear, cling tenaciously to the thrill of the moment, seeking it over and over again, compulsively, even desperately, 'like vultures fighting over a corpse', as a gay friend put it recently. We must allow the withdrawing. We must let go.

When Heidegger says, 'that which itself shows itself and at the same time withdraws is the essential trait of what we call the Mystery'[3], he is expressing a truth that all of us know at a deep, soul level. We also know it in our bodies. Perhaps the experience of orgasm is the clearest example of this for most of us. In that very moment of ecstasy, in that tasting, that bliss, that knowing, that briefest communion with that which cannot be named, as we are thrown over the peak of consciousness, at the burning 'white hot tip of sexuality'[4] as 'It' shows itself, it withdraws. We are left astonished, filled and shattered by sex, but still we *are* left.

What is going on here? Is 'God' playing games with us? (And there are names for games like this!) Are we being enticed, teased and abandoned? It is relevant to state that this precise question is also faced in the spiritual life of prayer, as the One who set our hearts on fire seems to abandon us and we are left 'on the streets', 'beaten', 'wounded' and 'stripped' like the bride in the Song of Songs.[5] This is a serious question, and in our longing we ask it from the depths of our heart.

Could it be that this showing-and-withdrawing actually reveals to us something of the nature of the Mystery itself, something of our own nature, and something of the nature of human transformation? Could it be essential to the spiritual journey? In the Book of Exodus, Moses, after receiving the Law, asks to see God's face. God tells Moses to hide in the cleft of a rock and as He passes, God will shield him with His hand, so that Moses can look out and see God's back (Exodus 33:18-23). It would be death to see God face to face – not in the sense of being punished, but because the encounter would be humanly

---

[3] F Browning, *The culture of desire*, Crown Publishers, New York, 1993, p. 88.
[4] R Burrows, *Ascent to love*, Darton, Longman and Todd, London, 1987, p. 115.
[5] Song of Songs 5:7.

overwhelming, unbearable; it would 'shatter the container' of the human.

To encounter the Mystery, the Unnameable One, 'God', is to go beyond words, concepts, images and doctrines. It is to stand naked, utterly vulnerable in the embrace of the ineffable essence of That Which Is, encountering It in ourselves, as ourselves, as All. This is that which 'no eye has seen, no ear has heard, nor has it entered into the mind of humans to conceive' (1 Corinthians 2:9). This encounter can only be borne in the briefest of touches; a full revelation of the Mystery is literally unthinkable, impossible for human life as we now live it. Even our fleeting glimpses baffle and stun us.

In the immediate *withdrawing* of the Mystery, even as it embraces us, as it licks our lips, we see its nature as utterly 'more', ultimately 'beyond', transcending all, just as in its *showing* we see its immanence; for it is closer to us than we are to ourselves – intimate and immediate in the depths of our humanness.

In our truly liminal experiences, in the depths of prayer and in the depths of sex, I believe we do indeed encounter this Absolute Mystery, showing and withdrawing, embracing and emptying, and we long for it with all our heart and soul. 'My *body* pines for you, like a dry weary land without water', cries the Psalmist (Psalm 63:1) and the mystic and the lover in us cry out with him. We know the yearning of those who 'are willing to make shipwrecks of themselves in order to gain the one they love'.[6] It is the withdrawing of the Mystery that kindles and re-kindles this longing.[7]

This, then, is the second gift of the withdrawing: we are seduced onto the spiritual journey, the human journey to maturity, union and transformation.

In every era and in every part of life there is a tendency for us to focus on 'experiences', ecstatic 'thrills' – the tastes and touches we have been discussing. This tendency is especially marked in sexuality and spirituality, where the tastes are so intoxicating, fleeting and profound. These tastes are essential; they are seeds, glimpses of that fullness to

---

[6] Saint Augustine, *Confessions*, translated by RS Pine-Coffin, Penguin Classics, Middlesex, 1961, p. 232 (Book X, Chapter 27).
[7] This 'showing and withdrawing' of the Mystery, the 'emptying and embracing' reflect the two great movements of the Christian spiritual life: the Apophatic (negative) Way and the Cataphatic (affirmative) Way.

which we are called. However, they are not the Journey itself, not transformation, not mystical union, not enlightenment. They set us on the road – perhaps they are even glimpses of the destination – but we have not yet arrived. Indeed we have hardly set out! If we become addicted to simply seeking more and more 'experiences', whether sexual or spiritual, we never will arrive. We all know this tendency in sexuality, but the seduction in spirituality can be more subtle, more compelling and more soul destroying.

So what is happening? Firstly, some element of this 'addiction' is probably inevitable in our yearning and longing, for the taste of ecstasy, however it comes, is so delicious, so overwhelming. Of course we seek it again and again!

'You shed your fragrance about me; I drew breath and now I gasp for your sweet perfume. I tasted you and now I hunger and thirst for you. You touched me and I am inflamed with love of your peace', says Saint Augustine,[8] and in our different ways we know what he means. However, we must allow the withdrawing to take place. It is the withdrawing that will draw us towards the transformation, to the abiding fulfilment of that which we taste so briefly in our ecstasies. How does this happen?

To become that which we taste

When we taste the Mystery we long to drink deeply of it, to take it into ourselves, to be possessed by it, to surrender to it, to *become* it in an abiding way, 'forever and ever'. To become that which we taste. I think of our images of sexual 'hunger' and 'thirst', not just our desire to 'do it' with this or that person, but to 'drink them in', 'gobble them up', nibble, lick, suck, swallow – all, the 'eating' metaphors and delights of sex. This is mirrored very powerfully in the images of spiritual communion, where we eat and drink 'the body and blood of the Lord', our very bodies merging and becoming transformed into the One who is the Beloved of our souls.

This is the heart of our yearning: to become that which we taste and hunger for, not briefly, but fully, totally, permanently, being utterly transformed into that which we desire so deeply. Union. Ecstasy. The

---

[8] Saint Augustine, op. cit.

'Lover with his beloved, transforming the beloved in her Lover',[9] the seeker transformed into that which she seeks.

This truly is to die to ourselves, to lose our life so as to find it (Luke 9:24), to enter into the mystery of death and resurrection. This is what we hunger and thirst for in our bodies, in our sexuality no less than in our spirituality, and this is what we taste in both. All that is deeply and authentically human is a pathway into this transformation, but sexuality and spirituality draw us most profoundly, most ecstatically. I think of Jesus speaking to the woman at the well (John 4:5-42), seducing her onto her spiritual journey with the promise of a spring of living water that would never run dry. We taste this spring and we thirst for the day when rivers of this living water will rise within us flowing out of our 'belly' and welling up to eternal life, eternal union, eternal love (John 7:38).[10]

The Mystery that shows Itself must withdraw. It must seduce us. It must play a game of 'now, and not yet' with us, enticing us, leading us on and on, inflaming our longing at deeper and deeper levels. It must also teach us that the taste of this 'living water' is not enough, and allow us to find both bliss and bitterness in the tasting (especially when we become 'hooked'). It must teach us to follow the withdrawing, to let go and go deeper, learning the lessons of how to *become*, in the abiding, ordinary, everyday reality of our lives, that which we taste and thirst for. Nothing less will satisfy our hunger, fulfil our longing, and transform our humanity into the divinity we seek.

How does this look in practice, in people's actual lives? Firstly, it is important to say that there are as many answers to this question as there are people to ask it. The human journey of transformation, while it has universal qualities, is profoundly personal and particular and will look very different in individual lives as each of us experiences growth and purification in ways we least expect, but most need.[11] Those of us

---

9 St John of the Cross, *The dark night*, st. 5, trans. K Kavanaugh OCD and Otilio Rodriguez OCD, ICS Publications, Washington DC, 1973, p. 296.
10 There are those who would applaud these words as applied to 'holy longing' and 'spiritual desires' of the soul, but would wish to accord sexual yearning a lower place. I refer them to the Mystery of the Incarnation. There is one hunger, one thirst, one longing, one love moving in the depths of all that we are. We feel this most powerfully, most physically in our longing for sexual intimacy and ecstasy.
11 R Burrows, op. cit., pp. 108-109. Burrows shows how the 'Dark Night' can look very different according to people's different needs and personalities

marginalised by mainstream society, both secular and religious, because of our sexuality need to remember this, as does anyone who seeks to guide us. The ways we experience and embody our deepest longings often look very different from the ways sanctioned by a heterosexist culture, and likewise our path of transformation will look very different.

In us the free, uncontrolled Spirit of God offers a gift to humanity, freeing others to embrace this journey so particular, so universal. We must dare to be different; we must risk becoming our true selves.

The heart of our longing

What then are the universal qualities of the transforming journey? They are many and there are many books written about them in all religions. However, the 'bottom line', I believe, is the fact that, in the end, we are all longing for the same thing. In our spiritual practices, in our sexual desire, in the lives and relationships we build, when all the fetishes, dreams and different 'shapes' our longing has taken over the years – when all these have run their course, worn out or faded away – we will find that we are all longing for communion with the Other, and self-transcendence in and through that communion. Communion and transcendence. Intimacy and ecstasy. From the first orgasm, and in every orgasm since, I have sought that ecstatic moment, and its allure colours so much of my life still. Seeking out its possibility, feeling its approach, surrendering to it and allowing the rigid sense of self to melt deliciously as it rises within me, letting myself be caught up in the juicy passion that draws me toward it. There is an aloneness in this, as I close my eyes, go deeply into my experience of pleasure and let the ecstatic flow become all that I am. There is a deep solitude in the drinking of this water.

However, I also long to share this ecstatic vulnerability with another person, and that which I seek to drink in ecstasy, I am drawn to in and through other persons. Put simply, I long to have sex with another person, however intense solitary sexual pleasure may be. At a conference on AIDS I once tried to persuade a Church group that we needed to reassess the potential goodness and grace in all kinds of sexual relating, including 'recreational sex'. An agitated woman finally snapped at me, 'Well why can't you just masturbate?' I snapped back, 'I do, don't you?' My real answer, however, would be that it simply is not the same. There is another whole dimension of life – and of ecstasy itself – present in my relating with another, or other persons, whether it is in a casual encounter or in a lifelong relationship. This other dimension is communion, intimacy.

As one matures, this desire for communion deepens and the ecstatic moment itself begins to seem somewhat incomplete, even empty, without this growing, broadening communion with another, with the other in others, in all the dimensions of one's life and personality. At the same time, it must be borne in mind that without the allure and ecstatic possibility of self-transcendence in and through our relating, communion itself can all too easily become complacent and tasteless. (And we go out looking!)

So, we long for communion and transcendence. We long for them, and sometimes experience them as separate and sometimes as intimately interwoven. At depth, however, they are two faces of the same Mystery: Love. It is clear that those we call 'lovers' seek the truth of this. We see it, too, quite graphically in the almost universal desire to 'climax together' with the person we are having sex with. We also see it in the Christian spiritual teaching that the saintly hermit and the saintly activist are both, at depth, ecstatically transcending self and Michael Bernard simultaneously in communion with God and with all beings. Solitude and union; communion and transcendence; intimacy and ecstasy: Love.

This longing for communion and transcendence is the essence of spirituality; it is what I seek when I pray, what I try to live out in service, what I call true holiness when it matures in a human person. This is the same mystery that I long for in sex, in the daily reality of my life, in my choices, relationships and dreams. It is not esoteric and exotic, but ordinary and human, like true spirituality. It is this ordinariness, this humanness, this embodiedness that opens onto divinity. We will find it at home, in our cells, in our sweat.

This opening onto divinity is the truth of all that is genuinely human, and it cannot be restricted by the dictates of Church and society. Often, indeed, it will happen most profoundly in people and in situations outside the approved norms where people are on the edge, seeking to follow their hearts, having only their thirst for their guide. Saints, lovers and mystics have never been fit for polite society. They drink from the same well, perhaps in different ways and at different depths, but it is the same thirst and the same water. Little wonder, then, that their passionate language of love so often sounds the same!

However, mystics and lovers also know, if they are honest, that the Mystery which shows itself in intimacy and ecstasy also withdraws. We have looked at one dimension of this withdrawing. Is there another?

The Mystery that must withdraw

We long for communion and self-transcendence. In our sex and in our prayer we taste this. Sometimes this ecstatic, intimate experience is especially deep and comes through a particular person or in a particular context. We feel profound allure. Here is the chance to drink deeply and abidingly of this water, to be possessed by and to possess the Mystery, to be transformed, becoming what I taste, having 'all my dreams come true'. And we make life choices on the basis of this liminal experience of allurement and possibility. We form relationships, join communities, serve the poor, get married, learn tantric sex, choose celibacy, take up a spiritual practice, move to the beach. All of these are 'shapes' our longing takes at certain moments, and sometimes throughout many years, and we embrace them hoping to drink deeply and become what we taste in and through this person, this practice, this path. We celebrate and send out invitations!

Sooner or later, however, the camellias turn brown, the honeymoon ends, and we ask, 'Who is this at the breakfast table? My God what have I done?' Sooner or later the Mystery withdraws. What now?

The first thing to say, again, is that the Mystery *must* withdraw. However holy or sexy this person, practice or path may be, the Divine Mystery lies both in and *beyond* them.

We cannot fulfil one another's deepest longings. In this sense I am not 'God'. I am not the Beloved of another's soul for I, too, am seeking that Beloved. When I 'fall in love', part of what is happening is that I am projecting my own longing for union with the Mystery onto another person. The poet Rilke says that lovers are close to the Mystery, 'it opens up to them behind each other'. However, they are 'blocking each other's view', and 'neither one can get past'.[12] Someday we obscurely realise this and we say things like 'you're not the man I married!', and in a certain sense that's right.

However, this realisation, this withdrawing of the Mystery teaches us to do what we *can do:* nurture, support, love and encourage one another on our own spiritual journey, recognising, too, that in our love-making we do indeed encounter the depths of one another – those depths that go beyond the individual and into Absolute Communion. And then we can, perhaps, join hands and go forward side-by-side rather than face-to-face.

Even in this, however, we must face the fact that this person or these people who we love will one day die, and yet our longing will go on and on beyond them and into death itself.

This is also true of spiritual paths, practices and teachings. They are all fingers pointing to the moon, as Zen has it. Even Jesus said that he was 'the Gate' (John 10:9) and 'the Way' (John 14:6). The finger, the gate and the way are not the destination! We must follow the direction of the finger, go through the gate, walk the way, trusting more and more and leaving behind all that is familiar, magical and safe. We must embrace the Mystery.

The shapes of my longing, the shapes the Mystery seems to take in my life must play their part, but they must also fail. A gracious 'letting go' is what we are called to, but this process is usually deeply painful, even shattering, and can feel soul-destroying. All that we cling to, all of our old ambitions, values and loves will be stripped away, sometimes gradually, sometimes violently. There is nowhere to hide, except in illusion. If we can be open enough, if we can wait, if we can slowly accept the gift of trust in the midst of darkness and desolation we will come to sense, in our loneliness and emptiness, a deeper, silent, 'dark' embrace of the Mystery. In the emptying is the embrace.

This can only happen in the depths of my true self, and there is profound solitude in this. The person or path 'out there' may have helped me 'come home' to my deep self, but as I do I must release them in order to be free to enter the silence of this dark embrace.

---

12 RM Rilke, *Duino elegies*, eighth elegy, trans. D Young, Norton and Co., New York, 1978, p. 73.

Furthermore, it is in the ending of the honeymoon phase of relationships, of love-making, of spiritual life, of sex itself that we glimpse what it might actually mean to become that which we taste. It is communion and self-transcendence that we seek. Sooner or later we must learn what it means to live this out everyday, in the ordinary, mundane, unexciting, 'non-liminal' reality of life. We must learn what it means to transcend self again and again, not just in ecstasy, but in taking out the garbage, in the boredom and interior anguish of prayer, in the stink of the poor, or of a dying lover, whom we once embraced so passionately because they seemed to us like heaven itself. We must learn the endless concern, generosity, sensitivity and forgiveness that living a life of communion with the Other demands. This is practical, down to earth, simple and incredibly demanding. This is the other side of losing one's life so as to save it, of death and resurrection, of becoming a lover. A transformed human being lives a real life of days, hours and minutes, of cleaning, cooking and recreation, of listening, speaking, laughing and crying.

There is a Buddhist saying, 'After enlightenment: the laundry!' One might just as truly add, 'before, during and on the way to enlightenment: the laundry!' We are not playing games here; we are not seeking just liminal thrills, for all their beauty and power. The Mystery must withdraw into the ordinariness of everyday, for that is the place of learning and of transformation.

In the midst of this hard work of becoming, however, there will still be tastes and glimpses of that which we seek. These refresh us, renew us and encourage us, and they are vital. As the years pass, however, these will have a different, deepening texture, perhaps quieter, perhaps more free, sometimes more searing and overwhelming. Gradually the intimacy and the ecstasy will become one. Gradually, too, we will begin to sense a quiet, abiding embrace in the foundation of our soul.

Spiritual maturity

In the maturity of the spiritual life, the sexual life, the human life, there is a peace, a surrender, and a still, abiding passion that runs gentle and deep. The fireworks are few; they accompanied the momentary collapse of the structures of self that allowed earlier tastes of the Mystery. Now these structures are simpler, softer, more saturated with the presence of the Divine. One thinks of the classic image of the old couple (at least as often gay or lesbian as straight) whose intimacy flows quietly, needing few words or thrilling experiences. They abide in and with one another, loved and known, knowing and loving.

One thinks too, of the wise old Indian Teacher to whom Ram Dass offered LSD in order to see what would happen. The teacher took it, smiled, and just went on sitting, meditating in unitive peace. He was already there.[13]

Old age, of course, is not essential in spiritual growth.[14] Randy Shilts, in his book, *And the Band Played On*, tells the story of Gary Walsh, a gay man in San Francisco who went through the different phases of 'AIDS is a spiritual gift' and 'AIDS is an ugly curse' to finally reach a simple, deep tranquillity before he died. On the day he died a friend told him of the effect he was having on others, that people were coming away from conversations with him 'like pilgrims leaving a holy shrine'.

Gary 'smiled his mischievous grin and interrupted her. "I got it, I finally got it", he said. "I am love and light and I transform people by just being who I am." Gary recited the words carefully, like a schoolchild who had struggled hard to master a difficult lesson.'[15]

Many of us have seen such simple, human holiness first-hand in our friends and lovers. Many of us are growing towards it right now.

This holy, human maturity is based on our readiness to respond to the deepest challenges of learning, trusting, surrendering, loving,

---

13 In the 1960s Ram Dass, with Timothy Leary, was one of the early experimenters with LSD. Disillusioned with the transitory nature of the experience it offered, he travelled to India in search of more abiding transformation. See Ram Dass, *Be here now*, Hanuman Foundation, New Mexico, 1971.

14 That remarkable contemplative, St. Therese of Lisieux, who died of tuberculosis in 1897 at the age of 24, is proof enough of this.

15 R. Shilts, *And the band played on*, St Martin's Press, New York, 1987, p. 425.

becoming open always to the embrace, but also to the painful emptying, to the showing and the withdrawing, allowing the shapes of longing to fail and fall away, leaving only 'love-longing'.[16] Becoming that which we taste.

Conclusion

We must pay close attention, then, to our liminal experiences, our sexual desire, our orgasms, our loving communion, our spiritual life, our times of wonder and awe, our tastes of quiet, holy presence. We must pay attention to our Christmas mornings.

Equally, we must be open to our emptying and to the 'school of love'[17] that is everyday life.

Most of all, we must listen to our longing, not simply our desire for this or that person, but to the longing that rises from the centre of our hearts and that leads us on and on through the years, into and beyond our loves, as familiar and profound as breathing. In the embracing and the emptying this centre will become our place of stillness and truth. In the moment of death, it is through this centre that our longing will pass, opening us to the 'first Alleluia! of my eternity'[18] and to the eternal dance of desire with the Absolute Mystery of Love in whom we will be transformed from Glory to Glory![19]

It is for this that we were born, it is this that we taste, it is to this that we are destined – lesbian, gay, bisexual, transgender, straight. It is our birthright.

> Unnameable God, my essence;
> my origin, my lifeblood, my home.[20]

---

16 Julian of Norwich, Showings, trans. Edmund Colledge and James Walsh, Paulist Press, New York, 1978, p. 318.
17 A Jones, Soulmaking, SCM Press, London, 1985, p. 1. This is an ancient term referring to the discipline of monastic life.
18 From the saying of Pedro Arrupe SJ regarding death. Quoted by John J. McNeil in his lecture, 'Drinking from our own wells', Berkeley, California, 1992.
19 St Gregory of Nyssa saw the life of heaven as an eternal progression into God as our desire is constantly kindled, fulfilled and rekindled at deeper levels. See, for example, his Life of Moses, quoted and translated by H. Musurillo in his From glory to glory: texts from Gregory of Nyssa, John Murray, London, 1962, pp. 142-148.
20 Psalm 19, verse 14, translated by Stephen Mitchell, The enlightened heart, Harper and Row, New York, 1989.

And it all begins in the honest, earthy, human desire for love, for sex, for communion and self-transcendence. It all begins in that moment just before a small boy opens his Christmas present.

This essay was first published in the anthology, Our families, our values: snapshots of queer kinship, *edited by Robert Goss, Haworth Press, Binghamton, NY, 1997.*

Selective blessings that sully the faith

On Monday 27 October I was refused Holy Communion in St Patrick's Cathedral because I am openly gay. Last Friday my sister rang me to say that the issue had been covered by Melbourne's most popular newspaper cartoonist, Michael Leunig. 'You know you've arrived when you make it into Leunig!' she quipped. It's a gentle enough cartoon – a priest holding the Communion plate asks a kneeling man if he is a 'practising homosexual'. The man replies that he doesn't need to practise, he has a 'natural genius for it'. Like most Leunig cartoons it has a hidden depth.

Catholic moral theology has long condemned homosexuality because it is 'unnatural'. However, more recent Church documents teach that homosexual orientation is 'innate' – or inborn – for many, that it is not chosen, that it is generally irreversible and that it may have a biological basis. Certainly this accords with the experience of very many homosexual people. Self-affirming gay and lesbian people have reached their sense of personal integration precisely by accepting that their sexual and affectional desires are deeply 'natural'. We just have a 'natural genius' for it.

However, Catholic teaching also calls the homosexual orientation 'an objective disorder' and an 'orientation to intrinsic moral evil'. Homosexual acts 'can in no circumstances be approved'. If this sounds harsh, well, believe me, it is!

Imagine that you have a young teenager in your family, your classroom or your congregation. He or she is just beginning to feel that exhilarating surge of the hormones, those first crushes, that frightening, wondrous taste of the erotic, romantic dimension of life. Problem is, said teenager is simultaneously discovering that he or she is 'innately' homosexual. Exactly when and how will you go about telling him or her of their 'objective disorder' and their 'orientation to intrinsic moral evil'? Let me quote from an American theologian and educator, Paul Giurlanda:

> But let us carry the argument further: if the Church's teaching is internalised what kind of life can he or she look forward to? This

youth must recognise that every sexual impulse he or she will have is dangerous and evil... There is no possibility of using one's sexuality someday in the service of love, since it is an inclination to evil. What other boys and girls are told, traditionally, is to 'wait until marriage'. What these teenagers must be told is 'wait until death'.

Small wonder that teenagers from religious homes are over-represented in youth suicide statistics, as recent studies suggest.

The Catholic hierarchy last week repeatedly said that the rules were the same for homosexuals as for heterosexuals. Since heterosexuals can marry and have active sex lives over many decades, this is hardly honest or fair. If only 'practising homosexuals' would repent and be celibate, the bishops pleaded, they would be welcome at Communion. They put this forward as if it were a simple matter. Lifelong celibacy is not a simple matter, even for the clergy. For your ordinary gay or lesbian person it is a cruel and almost impossible demand. A life lived in this spirit would hardly be likely to flower into peace, love and joy. Despair, isolation and self-hatred would be more likely.

Last week the Catholic hierarchy also said repeatedly that they were 'bound by Church teaching'. Significantly, what I told the priest on 27 October was that I was 'openly gay', not that I was sexually active. There is nothing in Church law or teaching that says that someone must be refused Communion for simply revealing their sexual orientation, even if it is homosexual. What is demanded, however, is that such a person make no public disclosure about his or her sex life – if they have one. Individual Catholics always have the right to make 'private decisions in conscience', whether they concern contraception, for example, or homosexual sex. These decisions must always be respected – but they must remain private. So, an openly gay person who accepts this contract of public silence may be admitted to Communion. Simple enough. After much blustering and confusion, the Church hierarchy admitted as much late last week. So what was all the fuss really about?

Writer and gay Catholic, Andrew Sullivan, says that 'homosexuality is not a new subject for the Roman Catholic Church. It is not a distant subject. It is at the very heart of the hierarchy, so every attempt to deal with it is terrifying.' Did we see an example of this 'terror' last week?

Yet homosexual people have always been present at every level of Church life. People as diverse as Native American tribes and psychologist Carl Jung have recognised the special gifts we carry for the spiritual and ritual lives of our communities. It is high time both our giftedness, and the sexual orientation underpinning it, were acknowledged and celebrated.

Of course, this would only be half the story. What of those of us who are public about being 'practising homosexuals' and who do challenge Church teaching? Are total silence or total exclusion the only options?

Father Maurice Shinnick, an Adelaide priest who recently published a book called *This remarkable gift: being gay and Catholic*, believes that 'a critique of (the Vatican's) teaching and method of imposing it on the whole Catholic Church must take place'. He calls for open dialogue on this issue, like the late Cardinal Bernadin of Chicago who said in 1996 'The Church must risk authentic dialogue…'

For myself, I would suggest the following course of action:

First, the hierarchy should give a guarantee that all priests, religious, teachers and Church workers can publicly reveal their sexual *orientation* without being sacked, suspended or having their careers derailed. Like unmarried heterosexual Church employees they would not be able to discuss their sexual lives. However, straight teachers, for example, are quite open about their orientation – why not gay teachers? And what could possibly be the problem with openly gay priests or lesbian nuns? They already have a public commitment to celibacy!

Second, an official diocesan ministry must be set up to provide education and pastoral care. It should be staffed by gay or gay-friendly psychologists, priests and teachers. Workshops, courses and counselling must be offered to counteract homophobia in classrooms and staff-rooms, and Catholic schools must be declared 'safe places' for gay and lesbian youth. Harassment and vilification must not be tolerated. The lives of our young people are at stake.

Third, the Church should set up an official 'Year of Listening'. Gay and lesbian people must be invited to share the truth of our experience. This would be a new moment in the life of the Church, for we have never been listened to. Such a 'Year of Listening' could prepare the way for an Ecumenical Council that would examine sexuality as a whole and homosexuality in particular.

The above measures could be initiated immediately, even by Bishops who are 'bound by Church teaching'. It is not that there is nothing to be done, it is whether we have the will. I remind the Bishops that there are also 'sins of omission': refusing to do that which is demanded by love and justice.

Published on the Opinion page of The Age *in November 1997.*

The road from Emmaus
the challenge of the future

I state right from the outset: Be not afraid! ... Of what should we not be afraid? We should not fear the truth about ourselves.[1]

Let it be said from the outset of this talk on the challenge of the future: 'Do not be afraid!' And these are words not of comfort but of challenge! Not a consolation, but a confrontation – a key to the future and the prophetic challenge it places before us. Do not be afraid of the truth! Do not be afraid of the truth of who you are and of who you are called to be. Do not be afraid of all the forces within and around us that seek to use fear to stop us from embracing this truth, living this truth, being this truth. Do not be afraid!

As a gay man, I hear these words with joy and with this sense of immediate challenge. I also hear them with a feeling of sad irony, because the person speaking is Pope John Paul II. Under the authority of this man I am also told that at the root of who I am as a relational being there is objective disorder, an orientation to intrinsic evil.

'Do not be afraid', he says. I look around at this gathering and I wonder how many of us – if any of us – come here with no sense of fear at all, fear not just of who we are, or who we might be thought to be, but fear simply of engaging in this forbidden conversation. Like many of us, I often wonder if there is any way of remaining engaged with the Catholic Church and still being and growing healthy and free. Does such involvement end up being, funnily enough, the true sin of self-abuse? Can I be healthy, joyous, loving and free as gay and as Catholic? Can I come fully into the truth of who I am and who I am called to be, can I openheartedly share the gifts and blessings of who I am and how I love, as gay and as Catholic? Is there a way forward? What is the challenge of the future?

To answer these questions I want to observe a time honoured tradition of returning to the roots of the Christian experience – to the Gospels – and engage in the prayerful process, practised in every age,

---

1 Pope John Paul II quoted in Andrew Sullivan's *Virtually normal*, Knopf, New York, 1995, p. 19.

of reading in them my own journey of faith and of discerning in them the call of God for me today. I will use some of the tools of scriptural exegesis – not as an academic expert, but as an informed student. I will do this as a gay man, refusing to be afraid of those who would deny me the right to reclaim Scripture for gay and lesbian people. I will try to do it in an honest and informed way, seeking to be mindful of the original meaning and the context of the text, but seeking also to find in it the voice of the Spirit for us today, as she calls us to love, to freedom, to life beyond fear. This is a crucial part of the process of discernment, for our uses of Scripture, like our theologies and our moral teaching, 'are accountable to justice', as theologian Carter Heyward points out.[2] In taking up the Scriptures I will need to be bold.

John McNeill says that all the spiritual wells from which we draw are polluted by homophobia,[3] and we might add, by misogyny and erophobia – hatred of women and fear of the erotic. It is impossible to engage with Scripture or with our spiritual heritage without tasting this pollution. Can we hope to find any fresh, life-giving water here? I believe we can, but we must be daring and imaginative, testing the water we draw, being suspicious. Suspicious of what?

Suspicious, like feminist scholars, that our place and our experience do exist in the heritage of Scripture and tradition, and that there is wisdom for us here, but that this has been obscured, denied and distorted. Leaps of imagination will be required, leaps that have some solid basis, but leaps nonetheless. So, we come to our heritage with a 'hermeneutic of suspicion', to use the technical term.

As we take up the Scriptures, we refuse to be afraid. In doing this new and untried reflection, we will make mistakes. We will also find that we are embraced, emptied, shocked, delighted – and sent forth. We will not be afraid; for that command, 'Do not be afraid!', is not only challenge and confrontation, it is Promise! Do not be afraid – for I am with you! So, confident that in every moment the Divine Lover is inviting us into the Dance of Love and Liberation, to life beyond fear, let's take up the Gospel of Luke. We are going to reclaim our heritage and seek within it a vision for the future, by 'playing in God's presence'

---

2 Carter Heyward, *Touching our strength*, Harper Collins, New York, 1989, p. 25.
3 3 John McNeill, *Drinking from our own wells*, lecture in Berkeley, California, 1991.

with one of the best loved stories in Scripture – the story of the two disciples travelling the road to Emmaus.

First, however, some context. Luke, we find, was almost certainly a well-educated, sophisticated Greek who writes in Greek for a Gentile Christian community. He has a special concern for outsiders, for women, for Gentiles, for the poor. This reflects the position of his community – the people he has in mind as he writes. These Christians are not part of the 'in' club. They are the 'new wave' of Christians, you might say, and they are looked at with concern and even disdain by many of the more 'traditional' Jewish Christians, especially those who looked to the Jerusalem Christian community as their foundation and guide. These Gentile Christians do not follow the full law of Moses – they are probably uncircumcised, and they don't follow the dietary and ritual purity laws so dear to the Jews, and to the early Jewish Christians. The Jerusalem community – and others like it – found this extremely hard to accept. These were issues of clean versus unclean, issues that had always been the dividing line between those who were 'God's people' and those who were not, issues that provoked a certain anger and revulsion amongst dedicated Jews who had become Christians. Many of them, for example, refused to eat with Gentile Christians who did not follow the law of Moses. They were 'unclean'. Luke's community would have known all too well the attitude of these Jewish Christians towards them, and they would have been struggling with this, feeling often like outsiders, like rejects, wondering sometimes, perhaps, if they were indeed 'unclean'.

These Gentile Christians also existed in the Graeco-Roman world, where they were considered strange and even dangerous. The idea of Christ's crucifixion was a key problem here: how to convey the idea that the brutal death of Jesus was not just an absurd, disgraceful tragedy. So, here is a group of people caught between two fairly hostile or at least unwelcoming communities, trying to understand the Good News of Jesus in their lives. (This may well sound like a familiar situation to many of us!)

It is against this background that Luke's gospel is written, as is his second book, the Acts of the Apostles. Indeed, these issues are not simply a background for Luke – they dominate his theology and the way he shapes his writing.

The particular part of his writing that we will consider is of a rather special kind – it is a Resurrection account. The Resurrection accounts across the four Gospels are often looked at together, partly because they present unique problems and issues. These accounts attempt to speak of an event and of experiences that transcend historical time and space – no easy task! The accounts do not fit neatly or chronologically together, in fact they conflict in some areas and in ways that the Passion narratives, for example, do not. It seems that each evangelist has taken the Resurrection accounts and fragments of accounts that were available to him, and shaped them differently, weaving into them some common themes and some themes particular to the individual Gospel. In such an organised and artistic writer as Luke we could expect that the way he shapes his account of the Resurrection will reflect and bring to a culmination the overall vision and theology that have shaped his Gospel, especially as these relate to the community he is writing for. And so it does.

A great deal more could be said by way of introduction, but let's turn to Luke's account of the day of the Resurrection. And a day it is – for in this Gospel everything happens on a single day: the women and the empty tomb, the disciples on the road, the appearance in Jerusalem, the promise of the Holy Spirit, the sending forth of the disciples and the Ascension. All occur on one day. Luke's account of this day is a beautiful work of art and of theology – carefully structured, short and economical, profound and spiritually rich. Every verse counts. We will not be surprised to find that women and outsiders have particular roles to play.

We are going to examine in detail the Emmaus story, but it, too, must be seen in its context, which is the whole Resurrection day. This day begins with the women going to the tomb. There they find the stone rolled back and the body of Jesus gone. Two angels tell them that Jesus is not there, but has risen. These women, the first disciples to hear the proclamation of the Resurrection, faithfully return and tell 'the eleven and all the rest' what they have seen and heard. However, this astonishing, ecstatic news is dismissed by the apostles – and Luke makes it clear he *is* talking about the *apostles* here – as 'an idle tale',[4] as

---

4 Luke 24:11 RSV.

'pure nonsense'.[5] It's not even important enough to make them get up from the breakfast table and go and have a look. Imagine the excitement, the amazement with which the women would have told their story – yet the witness of women did not count in that society, and, despite all their time with Jesus, it does not count with the apostles. (These officially appointed leaders of the community don't look too good in Luke's day of the Resurrection.) Peter, however, in many of the ancient texts, but *not all*, does leave his breakfast and go to have a look, and he finds that everything was as the women had said. Luke uses this response of Peter as part of his theological construct, as we'll see, but overall the apostles are simply not open to the witness of women and therefore not open to the first proclamation of the Resurrection of Jesus.

Luke immediately follows this with the story of the disciples on the road to Emmaus. (*At this point in my lecture, I read aloud the passage:* Luke 24:13-35.)

We'll pause here, since this is where most people tend to end the story, and return later to the following verses. What does this story have to say to us? A pedestrian enough opening to your average homily. What I am asking, however, is whether this story can speak to us as gay, lesbian, bi-sexual and transgender people today. Not quite so pedestrian.

Firstly, this story is unique to Luke. There is a brief reference in the second ending of Mark's Gospel to Jesus appearing to 'two of them as they were walking into the country'[6] – but that's it. Whatever information Luke was working with, he has skilfully crafted it into a theological work of art. Just as he worked creatively and imaginatively with the story he was given, let us work creatively and imaginatively with the story he gives us.

Two of them are walking to a village called Emmaus. Let's imagine that they are two of our people – two lesbian women or two gay men. Why not? We know that Luke is concerned with the outsiders, with those excluded because of ritual purity laws, with women, with Samaritans, with Gentiles. He lived in a Greek world where liaisons and even established relationships between people of the same sex were

---

5 Luke 24:11 Jerusalem Bible.
6 Mark 16:12

common enough. He has already told the story of the Roman centurion and his 'beloved boy'.[7] Later in Acts he gives us the story of the Holy Spirit descending on unbaptised, uncircumcised Gentiles in the house of Cornelius[8] and also the story of the Ethiopian eunuch whom Phillip met.[9] He, too, was someone outcast because of issues of sexual reproduction and ritual purity. Why couldn't Luke have had two members of our 'tribe' in the back of his mind when he wrote 6 Mark 16:12. the Emmaus story? More importantly, however, *we* need to learn to *see ourselves* and *our lives* in this story. Everyone else is invited to do this as a matter of course. Why not us?

So, they're walking along – not silently, but talking about everything that had happened – as we do. They are sharing from their hearts. They are sad and confused, yes, but still open to one another, finding comfort in their sharing together. Also, it seems they are still *wondering*. They have heard about the empty tomb, but the apostles' ready dismissal of the women's story has not settled things for *them*. They're still wondering what it could all mean. Jesus comes up to them and asks them what they're talking about.

Please notice: these two are already deeply reflective, seeking to listen with the heart, already 'in community' with one another in the midst of their sadness and uncertainty. Is it this open-hearted, reflective communion in the midst of disappointment and confusion that draws Jesus to them? If so, we can be deeply confident that he draws near to us this weekend. Notice, too, that Jesus comes up to *them*. So often we search and search to find God in our journey – especially as lesbians and gay men – yet the Divine Lover is always seeking us, walking with us whenever our hearts are open.

Something keeps these two disciples from recognising Jesus. This reflects a theme, common in the Resurrection accounts, in which Jesus manifests himself and yet some uncertainty or lack of recognition is also present – but here Luke uses it for his own theological purposes. These two have a journey to go on, a journey on which they will be called to reflect on the Scriptures and on the meaning of life and death,

---

7 Luke 7:1-10. See also John McNeill, *Freedom, glorious freedom*, Beacon Press, Boston, 1995, pp. 132-136.
8 Acts 10. This story covers a whole chapter.
9 Acts 8:26-40. See also Nancy Wilson, *Our tribe*, Harper Collins, San Francisco, 1995, pp. 120-134.

and called to an encounter beyond their dreams. It is crucial that they go on this journey – for their own sake, yes, but also for people yet unborn. So divine Love calls them forth gently, insistently, in a hidden way, moving at their pace but also opening them more and more to surprise, delight and epiphany. And so it is with us. The journey is essential.

So, Jesus asks them what they're talking about, as they walk along. Amazingly, they stop immediately. These two are not 'task-orientated'. It's not 'excuse me, we have a village to get to'. No, they stop dead. The encounter, the sharing with someone interested and concerned is far more important. Not only do they stop, however, they open their hearts to this person. They tell him all about their sadness, disappointment and pain. They do think he's a little out of touch – but they pour it all out. And who is this man? A Nobody. Just a bloke along the road who asks them how things are. I see here a profound openness – even a readiness to embrace the stranger – something many of us share, I believe. I also see here a hunger to share their story, to talk about their hopes, their bewilderment, their wondering. Yes, like us, there is a love of sharing and discussing in these two, but also the deep 'hunger-to-speak' of those who are never truly asked, those whose stories and questions and deep longing count for nothing, or are treated as 'not fit-to-be-named'. Yet, this stranger asks, this stranger listens, this stranger receives their wondering and their pain – and they pour it out.

Many of us have had this experience of pouring out our hearts when we finally find someone who actually asks! And this person is Jesus for us, wherever we meet him or her. We understand how these two disciples can pour out their hearts to this loving stranger.

And what is their story all about? It is a story of hope, and of hopes dashed. These two have had no doubt about who Jesus was – 'a prophet mighty in word and deed before God and all the people', and their hope had been that he would be the One to set Israel free. The hope of freedom, after all these centuries of waiting, in a time of ruthless and systematic oppression. However, their hope has been crushed. Their chief priests and rulers – the very ones to whom they might have looked to welcome and acclaim Jesus and his freedom – have betrayed him to crucifixion and death. 'We had hoped', they say, and they go away sad.

How often, how many times have *we* gone away sad, our hopes dashed. We, too, had hoped that Jesus would be the one to set us free, that the love, dignity, community and joy he proclaimed would touch us in the core of our love and our longing as lesbians and gay men, and set us free to be ourselves. How many Eucharists, sermons, sacraments, theology classes, profession ceremonies, ordinations, marriages, funerals, have we gone away from sad at heart, saying, 'we had hoped': we had hoped to be set free from oppression and condemnation, from hatred and self-hatred, from fear and isolation, freed to live and explore and play and make love and seek justice, freed to find and share our gifts and our grace with one another and the whole human family? It's as if we go to every Mass with a small part of our hearts still hoping to hear words of liberation in the name of Jesus. And year by year that part of us that still hopes has grown smaller and smaller and weaker and weaker. And the very people we looked to, to proclaim to us the liberation in Jesus that we have been seeking – our chief priests and rulers – have been the ones to betray both him and the hope he promised us all, the very ones to crush our hopes, again and again.

The beauty of these two disciples is that they *name* the betrayal. They face it. They do not excuse their religious leaders, they do not pretend. Jesus proclaimed radical human liberation and called people together into a new community of love and justice. Twenty centuries later, look around and see the level of fear and control that are peddled in his name. Think of the fear in so many of us here this weekend. Can we, too, name the betrayal?

The two disciples then go on to speak of the visit of the women to the tomb. Unlike the apostles, they do not dismiss their story as an idle tale. In fact, some of their group actually went to the tomb to check things out and found them just as the women said. These two are themselves still talking and wondering about it all. They are not closed off, they are open to the witness of the women and to new possibilities.

These two disciples, the women and those who also went to the tomb were not among the leaders of the community, were not apostles – they were just ordinary folk, the type of people some church leaders today might call 'the simple faithful'.

The two disciples tell the stranger how the women saw a vision of angels who declared that Jesus was alive, but of him they saw nothing. So, the women's story is very much on their minds – and undoubtedly they have also been discussing the apostles' reaction to this story. Here, we need to realise that the community back in Jerusalem must have found itself in the midst of a profound crisis. On top of the devastating grief and uncertainty following the execution of Jesus, there has been added the conflict between the women's story, the apostles' ready dismissal of it, and the later evidence of those who did visit the tomb. Anguish, confusion, conflict and bewilderment must have been thick in the air that Sunday morning. Significantly, it is right at this point of conflict and crisis that these two disciples leave. A strange thing to do, it would seem. Luke doesn't tell us why they are going to Emmaus, but it is clear that they are *walking away* at a painful and crucial time. Sometimes, in spite of everything, this proves to be the only way forward. The journey is essential, for us – as for these two disciples – but also for the whole community. It will bring a resolution to the crisis that could never have been imagined.

Please note, the two disciples are leaving a community in which the Resurrection *has already been proclaimed*. While the women did not see Jesus, they were the first to hear his resurrection proclaimed, and they were themselves the first to proclaim this to the gathered community. However, this is also a community in which the proclamation of the Resurrection, like the witness of women, could not and did not find a home. It is a community in which the leaders were the first to dismiss what their hearts were not ready to believe, treating the witness of others – less 'important' others – as worthless. Instead of the power and joy and freedom of the Resurrection, there is conflict and confusion and division. The response of these two, at least, is to hit the road. But they're still wondering.

We have also been part of just such a community. Many of us have spent most of our lives serving this community. In this community the Resurrection has been proclaimed over and over again, and yet … somehow the Risen Life has not been deeply received, celebrated and claimed in all of its liberating power. Somehow it has not taken root, not found a home, not been unleashed. It's been boxed in, constrained, even crushed. Some – no, many – of the people whose witness to the Resurrection has been most powerful and free have been dismissed, silenced, condemned, excommunicated. Sometimes executed. We have grown tired of watching and waiting and hoping for the freedom we have been promised.

Confused, bewildered, not knowing what to make of it all, some of us have 'left' the official community even as we recognise its time of crisis – and we walk away – sad at heart, yet not quite without faith.

I believe we must *walk away!* We must leave the official community. To stay would not only be unhealthy and abusive, it would mean we'd miss out on the journey to and from Emmaus – a journey that we need to make, a journey that the community needs us to make. As lesbian, gay, bi-sexual, transgender Catholics, we are called urgently to make this journey. Leave! Now, this 'leaving' can take many forms. For some it will mean severing virtually all contacts, leaving jobs and parishes, even rejecting the whole visible structure of the official community. For some others it may mean staying loosely within these visible structures, or maintaining some contact, but detaching, disengaging their heart and soul – and body – from the all-consuming demands and claims of the institution. Choosing to have a life! – with all its risks, joys and uncertainties, becoming open to a new and hidden road of faith and of loving, seeking to find the 'law written on the heart',[10] that sometimes means going against the 'laws written in the books'. The gay writer Paul Monette once wrote 'such obedient slaves we make with such very tidy rooms'.[11] To walk this road to Emmaus is to refuse to be a slave any longer, and to increasingly refuse to collude in our own repression or in the oppression of others. It is to refuse to pretend, to refuse to teach what we don't believe, to refuse to be afraid. Some of us will walk this road openly, even publicly – and, yes, some of us must be public! Some of us will walk this road quietly. All of us, I believe, *must walk* – we must leave the institution, in the midst of its crisis, and have the courage to walk the road towards a small and insignificant village.

We will name the betrayal. We will honour the lives of women and of gay, lesbian, bi-sexual and transgender people. We will face the pain of our dashed hopes. We will seek to walk in community – with a soul-mate. We will remain open and wondering as we walk, ready to welcome the strangers we meet on the road. All of this – but we must GO!

---

10 Jeremiah 31:33.
11 P Monette, *Becoming a man*, Harper Collins, New York, 1992, p. 2.

So, these disciples are making their journey *outside* the Jerusalem community. Here, I suggest, they take on the role of the outsiders, the Gentiles, in Luke's theology. As they leave and walk away they 'become' all who are outside the official Christian community, all outsiders – us. Interestingly, the distinguished Scripture scholar Xavier Leon-Dufour draws a very close parallel between the structure of the Road to Emmaus story, and the story of the Ethiopian Eunuch in Acts, seeing them as matching stories.[12] That story, too, is very much about the Revelation to the outsiders. The disciples on the road to Emmaus are on the margins of the official Christian community, walking away at time of crisis, and the eunuch is a ritually unclean foreigner. In both cases the revelation of God's love in Christ comes to meet them and transforms them with joy and hope. (Some also argue that the term 'eunuch' is a generic term or category and that it included people we would call gay.[13] If that is true, and if these are two matching stories, then these two disciples may very well be our ancestors in faith.) Having opened their hearts to this stranger, the two disciples now pause. Jesus says to them 'O foolish people, slow of heart to believe (not 'hard of heart', note, – a gentle rebuke, I feel) all that the prophets have spoken!' We need to hear this too. In our sadness, in our sense of betrayal and of exclusion we, too, are slow to believe, slow to recognise that we are part of an old, old story of life that comes out of death.

Jesus then goes on to explain to them the Scriptures – and everything in them concerning himself. Now, notice that these two disciples not only open their hearts to this stranger, they now listen to him! Remember, this man is nobody special – not an apostle, not a priest or a scribe, not a rabbi – just a bloke on the road, and yet they are profoundly open – 'heart-open' – to hear and receive his words, and to the unexpected and overwhelming transformation they bring. (Could we all have such openness!) And the rank, the status, the qualifications of this stranger, this teacher, are irrelevant. All that matters is the integrity and truth of what he says. On this journey that we are called to make, all that will matter is this kind of openheartedness, this kind of integrity and truth. We gay and lesbian

---

12 Xavier Leon-Dufour, *Resurrection and the message of Easter*, Chapman, London, 1974, pp. 162-163.
13 See for example Nancy Wilson, loc. cit.

people can be very skilled at seeing through status and rank and their claims to authority. Some people suggest this is because we are used to playing roles in order to survive. In any case, we need to exercise this skill. We also need to be open to the complementary challenge of embracing the truth – whenever and wherever and however and through whomsoever it is encountered – completely irrespective of the status of the truthteller, and irrespective of whether it is conveyed in words or in deeper levels of living and loving. There is no future in anything but the Truth – the truth of who we are and who we are called to be as fully alive human beings, as gay, lesbian, bi-sexual, transgender lovers imbued with the erotic power of the Risen Christ. This truth is all that really matters in our lives, and the key to it is learning to do what we have been told not to do: to listen deeply to our own experience. This is not easy. It will involve a lot of unlearning. It will mean the shattering of old images of self and of God. It will mean being vulnerable to the truths told in unlikely places by unlikely people – the strangers met on the road.

And what does this particular stranger say? 'Was it not necessary, ordained, that the Christ should suffer these things and so enter into his Glory?' Jesus then interprets everything in Scripture concerning himself. We may be confident that in Luke's mind as he is writing this are the words from the prophet Isaiah that he put on Jesus' lips at the very beginning of his ministry: 'The Spirit of the Lord is upon me … to bring Good News to the poor, to proclaim liberty to captives and to the blind new sight, to set the down-trodden free, to proclaim the Lord's year of favour.'[14] We can also be confident that he has in mind words such as these, also from Isaiah: 'Without beauty, without majesty we saw him – a man of sorrows and familiar with suffering. A man to make people screen their faces. He was despised and we took no account of him.' (This is, in fact, the passage the Ethopian Eunuch in Acts is reading when Phillip meets him on the road.)[15]

As Jesus and the two disciples walk along that road in the gathering twilight they are discussing the astonishing truth that is at the heart of the Pascal Mystery: the road to entering into 'Glory', to fullness of life,

---

[14] Luke 4:16-22.
[15] Isaiah 53:2-3; Acts 8:27-33.

to 'glorious freedom',[16] lies through the struggle for justice, and through the Cross, into death. So it was for the Christ. So it is for us.

Who wants to hear this? Is this the 'Good News' we were promised? We hear these words and we shiver. Here Luke is touching the mystery and scandal of the Cross, a mystery and a scandal that will always shock us and always elude our theological grasp. All we are really given is that the road to life lives this way, and that we walk it in good company.

There is one group of people, however for whom it *can* be good news to hear that the road to fullness of life lies through rejection, exile and death. (And it's not the apostles, still back in Jerusalem crying into their beer over their wasted career opportunities.) If the road to life lies in the company of the One who was despised, rejected, cut off from the people, surely those who will receive this *as* Good News are those who are *themselves* already despised, rejected, exiled! The outsiders. They have nothing left to lose! Blessed are the Poor! We hear it again and again, but still we don't believe it. Blessed – congratulations, oh, rejoice – you who are Poor!

So, in the company of Jesus we will struggle tirelessly for justice, we will defend the rights and the dignity of the oppressed including ourselves, we will overturn the tables of the money lenders in temples both ancient and modern, we will challenge those who use 'religion' to keep people in chains and to advance their own power and ambition, we will refuse to dance around the golden calves of mainstream society or of gay sub-culture, we will reverence and care for the birds of the air and the lilies of the field, we will proclaim freedom and new hope. Yet still, even beyond all this, we are called to walk in the company of the One who was crucified, to enter into poverty and exile, and, if we are faithful and trusting enough, we will be led into and through the Cross.

'Embracing the Exile', the gay writer John Fortunato calls this.[17] Beyond facing our exclusion and exile there lies the grace of embracing it, entering into it, learning its lessons, discovering its gifts. This is not a wallowing in victim-hood. On the contrary, it is about a passion for justice and for true life, born of the experience of marginalisation and

16 See John McNeill's treatment, op. cit., pp. 7-10.
17 J Fortunato, *Embracing the exile; healing journeys of gay Christians*, Harper and Row, San Francisco, 1987.

exclusion. As we open ourselves to this experience we are offered a startling and disturbing view, a perspective from the edge of society. As marginal people we are invited into the experience of seeing through the hallowed power structures and values of society and church in which we have no part, and, if we are able to face this, we are freed to see the injustice and corruption at their heart. This is the view of the poor, the poor who are blessed. We are blessed to find ourselves amongst them – yet here is the rub for us as gay people: we have a choice. Unlike most minority groups, many of us have the option of 'passing', of playing the game, of seeking to become, or to remain part of the 'in' crowd, the mainstream, the included. Sometimes this seems a matter of survival – but there is deep seduction here too. Deeper still, however, is the call of grace, the words and the living witness of the One who walks beside us on our own roads to Emmaus.

Each person, in the silence of his or her own heart, has to discern how to respond to this call. I don't intend to address directly the issue of coming out publicly, except to say these things: 1) blessed are the poor; 2) the call is to work for justice and liberation and to accept that this road will, ultimately, lead us to the Cross; 3) coming out, both within our hearts and within our world in not a state but a direction – and one that I believe the Holy Spirit will always be nudging us along; 4) in the end, the only worthwhile reason to remain involved in unjust power structures is so that we can help reform them from inside. If we're not actually committed to that, we have no business being there.

However we may respond, the first step is always to face the truth of our exile and learn to embrace its blessings. 'Was it not necessary that the Christ should suffer these things and so enter into his Glory.' We are in good company.

Now, when they hear these words our two disciples find that their hearts burn like fire within them. You usually only have that depth of reaction when something profoundly touches your own experience. Why did the hearts of these two 'gay' and 'lesbian' disciples burn within them when Jesus explained the Scriptures that speak of justice and liberation, of rejection, exile and condemnation? Because they know this place! We know this place! And here it is being named, being touched, like a raw wound, and at the same time being opened up as a road of blessing. What if the very thing that we had been told was a curse, the very thing we had hidden and feared and been told was intrinsically evil, unclean, unnatural, turns out to be Blessing, Gift, Grace. Jesus himself died, accursed and cut off from the people, a blasphemer condemned by the Sanhedrin itself – yet this turns out to be the path of blessing beyond imagining. Perhaps in his company there is blessing for us. Of course their hearts burn within them!

Well, they draw near to their village. The stranger appears to be going on, but he is awaiting, I believe, their invitation, honouring their pace and their freedom, never forcing himself on them. (How different from so many who will teach in his name.) The Divine Lover, the Divine Liberator waits on our invitation. (What a trip we will have if we invite this stranger in!)

Immediately, spontaneously, open-heartedly, these two disciples invite the stranger come and 'stay' – abide – with them, into their home, into their lives, to their table. How trusting they are of this stranger – or perhaps how hungry for his words and his company. We know this feeling – the bodily hunger for someone not just to listen to us, but to speak honest words to us, words of truth that honour and touch our deepest, most raw experience and reveal it as blessing. Of course they're not going to let him get away. Please, come in, stay with us!

So, he goes in to stay with them. Of course, this is what the loving stranger had been intending, even longing for all along – to be invited into the most intimate part of their lives. But they must *invite* him in. Without hesitation, without questions or conditions, he goes in to sup with them. All he has been waiting for is their invitation – and so it is with us.

At this point in the story, as night comes down, the two disciples reach the turning point in their journey. Here, in their home and at their table, they are at the farthest point *away* from the Jerusalem community. These two 'outsiders' are now in their appropriate place, as far 'outside' the official community as Luke can make them. The scene is set. The stranger goes home with them.

Now, we must note that Jesus goes in to their home and their table – he doesn't invite them to his place or to a restaurant down the road. No, it is their home, their table, their lives that are at issue here. And, as he sits at their table, he will take up *their* bread – not some special bread he brought from Jerusalem! In just such a way, on our journey, this loving stranger seeks to come in to the 'places' where we live, where we actually live, to stay with us, to take up in his hands *our bread* – the crushed grain of our lives and loves, our dreams and hopes, our struggles and our joys, our pain, the most vulnerable, intimate and tender parts of our lives: our 'bread'. And, as at Emmaus, he will take up this bread and will say the blessing. The Hebrew blessing is not a blessing *of* the bread, but a thanksgiving to God *for* the bread. Jesus takes up our lives, our bread in his hands, and he gives thanks to God for our lives. And then he breaks open our lives as sacred food, as himself, as Eucharist. Here, in this ordinary home, far away from the official community, with night all around, the Risen Christ is at table with his people. In all of the Gospels *this* is the most explicit scene of the Risen Jesus celebrating the Eucharist with his disciples. And look where it happens! So it must happen for us! The Divine Stranger has been seducing us onto the journey for just such a meal.

But we must invite the stranger in, trusting our hearts. We must allow him to take up and give thanks for and break open our lives and our loving – as they really are. This is Eucharist! And Emmaus is all around us, if only our hearts are open.

It is in this moment that the eyes of our two disciples are opened and they *see*: they are empowered to recognise Jesus, the one who has been walking with them on the journey all along. Unlike others in many of these resurrection stories, there is no hesitation, no doubt in their hearts. The truth of their experience is undeniable and it is utterly transforming.

In this same moment Jesus vanishes from their sight. He is with them now, in them, in the bread they share, in their lives together, no longer 'out there', but within them, in their very flesh as they share this bread and as they reflect on his words, words that set their hearts on fire.

And in this reflection on the journey, on word and on sacrament as they have experienced them, they know themselves as *sent* – and sent not so much out, or forth, as *back*. A little earlier there'd been weariness and a fear of the dark descending, but *now* there is no hesitation, no fear, apparently no concern for the kind of reception they might meet with back in Jerusalem (remember the response the women had met with). They get up that very hour and go all the way back to the Jerusalem community. The story of the Road to Emmaus becomes the story of the road *from* Emmaus, as they return to witness to the truth of their own experience within the heart of the official community. This is the second great movement of Luke's story and of our journey – the outsiders return!

This, I believe is the mandate we share! Following Luke's paradigm, we are called out onto our journey, a journey that will take us in some deep sense away from the official community. As gay, lesbian, bi-sexual, transgender people we are called to embrace our lives and to enter into the struggle for justice, the experience of exile and, ultimately, death to self. We are also called to live with passion, creativity, daring and freedom. As we do, we are called into living our Eucharists and into sharing our soulful reflection on our experience. This reflection is essential – and it is a reflection that has been forbidden us. On so many levels, we queer folks have had our lives blighted by this ban on deep and honest reflection, in the light of faith, on our actual experience of living and loving. I am thinking here particularly about our sexual experience – about embracing ourselves as sexual, sensual beings with all of our yearnings and desires and fantasies and joys and chaos, the whole mixed and messy wonder that is sexuality.

Here, of course, we touch a raw wound within the Body of Christ, a wound that afflicts all Christians, whatever their sexual orientation or experience. It is surely impossible to be fully human and not to enter vulnerably into sexuality, into this very fundamental dimension of human living. If we can't encounter the Divine here, where can we expect to? If the Incarnation does not involve this, then what does it involve? Yet when, in the whole history of the Church, has there been an honest, open, reflective embrace of sexuality with all of its lessons and its revelation? It's as if the Church has always been holding off from, even denying life, embodied life like itself, lest it soil its hands with the stuff of creation. We have a teaching on sexuality – one could hardly call it a theology – that has virtually always been based in distaste for and even hostility towards sexuality. We have so many rules and regulations based not in reverence and honest reflection but in rejection – and I am speaking here of sexuality per se, including heterosexuality. How much more is this the case with gay identity, desire, love and experience!

Crucial to our journey, then, is a journey into sexuality – into its revelations and its Eucharists. We then must reflect on this experience

– 'do theology' – together as it has never been done before, and come back to witness to our experience of the Divine in flesh, in our own flesh and in the flesh of those who journey with us. We gay and lesbian people, we who have borne most cruelly the brunt of the Church's rejection of the sexual, are especially called to go on this journey. If not us, then who? We bear a precious, irreplaceable gift.

Like those two disciples, it is when we encounter the Risen Christ blessing, breaking open and sharing the bread of our lives, as queer people, that we will see him in his glory, and know ourselves as sent – sent to share the truth that has set us free. And when we return we will speak with power and with humility and with an inner authority that comes from integrity. We will not sit down and we will not be silent. Our story must be told, for our mandate comes not from the institution but from personal, prophetic experience of Divine erotic energy in our lives. We will seek to speak in community, like these two disciples. We will speak, in some sense, for all those who are 'outsiders', for all those whose lives and loves have been ignored, dismissed, treated as 'an idle tale', for all those regarded as 'unclean', cut off, accursed. We will speak, but really it is the witness of our lives that will speak, calling the official community to listen in ways that it has never listened, calling it to conversion of heart, calling it to embrace all that is human and earthy.

I wonder what kind of a reception we can expect. When our two disciples return to the Jerusalem community, they are immediately met with a proclamation: 'The Lord has risen indeed and has appeared to Simon (Peter).' Peter, note, the leader of the official community – the one who will, in Acts, struggle with Paul over the issue of the Gentiles. Now, there seems to be an ancient tradition here – Paul, too, will include an appearance to Peter as part of his account of the early Kerygma.[18] But I think Luke is also weaving his theological threads together here.

There has been, on the one hand, a briefly mentioned appearance to Peter, the 'foundation stone' of the official community. On the other hand, there is this fully developed story of the appearance to these two disciples outside the official community. What happens now?

---

18 1 Corinthians 15: 3-8.

In Luke's account the two disciples hear the brief proclamation of the appearance to Peter. They then tell their story of meeting Jesus on the road, and how they recognised him in the breaking of the bread (this is explicit eucharistic language.[19]) So, these two stories are now together, proclaimed and heard in the midst of the whole community.

We need to note that up to this point there has been no appearance of Jesus to the whole gathered community nor to any of the apostles except Peter. Almost the whole of the day has gone by, and the community in Jerusalem has still not seen Jesus. However, it is at this point, as the two disciples tell their story of meeting Jesus on the road ('as they were saying these things') that Jesus himself stands amongst them all and says, 'Peace to You'.

This is clearly the moment that Luke has been leading up to on this day of the Resurrection, and we may be sure that every element of his account has been carefully weighed, every word matters. So let's recap: we have the gathered 'official' Christian community who have not yet seen Jesus, we have the brief account of Jesus' appearance to Peter already proclaimed in that community, and we have the two 'outsiders' – the two disciples who had walked away from the community and who had their own experience of the Risen Christ – now back in Jerusalem and telling their story within the official community. Only *now* does Jesus appear. It is *only* when these two accounts are brought together, only when the witness of 'Peter', the leader of the official community, *and* the witness of the 'outsiders', the two disciples, are shared and received within the gathered community, that the Risen Christ can appear to the *whole* community. *Only now* can he reveal himself, bring the promise of the Spirit, open their minds to understand the Scriptures, send them as witnesses to all the nations and then ascend – all of which happens in the next few verses.

So, this coming together, this speaking and listening to the Resurrection experiences of both 'Peter' and of the 'outsiders' is absolutely crucial. It was then, and it is now. Luke has written for us not just an account of a wondrous day, long ago. He has passed on to us all a pattern, a paradigm, a model, a mandate for all who would walk

---

19 Even today we can recognise the liturgical formula 'he took the Bread, blessed it, broke it and handed it to them'. It is clear that Luke is deliberately evoking the Eucharist. See also Xavier Leon-Dufour, op. cit., pp. 160-164.

in the way of Jesus. His whole gospel has led up to this moment, and the unfolding of this moment will not only shape his next book, the Acts of the Apostles, but its power will resonate down the centuries to us, gathered here today. If we long to see the living power and love of the Spirit of the Risen Christ unleashed in the community and in the world, then we must come together with open hearts, on all sides, and share the revelation of God's love and freedom that we have come to know. The experience of the 'outsiders' is no less real, no less precious, no less essential than the experience of 'Peter'.

Can we come together and share the Truth we have come to know? If we do, how will our story be received? (Luke does not say how the apostles responded to the two disciples' story.[20]) We cannot answer for 'Peter' or for the official church, but I believe our mandate, as gay, lesbian, bisexual and transgender people, is clear. We must go on our journeys, open our hearts, live our lives, enter into our eucharists – *and* we must also come back and speak the truth of our experience. This will take courage and great generosity. For myself, I would much rather stay at 'Emmaus' with my friends and share the eucharist there. I feel no great personal desire to engage again with the institution of the Church. Yet the call seems clear and utterly compelling. Why?

This call to return is not given simply for our sake, nor, I suggest, simply for the sake of the Church.

Why are we called to return? In Luke's day of the Resurrection the two disciples return, and as they tell their story to the gathered disciples, the Risen Christ appears. Central to this appearance to the whole community is the promise of the Holy Spirit and the commission to preach the Good News to 'all nations'. This community is called into being not simply for its own sake, but for the sake of all the world. In this moment, when the Risen Christ gives his mandate and promises the power of the Holy Spirit, the little community in Jerusalem is called to become the Church. The witness of the 'outsiders', proclaimed in its midst, is essential in that process. In our day, too, the witness of the 'outsiders', proclaimed with courage and love, is essential if the Church is to become what she is called to be – a

---

20 In Mark 16:12-13, however, we are told that the witness of the two disciples was not believed by 'the rest' when they returned.

light to the nations, a sacrament of the liberating love of Christ for all people and for all of creation.

We look around, however, at the contemporary Church, and it is hard to say those words, let alone believe them. What could it mean to imagine the eruption of the power and love of the Risen Christ in our midst today?

Various social commentators have spoken of the extraordinary failure of the Church in our day. We live in perhaps the bloodiest era in human history. We certainly live in the most ecologically destructive. It is a time of great human liberation, but also of great chaos and uncertainty. Vistas never before imagined have opened before us, dilemmas never before faced, challenge us. In such a time of crisis and of Kairos, where is the official Church? Some fine words are spoken and written, perhaps, and many not so fine, however, as a whole the institutional Church seems without juice, without power, without a vision to engage modern people. Within the Church itself many move in ever-tightening circles around the 'throne' of Peter, facing inwards, while many others who know better have fallen silent, given up, or been marginalised. On the other side, how many sincere, reflective people have walked away completely, finding the official Church no longer credible or even worthy of respect?

This failure of the official Church is based, I suggest, in two great sins. The first is its reliance on, even idolatry before its own power and control and the concomitant refusal to truly listen to any voices other than its own, lest that power be compromised. This is also a great failure of trust in the Holy Spirit and in the people of God. If ever there was a time in human history when searching, open, spiritual and moral dialogue was needed, it is today. Physicists, cosmologists, medical researchers, biologists, philosophers, genetic engineers, environmentalists – the list could go on –all call for dialogue. An institution that refuses to genuinely listen and search with modern people is of no help today.

The second sin is the rejection and trivialisation of matter, of earth, of flesh, of sexuality, and therefore of women and gay men. This sin, in effect, denies the Incarnation, denies the sacramental, revelatory dimension of Creation itself. It teaches us to fear our own God-given bodies and the delight, wisdom and holiness they are for us. This sin de-sanctifies earth, animals, forests, oceans, air – and it plays a foundational role in a culture that is destroying the ecology of the planet. This sin is at the heart of the most profound crisis faced on earth since the advent of *homo sapiens*. The environmental scientist David Suzuki says that many scientists already privately believe it is too late to turn back the tide of massive destruction. Where is the Church in the midst of this crisis, a crisis based primarily in Western culture?

And who can we look to as a voice of spiritual and moral vision in this culture if not the Church? Where is the power and the promise of the Holy Spirit, breathed into us by the Risen Christ? Are these just words, after all?

While the Church refuses to *listen* to the wisdom, the experience and the searching – and to the Spirit of God – in all people, it will be unable to speak to or with contemporary women and men. While the Church continues to view with disdain, or even subtle hostility, matter, flesh, earth, sensual pleasure and erotic power – and therefore alienates and even condemns those of us free enough to delight in our bodyliness, our sexuality, our earthiness – it will be unable to engage with power or authority in the crucial issues of our time. And the crisis will deepen.

We have a vocation. We will challenge the Church to listen. We will tell the truth of what we have known of life and love and freedom. We will bear witness to the power of the Risen Christ in our lives, our relationships, our bodies. We will not be silent. We will not be afraid. We will challenge the Church by our embodiedness, our erotic delight, our holy, earthy pleasure. We will celebrate our sexuality and embrace the earth as sacraments of the living God.

In Luke's day of the Resurrection the Risen Jesus has to convince the apostles that he has a body, so he has them touch him and give him something to eat. I'm tempted to say, 'Typical, they still can't believe he had a body'!

This is perhaps the primary Christian heresy. It is also, perhaps, the primary Christian truth: the Love of God is embodied in Creation, in Christ, in us. This is the sacrament, the tabernacle, the holy Communion upon which all other sacraments, tabernacles, and holy communions depend. And perhaps we are called to be, in our day, its witnesses, its ministers, its prophets. If we can be faithful and honest enough, perhaps we will come to see the power of the Risen Christ present in the Church, present for the world in this critical age.

The road to Emmaus lies before us. We must not remain fearfully secure, silent and depressed back in Jerusalem. Try to imagine the Gospels without the story of the road to and from Emmaus! Now imagine the modern Church without our stories! This is the challenge of the future – a future already upon us.

And as we set out, we hear again – Do not be afraid! Do not be afraid of the truth of who you are. Do not be afraid, for always I am with you. And we hear this as challenge, as promise, and as infinitely tender lovemaking.

Amen, Amen, Come, Lord Jesus!

This is the edited text of a keynote lecture delivered at the First National Symposium of Acceptance, held at Treacy College, Melbourne, in 1997. Acceptance is an Australian association of Lesbian and Gay Catholics. The lecture was based on Volume 6 of my video lecture series The Erotic Contemplative: the spiritual journey of the Gay Christian, *published by Erospirit Institute, California, in 1995.*

Open letter to Pope John Paul II

Dear Pope John Paul,

I am writing to you as an openly gay man who embraces and celebrates his sexuality as a Sacred Gift. I am also writing as a member of the Church and as a person who, like so many others, longs for a just and more loving society.

I am writing to ask you to publicly welcome and embrace gay and lesbian people, including those who are members of the Catholic Church, and to enter into open dialogue with us. Surely the time has come.

After many centuries of persecution, gay and lesbian people are finally finding a voice, claiming a place, celebrating the hope of freedom. Increasingly, people of good will around the world are encouraging us in our struggle for liberation and justice.

In the Church, too, there are signs of hope. Catholic teaching now says that homosexual women and men 'must be accepted with respect, compassion and sensitivity', that they 'should have an active role in the Christian community' and that 'every form of unjust discrimination in their regard is to be avoided'. In some dioceses there are also genuine efforts being made to develop dialogue and pastoral care.

Despite these signs of hope, however, lesbian and gay people continue to face entrenched hostility and discrimination in both society and Church. In families, schools, parishes, workplaces, secular institutions and Church structures we are still routinely silenced and excluded. Both the teachings and the attitude of heart of many in the Church continue to provide a foundation and a justification for those who condemn, reject and harass gay people.

Within the Church community itself there is still real oppression and deep-seated fear. It remains true that reputations, careers and lives can readily be destroyed if people are named as gay or even gay-friendly in our Church, despite official claims of tolerance. The imposed silence, the invisibility, the neglect, the exclusion and the active rejection that lesbian and gay people continue to endure in our Church are an insult to the Heart of Christ and a scandal for the People of God.

A stark and deeply symbolic example of this rejection occurred late last year. In both Melbourne and London two Catholic men, one a priest, were officially refused Holy Communion because they came forward in the Church proclaiming that they were gay. The symbol they wore was a Rainbow Sash.

At the time, Archbishop Pell and Cardinal Basil Hume gave different reasons for this refusal, but the message was the same: those who come forward in the Catholic community proclaiming that they are gay will be met with one of the Church's strongest sanctions, they will be refused Communion. This rejection is a blow to the heart for gay and lesbian Catholics and Christians, and for all who seek a more just and loving society. It will encourage those who oppress gay people. It will crush the spirit of lesbian and gay Catholic youth. What future will they see for themselves in a Church that condemns them to silence and invisibility or to public rejection?

The time has come to break this silence, to challenge this rejection, to call for a change of heart in the Church. If not now, then when?

We are therefore writing to you to ask you, to call you, to offer leadership and loving service. You are called the 'Servant of the Servants of God'. Will you be a servant for gay and lesbian people? Will you dare to do something new for love and justice?

We ask these things of you:

Will you publicly welcome openly gay and lesbian Catholics to Communion, and will you call the Bishops of our Church to do the same?

Will you encourage gay and lesbian clergy, religious and laity to come out, namely, to openly acknowledge their sexual orientation, so that our young people may have mentors and role models and so that the rich gifts of all of God's people may be honestly celebrated? Will you guarantee that the ministries, careers and reputations of those who come out in the Church will be protected?

Will you call all Bishops to set up diocesan ministries to lesbian and gay people and their families, along with education and support programs in schools and parishes, so that intolerance, prejudice and hatred may be overcome by the Love of God?

Will you meet with lesbian and gay people from around the world, with Bishops and theologians, and set up 'Structures of Listening' in dioceses and in the Universal Church? Will you let our voices be heard and our wisdom and experience be honoured?

Will you seek, with us, a new appreciation for human sexuality in all of its diversity and beauty?

We ask you to consider prayerfully all that this letter puts before you. We realise this may take some time. However, Love and Justice call incessantly, and so we hereby inform both you and the whole Church that:

We will continue to come forward in the Church, proclaiming publicly that we are gay and lesbian people who embrace and celebrate our sexuality as a Sacred Gift. We will continue to call the Church to be a voice of justice, a promise of liberation and an advocate for those who are oppressed and silenced.

We will wear the symbol of the Rainbow Sash with dignity, hope and pride.

For the Love of God, please listen to us.

This letter was signed on 6 May 1998 by myself and the convenors of the Rainbow Sash Movement. It was sent to Pope John Paul II. No reply was ever received. The letter has become one of the foundational texts of the Rainbow Sash Movement. See Appendix – The Rainbow Sash Movement, for a more extensive history and discussion of the group and its objectives.

The radical ministry of Jesus

The radical Ministry of Jesus of Nazareth always has been an embarrassment to the religious establishment. From the first moment of his preaching, Jesus made clear that things would get interesting: 'The Spirit of God is upon me: for God has anointed me. God has sent me to bring good news to the poor, to proclaim liberty to captives and to the blind new sight, to set the downtrodden free, to proclaim God's year of favour' (Luke 4:18).

Jesus claimed this text as his charter. He then went on to give two provocative examples of how the Spirit of God specifically goes out to the rejected and the outsiders before anyone else. For his troubles, the local worshippers tried to throw him off a cliff.

So, you see, it can be risky, but if the Church is not living out this same mission, then it should shut up shop. It might be a nice religion with nice liturgy, but it is not Christian.

One of the most graphic ways Jesus lived out his Ministry was by attending and hosting what we might call dinner parties. Honestly, the man would eat with anyone! In a Middle Eastern society this was scandalous, especially for a religious leader. He ate with the learned, the religious upper-class, the rich, the poor, the prostitutes, the homeless.

He ate especially with the ritually unclean, those who were refused full participation in the religious life of their society because they were seen as impure, chronically sinful, spiritually inferior. The religious establishment was always attacking Jesus because of the company he kept, especially at dinner. Yet these open-hearted, welcoming dinners were seen by Jesus as models of the banquet in the kingdom of God, where the poor and rejected would have pride of place.

The spectacle, then, of a Christian Church refusing to share its sacred meal – Communion – with people who come forward in faith, honesty and love is shameful. It is even more so when these people come from the religious and social fringe, where they routinely meet with condemnation and abuse, as gay people do. These are the people Jesus told his followers to invite to dinner before anyone else. How times have changed. Jesus' radical table-fellowship caused such a stir because it was deeply symbolic. It was a tangible sign of the liberating embrace of God that he claimed would recreate not only human hearts, but also relationships and society.

In the sad, upside-down world of the institutionalised churches, the refusal of the sacred meal is also deeply symbolic. This is precisely why our group of gay and lesbian Christians and supporters have brought our call for justice to the table of the Eucharist.

Discrimination has no place at this table, or in the life of the Church as a whole. It has no place in Catholic families and schools where gay teenagers face their struggles alone and hear all too keenly the inflexible pronouncements of the Church. It has no place in the Ministry or religious life, where those who keep their sexuality hidden and secret can rise to great heights, while those few who dare to be open are sidelined or silenced. It has no place in the formulation of the Church's moral teaching, when men committed to never having sex claim to have privileged access to 'the truth', which they alone dispense.

Our action in the Church is not simply about receiving a Communion wafer. It is a call to the Church to embrace profound conversion of heart. That's why it is so threatening to so many. Modern Scripture scholarship is gradually revealing the features of the community of radical equality and freedom that Jesus sought to form. It doesn't look much like the Church we know, yet the same gospel lies at the source of both.

We stand on that gospel and call on the Church to follow the example and to open itself to Jesus' spirit in new ways. This will mean change and growth, but isn't that the infallible sign of life and of the spirit of God?

In the process, the Church will need to learn to listen rather than judge, to embrace rather than exclude, to serve rather than control. It will also need to explore a whole new understanding of human sexuality in all of its diversity and beauty. It will certainly need the courage, the witness and the honest challenge of lesbian and gay people.

We will continue to come to the table.

This article was published on the Opinion page of The Australian *newspaper after the Pentecost Sunday action by the Rainbow Sash Movement in June 1998. An opposing article by Rev James Murray was published alongside it.*

Rainbow warriors

A picture, they say, is worth a thousand words. On Pentecost Sunday the Church was offered a startling image. That day the Archbishop of Melbourne publicly refused communion to fifty people who were wearing brilliant rainbow-coloured sashes. Old and young, gay and straight, celibate and sexually active – all were refused. The Archbishop then formally rebuked them, and the congregation applauded. This vivid image continues to disturb hearts and minds both inside and outside the Church.

Daniel Madigan, in his article 'Telling it straight' (*Eureka Street*, July 1998) is clearly disturbed by it all. Like many liberal Catholics he shows considerable sympathy for the discrimination gay and lesbian Catholics face, and yet well, this is the 'family dinner table'. You don't arrive 'spoiling' for an 'argument'. This is not the time 'to turn up, fight with your parents and dare them not to feed you'. Many people have echoed these sentiments: 'We support what you're trying to do, but we don't like your methods.' Well, what about our methods? The 'methods' the Rainbow Sash Movement uses are simple, dignified, reverent and clear. We attend Mass. During the opening hymn we put on our rainbow sashes, which proclaim that 'we are gay and lesbian people who embrace and celebrate our sexuality as a Sacred Gift'. We then take part in the liturgy like everyone else. At communion we go up and quietly, but resolutely, claim our place at the 'family dinner table'. We are refused communion. We return to our places and stand silently. Family members and friends wear the sashes with us, becoming 'lesbian and gay for a day', enduring our rejection for the sake of love and justice. People who are not Catholics wear the sash and stand silently with us. After Mass we talk honestly about what has happened and about our call to the Church. That's it. These are our 'methods'.

Archbishop Pell calls such methods an 'inappropriate ideological demonstration'; Cardinal Clancy says they are 'futile'; Daniel Madigan suggests they will 'set back the cause of gay people in the Church'. We disagree.

The Catholic Church is not a discussion group, a theological academy or a debating society. It is a Church, and its lifeblood is the Eucharist. All that we are and all that we do finds its 'Source and

Summit' in this sacred meal. 'The Church makes the Eucharist; the Eucharist makes the Church', as the early Christians put it. To 're-make' this meal is to 're-make' the Church, which is why the bishops guard their control of it, why women are marginalised at it, why openly gay people are refused a share in it. Yet this meal is meant to express the depths of who we are as a Gospel community of love and justice. The Eucharist, then, must be accountable to love and justice. It must be answerable to the Gospel. The very idea of an unjust or oppressive Eucharist is a betrayal of everything Christ stood for. We have lived with just such a betrayal for far too long.

It is true that the Eucharist 'celebrates the unity that underlies our diversity', as Madigan says. However, at this table we celebrate heterosexual marriages, wedding anniversaries, religious professions, priestly ordinations, the legal profession, the racing fraternity, ethnic cultures and football teams. Everyone dresses up and celebrates! Yet gay people must not wear rainbows. No symbols, prayers or processions for us. We must be anonymous, lest we disturb the 'unity'. The silence and invisibility demanded of us at the Eucharist reflect, deepen and perpetuate the discrimination we face in the rest of Church life. This is the place where we must make our call for justice. This is the heart of the Church, a heart that needs radical conversion. Well then, are our methods 'futile'? Firstly, no action on behalf of love and justice is ever futile. Secondly, as Madigan points out 'Church moral teachings do in fact change'. Central to this process of change is the challenge and lived experience of those the Church refuses to hear. These people must speak. In our 'Pentecost letter' we call on the Church to 'honour our wisdom and experience', to seek with us a 'new appreciation of human sexuality in all of its diversity and beauty' and to work towards an Ecumenical Council with this focus. However, there are no public forums, no 'structures of listening' in our increasingly authoritarian Church. How are we to be heard? Within two weeks our movement had engaged six Archbishops, made headlines around the nation and provoked intense discussions in the media, in homes, schools and parishes. Bishop Power in Canberra has even begun to explore open dialogue with gay people in his diocese. Our methods are not futile. The furor they have caused suggests, rather, that we have indeed touched the very heart of the matter.

Furors, of course, can also cause damage. Have we 'set back the cause of gay people in the Church'? A woman outside St. Patrick's thought so. My sister, a heterosexual mother of six, was still wearing her sash when she heard an exclamation behind her: 'Whatever sympathy I had for gay people is gone now!' My sister snapped back, 'This isn't about sympathy, it's about justice!' Precisely. Polite discussions in closed rooms have their place, but so do clear strong actions. We have held up a mirror in which the Church must face the ugliness of what it is doing to gay people. Even more importantly, the Rainbow Sash offers a 'call to consciousness', as feminist theologian Carter Heyward commented, 'that things really are as bad as they seem. The only ethical way to be a Catholic in that kind of situation is to be a resistor.' This is the painful experience of 'Conscientisation', that first crucial step on the road to liberation. Gay people are waking up and standing up for themselves after many centuries of persecution. We refuse to be 'non persons', rejecting that fate which liberation theologian Gustavo Gutierrez claims is the worst oppression of all. This 'waking up' is the only true way forward.

The real question in all this is not how gay people can dare to upset the Eucharistic meal. It is how our brothers and sisters can continue to eat at this table when we are refused. Yet there was another woman on Pentecost Sunday who drew my mother aside. Mum had worn the sash and was still shaking from the palpable rejection. 'I am so sorry', she said, 'but I want you to know that when I saw you rainbow sash people being refused I said to the priest, Well in that case I won't take communion either!' We must make the journey to justice together. Please, join us.

Published in the Jesuit publication Eureka Street *in September 1998, a response to a previous editorial piece by Rev Daniel Madigan S.J.*

James: who's to blame?

Many people were distressed by last month's brutal murder of Matthew Shepard, a young gay American student. Yet gay youth in Australia also face high levels of violence and abuse, as a study from La Trobe University reported last week. We also have our own gay tragedies. The story of James Anderson is one.

James was a shy, intelligent, quick-witted young man. A student at a Catholic college in a Melbourne outer suburb, he grew up loving school and showing great promise. In the middle of Year 11, however, James became moody and withdrawn. He started saying he hated school and sometimes refused to go. His mother, Joy, got him to admit he was being 'hassled' and she noted his growing fear and anxiety. At the start of Year 12 he became too frightened to travel on the bus, so she drove him to and from school. At lunchtime he often took refuge in the office of a friendly teacher, but he kept silent about what was really happening.

Halfway through Year 12, James said he could no longer stand going to school, and such was his terror that his mother let him leave and study at home.

Later Joy Anderson would investigate what happened in these months. It seems one of James's close friends had let it slip that James was gay. From that moment he was subjected to vicious and relentless harassment by a group of students. He was verbally abused and physically accosted on his way to school; he had rubbish thrown at him; threats of bashing were commonplace; human faeces were left on his doorstep; abusive phone calls were made to his home.

One day an entire class stood up and moved to the other side of the room when he entered – a full battery of teenage intimidation techniques was brought to bear. One of James's friends says a group of boys forced him to do sexual things for them, claiming that as he was gay he would enjoy it. In the face of this abuse most of James's close friends deserted him. One can hardly blame them. Nothing in the schoolyard is as frightening as being associated with a 'faggot'.

James's teachers told his mother that they saw and heard nothing of this. She is careful not to blame them, but sometimes the tears and anger break through. 'How could they not have known! I sent my children to Catholic schools so they'd be loved and nurtured and cared for. How could they let this happen?'

James completed Year 12 at home and did well. At university he came out as gay, met a young man who became his boyfriend and began to breathe freely at last. As his nineteenth birthday neared, James made a brave attempt at reconciliation. He invited both his new friends and old school friends to a party to celebrate his new life. Only one of his old friends turned up. James was finally defeated. Two weeks later, in September last year, he fitted a hose to the exhaust pipe of his car and ended his life. He left behind a list of all the people he had been close to. The names of those who rejected him had been crossed off.

Homophobia killed James Anderson. It is also behind countless other youth suicides, often masked by terms like depression, low self-esteem, social isolation, and family problems. Repeated studies by universities in North America, Europe and Australia show that gay-related suicides account for around 30 per cent of youth suicides, and that gay youth are between 2.5 and five times more likely to attempt suicide than heterosexual youth. In rural areas the picture is even worse.

How has society responded? Earlier this year the Institute of Family Studies surveyed 853 youth-suicide prevention projects in this country. Only 300 mentioned the gay issue and only 12 addressed it in their programs. Last year the then Family Services Minister, Judi Moylan, censured one such project in Perth that used a poster to reach gay youth at risk. Beneath a photo of two fully clothed young men kissing, it carried a simple message for youth who thought they might be gay. Moylan said this was 'promoting homosexuality' and banned the poster.

At a Catholic Education Conference two years ago, organisers prevented students from presenting a role-play about a gay student contemplating suicide. Other issues were allowed, but this was deemed 'inappropriate'. Earlier this year, Melbourne teachers reported that in-service programs on youth suicide did not even mention the gay issue. Perhaps worst of all, at an August meeting with the Victorian Shadow Minister for Education, Bruce Mildenhall, many teachers spoke of their fear of being seen as 'too supportive' of gay students, or 'too concerned' about gay issues. They knew their jobs and careers would be in jeopardy. And so gay students are deprived of the role models and advisors they desperately need. Victoria, like most states, has no systematic programs in schools to address homophobia among students or staff.

Despite the gains made by lesbian and gay people in the past few decades, homophobia still infects families, schools, churches, and social and political structures. The death of James Anderson, and of so many like him, raises questions that demand honest responses from us all.

'How can they not have known? How could they let this happen?' This is the cry of one grieving mother. May it confront everyone who claims to care for young people.

This article was written with the support of Mrs Joy Anderson. It was published on the Opinion page of The Age *in November 1998.*

Ash Wednesday and the tears of things

There is a church in New York City that is situated right near the end of one of the subway lines. Every year on Ash Wednesday one of the old priests would dress in his purple vestments, take a huge bowl of ashes, and stand on the bottom step in front of the church. Morning and evening rush hours were his favourite times. Hundreds of New Yorkers would take a moment off from the frenzied pursuit of happiness to stand quietly and have their foreheads marked with the traditional cross of ashes, and to hear the old words, 'Remember that thou art dust, and unto dust thou shalt return'. One year the priest actually went down the subway escalators and 'ashed' scores of people as they came through the turnstiles. Another time a bus driver pulled up in front of the church, opened the doors and called out, 'Come on, Father!' So on to the bus he hopped, then went down the aisle anointing everyone with ashes. Over the years he became something of a fixture, and every February people of all faiths and none would look out for him, with his purple and his ashes, and accept his sombre blessing. Executives and housewives, beggars and gang members, prostitutes and office workers, cab drivers and artists, the fashionable and the forgotten – all would line up together to receive the holy ashes.

Sometimes, it's the eccentrics who teach us about faith. This old priest broke all the rules. There were no scripture readings, no Mass, no prescribed prayers – just the ashes in the marketplace, just the cross and the memory of dust in the midst of all those monuments to consumerism and corporate greed on the island of Manhattan.

Unlike so many religious observances, Ash Wednesday retains a poignancy and power. I don't think it really has much to do with the season of Lent, or personal penance, or even the call to 'Repent and believe the Good News', as today's revamped ritual puts it. I think it's the ashes.

Ashes are a stark symbol. They speak of devastation, loss, pain and death, and our society has no place for them. In a world that glorifies shiny gym machines, personal-power training systems, market forces, ambition, luxury and excess, what can it mean to be marked by ashes? What can a ritual of ashes possibly say to people of our time?

Behind our facades and all our bright striving, every one of us knows the taste of ashes. Broken hearts, crushed dreams, grief, tragedy, anguish and despair – these are part of the stuff of life. Somehow, the ashes honour the dark paths we all must walk, somehow they tell the truth. They cut through the hype, vanity and pretence and allow us to be human. We receive them almost with relief, like a sigh of understanding, a secret handshake, a tear shed for someone else's pain that we know is also our own. We all suffer. We are all broken. The ashes tell our story.

The black ashes also honour those who live and die in the long shadows cast by our Grand Civilisations. The families scavenging on rubbish dumps in Manila, the Brazilian street kids being exterminated, the nuns tortured in Tibet, our own Stolen Generation, the prisoners who go from ghetto to death row in the USA, the women in sweatshops, the gay youth bashed to death, old people living in loneliness, abandoned by their busy families – these are the people of the shadows and the ashes. If we dare to receive the mark of the ashes we must do so in solidarity with them, and we must commit ourselves to getting our hands dirty, not just our foreheads. Receiving the ashes is – or should be – a profoundly revolutionary act, both personally and communally, not simply an act of private piety.

Finally, the ashes speak of death. We worry about our personal deaths, of course, but we need to look around! Countless living species are being lost every year in this, one of the greatest eras of extermination in the earth's history. The ashes demand that we grow up, face this awesome planetary dying and ask what really matters in our living.

These have been hard words, but then Ash Wednesday is hard. The old philosophers spoke of the *lacrimae rerum*, the tears in the very nature of things. The holy ashes honour these tears. They draw us, heart and soul, into life's deep weeping. They teach us to work and to wait, there amid the tears and the ashes, for the gentle, inevitable dawning of hope.

This essay was published in The Age *as a Faith column in February 1999, just a few days before Ash Wednesday.*

Over the rainbow

Tomorrow morning, in St Patrick's Cathedral, I will be refused Holy Communion. I will be wearing a brilliant, rainbow-coloured sash, and standing up for myself as a gay man. Because of this, I will be denied the body of Christ, the sacred meal of God's people.

Wearing the rainbow sash is hard work, and we do not wear it just for ourselves. I think of Catholic kids trying to sort out their sexuality, of gay people who've suffered breakdowns or committed suicide, of all who've had their hearts broken by the church.

Amid the hostility, support and misunderstanding we routinely face, there is one question that is asked by people on every side: how can anyone bring together Catholic faith and gay sexuality?

The answer lies in the living. I have been a member of the church from the day I was born. My mother says she secretly baptised each of her children the moment we were put into her arms in the hospital, using a glass of water on her bedside table.

She also tells me I was three years old when I first announced I was going to be a priest. At five, I remember my parents taking me through the midnight darkness to my first Easter vigil. When choir and organ and bells burst forth into the 'Gloria' of Easter, I closed my eyes and imagined Jesus rising from the tomb that very moment.

I was entranced, God-struck, seduced into a life-long love affair – not with the church, but with the Mystery that the church, like a finger pointing to the moon, is meant to lead us towards. Still, with its ritual, music, incense, symbols and sacred teachings, the church awakened my spirit, giving me my 'mother tongue' of the mystery, my 'native language' of the silence of God.

The language of faith filled Catholic primary schools in the early 1960s, and I soaked it all in. I loved being an altar boy, and I remember sweating religiously under my robes as I followed Father Coughlan round the Stations of the Cross on sweltering February nights in Lent. Old parishioners used to whisper: 'I think that lad has a vocation.' I didn't doubt it for a minute.

This sense of vocation deepened in Year 8, when I fell in love with St Francis of Assisi, who became my hero, inspiration and guide. Through St Francis, I absorbed a spirituality of the heart that was radical and demanding, yet joyous and free; filled with beauty and delight, yet identified with the oppressed; grounded in simple integrity, yet strong enough to challenge the corruption of the Catholic Church at its very core.

This was a potent brew for a boy of thirteen. It also became the foundation for the Catholic faith that sustains me today.

At seventeen, I joined the Franciscans. Two years later, I took off the brown habit, returned home dazed, disillusioned with formal religious life, defeated by another force that no pious structures could keep in check. That force was, of course, my sexuality.

My Catholic faith had left me completely unprepared for the sheer power and pleasure of sexual energy. For me, as for any unmarried person, every sexual feeling, thought or act was a potential mortal sin that could sever my relationship with God and send me to hell if it were wilfully enjoyed. And so I fought and struggled against every sexual impulse.

This battle blighted my teenage years, but it was in the enclosed hothouse atmosphere of the Franciscan novitiate that the tension between my faith and my sexuality began tearing me apart. Eventually, seeing no way forward out of impasse and facing despair, I left the order.

Within six months, I was plunged into a crisis of faith. Not knowing who I was, or what I believed, I took refuge in one word – *fiat* – which became my life's touchstone. It is a Latin word meaning 'yes' or 'let it be', and, for me, it expressed a stripped-down, essential faith in the goodness of being alive, a 'yes' to whatever would come.

I know now that this word is at the core of Christian faith, and when the structures of religion collapse, as they must if faith is to truly mature, this core remains – the one thing necessary.

During this year I worked as a factory hand and a shipping clerk, and though I gradually made my way back to the church I would never see it in the same way again. I had touched my own truth.

For the next thirteen years I worked in Catholic secondary schools, teaching religion, running retreats, directing musicals, pouring myself into school life. I learned to make a home for myself and enjoy life in the suburbs. I also continued my theology studies as a lay student, revelling in the church's diverse, vibrant intellectual life.

Throughout these years, though my faith grew more radical, I remained celibate. It's hard to say why. It's as if I was trapped, as if there was a language I couldn't speak, while beneath the surface of my life, a silent sexual struggle was inexorably crushing my spirit. I would have to find a new way forward; I would have to face the fact that I was gay.

In the journey ahead, I would be guided by one conviction: that Christian faith is about real love and true life. Through 'love and life' I would sift every experience and every church teaching.

When I was twenty-eight I began long-term counselling. Many gay people, having grown up in a homophobic culture, need help to claim their dignity and freedom, but I also needed to deconstruct a religious faith that had opened me to the Love of God, then imprisoned me in shame. A few years later, I quit my job and moved to the Mornington Peninsula to rest and heal. That silent year by the ocean set me free.

In 1989, embracing this freedom, I travelled to San Francisco. During my four years there I completed a master's degree in Spirituality, worked as a university chaplain and let the city of St Francis lead me home to myself as a gay man.

This wasn't easy – I had a lot to unlearn. Yet I treasure the memory of the first time I took a handsome man to a formal dance, the shock of a passionate kiss, the ecstasy of erotic play, the discovery that the blissful bodily aftermath of love-making could lead me into deep prayer.

I treasure, just as dearly, memories of sharing a dawn Eucharist with protesters at a nuclear test site, of helping Franciscans run retreats for people with HIV/AIDS, of discussing the 'Gospel of Liberation' with *campesinos* in a village in Nicaragua called, yes, San Francisco.

Bishops sometimes claim people like me are not in 'full communion of faith' with the Pope in Rome. I am more concerned with being in communion of heart with Catholics like these, for it is love and justice that bind us to one another and to Christ, not rigid doctrinal purity.

It was love and justice that would guide me in early 1993.

A priest in Berkeley had been receiving death threats because of his ministry to gay Catholics, and a local newspaper asked if I would support him by sharing my own story of being gay and Catholic. At the end of a long, intimate interview only one question remained: did I want my name published?

I knew my career was on the line: the church does not employ 'publicly avowed homosexuals' as teachers and chaplains.

I remember sitting in the dark in our chapel, watching the moon rise over San Francisco Bay, and wondering at the paths of blessing and change that had lead me to this moment.

I took up the scriptures for the day, and smiled. It was the vigil of the Annunciation, the feast of *Fiat*, which is not only my sacred word, but the Latin version of the 'yes' the Virgin Mary answered when the angel asked if she would consent to be the mother of Christ.

I read the old Gospel story then prayed the accompanying psalm: 'Your justice I have proclaimed in the Great Assembly. My lips I have not sealed. I have not hidden your justice in my heart, but declared your love and your truth.' The next day I rang the reporter, said yes, and my life changed.

In the past five years, I have lived alone on the Mornington Peninsula in a quiet, contemplative way. I've walked down some rough roads, but I've also found peace and joy and learned to rest in the gentle silence in the centre of my soul. I've remained on the fringes of the church, sometimes drawing people together to create community and ritual that are close to the earth and to the Gospel, exploring new ways of being Christian.

Two years ago, a young man asked me if I would wear the rainbow sash, and become visible as a gay man in the heart of the Catholic Church. The question wasn't greatly welcome – I had no desire to re-engage publicly with church structures.

And yet, as we talked and prayed and argued, I suddenly found myself telling the story of Mary's *Fiat*, and I laughed out loud: another 'yes', another surrender to the hidden God of the road.

Tomorrow is Pentecost, the feast of the fire of the Holy Spirit. Looking back over my life, I can see that it is my body, no less than my soul, that has drawn me into that fire. In trusting my body, I have learned to trust the Holy Spirit, and so I have been led into the heart of life where all is grace.

Tomorrow morning a whole community of people will wear the rainbow sash, confronting the church's shameful treatment of lesbian and gay people, and standing up for justice and freedom. I will stand with them, wearing the rainbow and coming back into my church to share not only my challenge, but my joy. I will call my church to learn new songs of celebration that emerge from the sacred language of our bodies, the wisdom of our passions, the goodness of the earth.

For all of us must, when our moment comes, be free to say the 'yes' we were born to say, and allow divine love to become flesh once more.

This article was published in The Age *in May 1999, as the first in a series of autobiographical essays entitled First Person Singular.*

Light in our darkness

the gift of the winter solstice

A steep, green ridge rises up from the River Boyne, about sixty miles north of Dublin. Some 5000 years ago, an unknown people of unknown faith, for unknown reasons, built a large, stone cavern on top of the ridge, surrounding it with a vast circle of standing stones. The cavern's design is complex and precise. It was built of boulders and large sheets of stone transported from all over Ireland, then shaped and positioned with mathematical delicacy. The design is like a circular mound, within which there is a central stone chamber that is reached through a long, narrow passage. Above the chamber soars a roof of interlocking stone slabs.

Carvings, especially of spirals, cover the cavern's walls. Worthy of particular note is the outer entrance to the passage. Above the stone doorway is a kind of window made of much smaller slabs. Although scholars agree that the purpose of the structure, known today as Newgrange, is lost to history, this tiny, stone window surely provides a key.

The inner chamber of Newgrange is hidden and dark – and never more so than on the long nights of midwinter. Yet at dawn on the winter solstice, a few moments after the gold edge of the sun rises above the horizon, a thin shaft of direct sunlight shines clearly and precisely through the stone window and along the entrance passage. It reaches right across the floor of the inner chamber, widening, and illuminating the whole cavern. After seventeen minutes the direct beam is cut off as the sun rises higher into the sky, and the amber glow subsides.

Whoever the builders of Newgrange were, they loved the light – yet they also honoured the dark. They certainly knew how to work with both. We could learn from them.

Back in the early 1990s, when I was living in San Francisco, I led a winter solstice retreat for people living with HIV/AIDS. These were the days before the new combination therapies, and every week local gay newspapers published pages of photographs of people who had just died. I remember that one cold afternoon we sat around a log fire and I told them about Newgrange. We talked about the fear of the dark, and of pain, about abandoned hopes and the raw yearning for life and love that comes in the night, in the grim angels of loneliness and grief. We talked of how, in our modern preoccupation with light, we miss the richness of night, the depths of unknowing.

Then we lay on the floor and dreamed together, imagining the caverns that sickness and despair had carved out in our hearts. We asked ourselves whether we could dare to feel our way through the narrow entrance passage and into the secret inner chamber. There, in that silent, empty space as dark as the grave, we came gently to rest. We waited, we breathed, we opened ourselves to whatever our personal and communal midnights might bring. The waiting was hard, but it helped that others waited with us.

Almost imperceptibly, the palest greyness began to soften our darkness, and then, in the centre of ourselves, we imagined... light! A thin, sharp finger of sunlight pierced the waiting dark and, with fragile brilliance, illumined our cave. All we could do was open and receive its radiance. Nothing could have hastened its coming, nothing could have earned it – and nothing could hold it. Kissing the 'joy, as it flies', letting it go with thanks, we opened our eyes and sat up.

Quietly, by the fire, we shared our dream-journeys, wondering at the joy and love that only the dark chamber of the heart can receive.

There were plenty of tears and hugs and silences – we all knew some of us were facing dark times ahead. As the afternoon deepened into the longest night of the year, we sang a soft chant about dancing in the darkness, then shared a candlelit dinner.

As the winter solstice returns each year, I remember the words of the poet Rilke: 'You, darkness, that I come from, I love you more than all the fires that fence in the world... I have faith in nights.' I also think of the builders of Newgrange, and of my fellow dreamers on that retreat.

Ancient peoples celebrated this solstice not as the death, but as the *birth* of the Sun, for it is from the fertile darkness of the womb that life comes forth. To refuse darkness is to refuse life. With its beauty and pain, love and loss, Life is forever drawing us into its dance, entering the darkness, opening to grace.

This essay was published in The Age *as a Faith column in June 1999, a few days before the winter solstice in the southern hemisphere.*

What is it about the Catholic church and homosexuality?

When I was about thirteen I went to see an odd play called *Hadrian VII*. It was based on a book by an English eccentric, Frederick Rolfe, who wrote around the turn of the century. The poor man had been ejected from several seminaries, and in this literary fantasy he has himself miraculously chosen as Pope. At a climactic moment in the play numerous Cardinals – one of whom was Frank Thring – processed down the aisles chanting *Christus Vincit* ('Christ Conquers'). Glorious ostrich feather fans flanked the stage and clouds of incense descended on the audience. In front of me sat two men who were not exactly 'straight acting', shall we say. As Cardinal Thring swept by in his gorgeous red-watered silk 'cappa magna' with its forty foot train, I heard one man lean over and hiss, 'Oh my God! I've just got to have one of those!'

Quite apart from the author's eccentricities, the play had the touch of authenticity. Swathes of red-watered silk, forty foot trains, brocaded vestments, ostrich feather fans, hunky Swiss guards in their stunning uniforms, exotic incense, huge jewelled Bishops' rings, all male choirs, solid gold chalices – all these and so much more were part of the daily life of the Papal court at the time.

In this same Church, women were totally excluded from positions of authority, being either consecrated as virgins and robed in black, or consigned to the kitchen and the nursery. The sexual lives of married couples were rigidly controlled, every detail being subject to Papal decree or the 'Tribunal of the Confessional'. Castrati still sang in the Vatican's choir. Boys as young as eleven joined all male 'Minor Seminaries' to protect their vocations. Monks regularly whipped themselves as part of their spiritual practice. The slightest sexual feeling or fantasy – homosexual or heterosexual – could condemn a person to Hell for all eternity.

Now consider this: at the centre of this Church, as God, as Lord, as the object of love and adoration, was the image of a naked man, His arms flung wide open, His body fully exposed. I wonder if all this was connected?

When friends ask: 'What is it with the Catholic Church and homosexuality?' I am flooded with memories and theories, with past history and present emotion. The Church, 2000 years old and 900 million strong, is an enormously complex phenomenon. Its history with sex, eroticism, the body and homosexuality is just as complex. Can one say anything helpful or insightful?

Let's see. We're going to be covering a lot of territory, so for the sake of clarity I'll use three headings before returning to that central image of a naked man.

Virgins and martyrs vs housewives and husbands

Christianity was born in torture, blood and death. The death of Jesus itself was shameful and agonising, most of the Apostles were brutally murdered, and for three centuries anyone becoming a Christian did so with the terrifying threat of martyrdom hanging over their heads. Not only did the early Christians have to make sense of Jesus' death, they had to find meaning for their own dire predicament. In their quest they were aided by the pagan philosophy of Stoicism, with its deep antipathy to pleasure, and Gnosticism, with its condemnation of the body and matter as evil. Added to this was the early Christians' passionate belief that the present world, including the human body, was about to be swept up and transformed at any minute by the power of Christ's resurrection. Present sufferings – and pleasures – counted for nothing in the face of this. Not surprisingly, those who showed courage, joy and hope in the face of death became their heroes and models.

Around 110 AD Saint Ignatius of Antioch, on his way to be martyred, wrote: 'Now I begin to be a disciple… Let fire and the cross; let the crowds of wild beasts; let tearings, breakings, and dislocations of bones; let cutting off of members; let shatterings of the whole body; and let all the dreadful torments of the devil come upon me.' Such enthusiasm proved to be inspirational – martyrdom became the explicit desire of radical spiritual adventurers both ancient and modern.

The trouble is, martyrdom is not always available – even in those early centuries there were times of comparative tolerance. In these periods we find increasing admiration for perpetual virginity as a heroic spiritual call. It was the 'white martyrdom'. The untouched body of the virgin – male and female – showed that the 'present age' with its cycles of birth, reproduction and death was at an end; it recaptured the original state of Adam in paradise and it made the power of Christ's resurrection physically manifest. Virgins and martyrs were Christians par excellence. They were the 'Holy Ones'. They even impressed pagan philosophers – providing much needed PR.

However, the early Church hit a snag. As the exaltation of martyrdom and virginity increased so did the rejection of all pleasure, the fear of women and of the body, and the near-hatred of all things sexual. At the same time, most Christians had always been ordinary householders, most Church leaders were married, and wealthy women had wielded great influence since the time of St Paul. Whatever the radical ascetics might say, family life and civic order had their place.

By the end of the Roman era the Church has struck a fateful deal. Virginity, celibacy and sexual abstinence – even within marriage – are always and everywhere to be honoured and preferred. (Not surprisingly, as early as 304 AD all Catholic clergy were ordered to refrain permanently from any sexual activity. Total celibacy would be imposed more and more ruthlessly as time went on.) However, married lay people could have sex – but only for procreation or to prevent one's spouse committing adultery. They should strive to take as little pleasure as possible in sexual intercourse. Their model is to be the elephant (no, I'm not making this up): 'Out of modesty elephants never mate except in secret… They do it only every two years and then, it is said, never for more than five days. On the sixth day they bathe in the river. They are unacquainted with adultery.'

Although the early Christians did not focus greatly on homosexuality *per se*, condemning it along with all non-procreative sex and erotic pleasure in general, gay people were clearly in for a hard time.

Sacred celibacy and clerical culture

For the past 1700 years every Catholic teaching, policy and regulation on sexual matters has been made by males officially committed to renouncing all sexual activity, and even sexual thoughts. Paralleling this, since the Early Middle Ages the Church has seen the rise of an elite clerical/monastic culture. This culture could offer young men sacred wisdom, but also education, status, secular power, high culture, the company of like-minded males, security – and exotic costumes. This culture gradually became virulently, outspokenly homophobic – almost as if there were something to prove. Perhaps there was. For centuries saints and theologians would rail against the 'sin of the Sodomites' which they repeatedly claimed was especially prevalent amongst monks, priests and bishops!

The modern gay writer, Andrew Sullivan, referring to the harshness that characterises the Vatican's approach to gay issues, said recently, 'Homosexuality… is at the very heart of the hierarchy, so every attempt to deal with it is terrifying'. It's terrifying, I'd also suggest, not just because so many Catholic clergy are themselves gay. Historically, the hierarchy's prestige and sacred power has come to depend upon their being seen as renouncing sex, as being 'above sex', as being 'the Holy Ones'. Associating with women could be strictly controlled but in this all-male society sexual feelings for other men were always lurking – even for straight clerics (just like in prisons or in the military). The denunciations of homoerotic feelings had to be strenuous to throw the married laity 'off the scent', but also to convince the clerics themselves. The old Shakespearian saying, 'the lady doth protest too much' has never been more apt.

Ultimately, this culture of 'sacred celibacy' produced the rigid, homophobic, misogynistic, high-camp Church that so fascinated the author of *Hadrian VII*.

New changes and old fears

No institution, not even the Catholic Church, could have survived the turmoil of the twentieth century without change. (Those forty foot trains have gone, the ostrich feather fans are packed away, and the Papal tiara – a triple tiara, actually – is now defunct.) The hierarchy has not relinquished its 'right' to regulate the details of everyone's sex life, but in the past forty years even sexual teachings have progressed – despite the propaganda that Catholic teaching doesn't change. For the first time in history sexual intercourse is said to have a dual purpose: both procreation and the unitive love of the couple. Spouses are allowed to enjoy pleasure in the sexual act – provided it is 'sober and moderate'(!). Infertile couples are finally allowed to marry and have sex, and fertile couples may make use of the woman's infertile periods to actually avoid conception! (St Augustine called such people 'adulterers' and 'whoremongers' – my, how things change!)

Despite some softening in the Church's position, however, homosexuality remains 'an orientation to intrinsic moral evil', and every official document condemns all homosexual activity in whatever circumstances. For us there is to be no sex, no pleasure, no marriage – and, it now seems, no Holy Communion if we come forward proclaiming our orientation. The Church calls for 'compassion, sensitivity and respect' for us, but sacks lesbian teachers, seeks to limit our civil rights and silences theologians who support us. What is the problem?

Hopefully our quickstep through Church history will have indicated some possible reasons for this continuing hardness of heart, yet I suspect there remains another ancient fear.

At the centre of traditional Catholic devotion is that naked, vulnerable man – the Crucified Christ. The deepest longings of the heart and of the soul are to be centred on this man, upon intimate, loving union with this man. It is a profoundly erotic image. I think of a scene from the film Priest where the young gay curate, Father Greg, is striving to repress his sexual urges. Tortured and desperate, he argues with God: 'I turn to Christ for help, and what do I see? A naked man, utterly desirable!' I wonder if the Catholic hierarchy's bitter, enduring homophobia is a measure of its inability to face the erotic allurement, the sensuality, the scandal of this most physical, most vulnerable God – even as they adore Him.

I used to teach religious education to Year 12 students in Catholic schools. Every year I would ask them to tell me about the physical characteristics of Jesus. They were fine with the long hair and the beard, but became markedly uncomfortable around issues like his digestive and reproductive systems. Something in Catholicism had inculcated distaste, even shock in these twentieth century students when confronted with the raw, physical, sexual humanity of Christ. Some flatly refused to accept it. We hear echoes, here, of that ancient distaste for the body – as if God couldn't be so tacky as to become truly human. We also encounter the enduring fear of mixing the sacred with the sexual, despite the fact that this is exactly what happened in Jesus.

And so we see the Church focus on the 'Virgin Birth', the 'Glorious, Risen Body of Jesus', and the exaltation of suffering, self-denial and sacrifice – anything but a joyous embrace of embodied life and physical pleasure.

It is no secret that many great Churchmen throughout history would have liked to have forbidden sex altogether, but the realities of human biology defeated them. They had to find a way to 'justify' procreative sex. When it came to lesbian and gay people, however, no such concessions were needed, and so the full force of the Church's sexual negativity – combined with the bitter energy of repressed erotic desire – fell upon us. It still does. In oppressing us, I believe, the Church betrays its inability to accept its own teaching that 'God became fully human in Jesus'. We could teach the Church much about being fully human – about pleasure, erotic delight, sensuality, play – about the sheer enjoyment of physical being in all its earthy goodness. No 'justification' is needed, except the grace of living itself! We are a gift to the Church, whether it can cope with us or not.

Modern gay and lesbian Catholics are inheritors of an extraordinary, shameful, holy tradition. We are also its victims. We need to break free, to live our lives with imagination and daring, to find life in ways that were impossible for our ancestors. Hopefully articles like this, for all their brevity, can help us make some sense of the past, find freedom in the present, and re-shape the future. The Church – the 'Body of Christ' – has been sexually sick for a very long time, and the sickness is especially acute in the area of homosexuality. This sickness has infected the whole of Western society, distorting and souring the way we treat ourselves, one another and the Earth. If there is to be any healing then it must begin with lesbian and gay Catholics, with an opening to the deep truth of our lived experience.

It's quite a vocation! May all the lesbian and gay saints – virgins and martyrs, housewives and husbands, dreamers and lovers – come to our aid!

Campaign Magazine, Sydney, October 1998.

Out of great evil, grace

'I need to know. What do you teach about redemption?'

The question came as a shock to me. The man voicing it had sat quietly all evening, his elbows resting on the arms of his chair, his hands clasped in front of his mouth.

'I did three terms of service in Vietnam. I volunteered for them. I was a trained torturer and an assassin.' His voice began to break, his knuckles whitening. 'I've watched the life draining from the eyes of men as I tortured them to death. I've seen how precious life is. I've held it in my hands.' He wept silently, tensely. 'Somehow – God – somehow I made it back. So I need to know: what do you teach about redemption?'

Like the other men gathered in this retreat house in Northern California, this man was both a Vietnam veteran and a priest. Some were chaplains during the war, but most had been ordinary young soldiers whose experiences had later led them to faith, then into the ministry. Every year, like so many other vets, they would gather from all over the United States to share memories and support, but they also gathered to pray and to ask, again and again, what life and faith could mean after what they had seen and done in Vietnam.

This year they had decided to invite some theologians to search with them. Northern California is awash with theological institutes of all kinds, yet only one professor had agreed to come. Reaching further afield, they invited the chaplains from a local Catholic University – and the call came to me. It was an invitation I could not pass up. As I drove to meet them, I reflected that so much theology is about theology itself – religious talk about religious talk. Life becomes a footnote. This evening, I sensed, would be about life and raw faith, but nothing prepared me for what was to come.

As the priest asked his question, the room was still and silent. I sat stunned. Another man spoke, shyly, looking at the floor. 'I was one of the fifty soldiers at My Lai.'

For just a moment he looked up, straight into my eyes, then down. As he told his story of suicide attempts, alcoholism and drug abuse, I strained to hear it through my own memories. In the 1970s I had taught my students about My Lai, how the soldiers had entered this peaceful village and battered, raped, mutilated and murdered hundreds of villagers at the order of their commander, who suspected that these farming people were Vietcong sympathisers. Old people, children, pregnant women – all unarmed, all 'wasted' and left to rot. 'What would you have done,' I asked my boys, 'if you'd been a soldier at My Lai? Would you have followed orders?' Here was a man who had.

As I surfaced from my own whirl of emotions, he was surfacing too. 'Finally, when I couldn't get any lower, Christ found me. Now I set up halfway houses for homeless people hooked on substance abuse. I train some of the people and when they're ready I hand the house over and start another one.' He paused, then quietly added, 'So far I've started fifteen'.

I looked at these men as they waited for me to say something. I looked at them in horror and in awe. They did not want easy absolutions or cheap grace. These men knew who they were, and they spoke out of a guilt and a brokenness so deep that only love could fathom it. And love had. All at once I realised they were sharing their amazement as much as their shame, inviting me into their wonder as well as their anguish and asking, from their hearts and souls and guts, 'How do we speak of this?'

I hardly dared respond. What gave me permission, I told them, was my belief that the heart of darkness is found in the human heart – mine no less than theirs. They had gone beyond the edge of evil, but they went at the behest of other human beings like them and like me, and now they carried the agony and the stigma and the lesson of that evil. The miracle was that they had become servants of love. Somehow the crucible of evil held the fire of grace.

So much of what passes for religion, I suggested then and I know now, is about 'being nice', about self-justification, about reciting doctrinal formulas and following rules that make us feel safe, righteous and good. Perhaps there is a place for all this, but it has little to do with God. God is found in life, where our securities are undermined and our illusions shattered, where we are forced to face reality, with its terror, beauty and infinite possibility, where we are stripped down to the naked truth of who we are. As the witch Starhawk, condemned by the Vatican, puts it, all that we truly are, but believe we should not be – angry, cruel, vengeful, lusty, rebellious, sadistic, sensual, brutal, proud, lazy, and also beautiful, creative and good – squats in our spiritual doorway, refusing to let us pass until we face our essential humanness.

Most of us, of course, will never be torturers or murderers, but all of us have the capacity for great good and great evil, and all of us have depths in ourselves that we fear to face.

St Cyril of Alexandria addresses this fear simply and sharply: 'We go to the Father of our souls, but it is necessary to pass by the dragon.' The dragon is the truth of who we are. It is only in facing that truth that we discover how absolutely we are loved. It is in that part of ourselves that we most fear, the place of our deepest shame, that the eyes of divine love open and gaze into our own. It is there that God waits for us.

These men have entered that place, and they carried in themselves the grace. I had to tell them that. 'All my life I have heard words about love and forgiveness, about Christ saving us from our sins, about life coming out of death – but tonight the reality of 'redemption' has finally touched me. I am shaken, humbled by the extremes of human experience where you men have walked, extremes where God has met you, extremes where love and truth have set you free. Do you realise the treasure you carry? You speak of what you know.'

I turned to the man who had asked the question. 'You ask me about redemption. You ask, and you strike me dumb. You are a torturer, assassin, servant and priest, and it is you, father, who must tell me about redemption. It is you who must teach.'

Published in The Age *as a Faith column in September 1999.*

Gay and Christian: why bother?

It had been a long weekend. I had been helping lead a spiritual retreat for people within an HIV/AIDS centre about an hour east of San Francisco, and now I was exhausted. A friend had coaxed me into winding down over a long, leisurely dinner in the Castro.

We ended up at *The Patio*, a favourite haunt just down from Castro and 18th streets. As we sat down, an old flame of my friend's came over (people are always running into old flames – or at least brief flickers – at *The Patio*). I was happy enough for him to join us. The last thing I needed was to rehash the weekend and, besides, he had an easy, juicy sexual energy about him. As my friend went off to get some drinks 'Greg' sat down and said, a little saucily, 'So, tell me all about Michael. What do you do when you're not cruising at *The Patio*?'

I took a deep breath. Would I say 'Counselling', as I so often did? What the hell. 'I work in the area of spirituality and religion – kind of helping gay people who are trying to integrate their sexuality and their faith.' 'Oh', said Greg coldly, not missing a beat, 'that bullshit. Why do you bother?' I winced and changed the subject.

Scenes like this are pretty familiar to gay and lesbian Christians, especially those who are 'out' about both their faith and their sexuality. Awkward and painful as they are, there is a sense in which I welcome them. Any gay or lesbian person who dares to remain within the Christian Church must ask himself or herself some pretty tough questions. Is it all bullshit? Why do we bother? Are we colluding in our own oppression? What kind of Christianity is not destructive but life enhancing? Why not just get out and get a life? And on it goes.

I must admit that some 'gay Christian groups' do not help either our reputation or our personal growth. Too often they feel like gatherings of lost children still anxious about their parents' approval. One is sympathetic but hardly inspired. Then there are those covertly 'gay friendly parishes' where you can go each week to get a spiritual fix provided you don't say 'gay' too loudly, don't agitate for justice, don't confront the hypocrisy or the bishops, and don't expect your sexuality to be celebrated or even mentioned. Be nice, be quiet, be discreet and you too can have an active role in the Catholic/Anglican/Protestant Church! Karl Marx called this kind of religion the 'opium of the people'. It numbs the pain of exile and rejection and even makes you feel good for a while – till next Sunday when you can get another fix. As far as I'm concerned this is not Christian, not healthy, not just, not spiritual and not the way forward. So where do we turn?

Let's return to Greg's blunt question: why do you bother? I'd like to explore this and then consider the 'how' – how can someone be gay or lesbian, Christian and healthy?

When you ask gay or lesbian Christians why they don't just leave the Church they will often say, 'But why should I? It's my Church too!' There is a way of remaining in the Church that is defiant, that proclaims the right to a place and a voice, that refuses to surrender to the bigots this complex and rich phenomenon called 'Church'. Being part of the Church means being part of a people, a culture, a network of values, ideals, rituals, traditions, symbols, stories, history, music, art and literature as rich as any that human civilisation has produced. It means being at home in an ancient and worldwide tradition, and also intimately involved in a local community where many enduring and intimate relationships have developed. It is within this context that people have developed their sense of themselves, of the world and of life itself. In saying 'It's my Church too!' they claim their right to belong and to have an active role in shaping and handing on this culture to future generations. Why should they get out? Why should they allow the bigots and the bishops to claim total ownership of the Church and use it and direct it in the service of prejudice and oppression? Why not defiantly claim one's membership and bring into the Church the experience of gay and lesbian Christians? God knows it needs us – and so does the next generation of gay teenagers growing up in the Church. As Michelangelo Signorile has said, some gay Christians 'have chosen to stay in there and fight. They are activists in every sense of the word'.

The key words here are 'and fight'. Simply staying in as a passive agent is a cop out. This 'fighting' can be done subversively, using one's position and access on behalf of gay people, or it can be done confrontationally; but it must be done.

Gay and lesbian Christians 'bother' because they believe the Church has both the call and the potential to be a critical voice for justice and freedom in our society. They are not satisfied with pious, feel-good Christianity, nor are they satisfied with the values of consumerism, materialism, success and individualism that characterise both secular society and so much of the gay sub-culture. The Gospel provides a charter for justice, freedom and authentic human values that continues to inspire both individuals and communities to dedicate their lives to the poor, the oppressed and the marginalised. The Church itself has immense resources, prestige and influence – it still has the clout to call governments and corporations to account. Whether it's the rights of indigenous people, homelessness, social welfare or the rights of workers, the Church has the potential to be a major player – and it also has some impressive teachings on social justice and human dignity. Gay and lesbian Christians want to call the Church to be true to its vocation to work for justice, and they also want to apply its teaching to the rights and freedoms of gay people. Those who think they can ignore the Churches when it comes to justice and gay rights are fooling themselves. Not only is their power too great but their social teachings are too good. Self-affirming gay and lesbian Christians know this and that's why they bother.

Underlying all of this, however, is something deeper, something that has to do with love and faith. In the end, those of us who go through the struggle of integrating their faith with their sexuality do so because they believe in both. I don't mean they necessarily subscribe to every dogmatic formula propounded by the Pope or every line written in the Bible. True faith is more simple and more profound than that. In spite of the hard-heartedness of the Church and the cynicism of the gay community, lesbian and gay Christians have come to experience deep in their hearts, and in their sexual loving, something of the love and inner freedom that Jesus spoke of. In living out our faith and being true to our sexuality we believe that we have known, however tentatively, the gracious, guiding presence of Divine Love. Empowered by this love, we believe in the community of justice and peace that Jesus sought to build; we believe that his liberating Spirit lives in us still; we believe that in deeply celebrating our humanity we encounter divinity. We believe in the Truth that sets us free and the Love that casts out fear, and the Light that triumphs over death – and the oppression of the Church itself has not been able to crush that belief. This, in itself, is a miracle of grace.

And so we 'bother'. It may be foolish, it may be wishful thinking but the courage and determination of lesbian and gay Christians is worthy of admiration, not scorn. We have chosen to challenge one of the greatest and most oppressive institutions on earth, and to critique it on the basis of our life experience and of its own Gospel. That's quite a call.

So, then, how are we to do this? How are we to be gay/lesbian/Christian – and still be truly healthy and free?

There are few precedents in Church history for what we are trying to do. This is a radical experiment. It is not surprising the Churches are unnerved by it – we are as well. However, there is another movement within contemporary Christianity that has also unnerved some major religious institutions, a movement that can teach us a great deal. It's called Liberation Theology.

Liberation Theology

Liberation Theology developed over the last few decades among the desperately poor Christian people of Latin America. They have been brutally oppressed for centuries by political regimes routinely supported by the Church hierarchy. They do not back away from this fact. As the leader of a Christian Liberation community in Nicaragua said to me some years ago, 'The Church has always been in bed with The Empire, but we do what we have to do. We follow the Gospel'.

For them this has meant developing small, radical communities that support and care for one another, that explore both politics and theology, and that actively challenge structural injustice in secular society and in the Church. These communities passionately believe that the Gospel is about fullness of life, experienced, not just dreamt of; and about liberation from unjust political and economic structures as well as internalised oppression; and about human dignity, bestowed not by any external authority but inherent in every person. They claim and draw strength from the constant Biblical teaching that God is especially close to the poor and marginalised, and is always seeking to lead them to freedom. These grassroots communities, loosely organised and frail in many ways, have had such a widespread impact in Latin America that some of the most powerful forces in the world have, for their various reasons, determined to crush them: Pope John Paul II, Ronald Reagan, the CIA and the Tri-Lateral Commission spring to mind – an unholy alliance if ever there was one!

Both the commitment and the methodology of these communities of liberation have much to offer lesbian and gay Christians. It's significant that both groups use, as their central image of freedom, the story of the Exodus from slavery in Egypt – the ultimate coming out story. If we doubt that Christian faith can be a force for liberation we have only to look to Latin America. These people can show us how.

Another place we could look is Australia. Over the past six years the lesbian and gay network of the Uniting Church has held two national conferences, with a third planned for June this year. The titles of these conferences offer us a model for the journey of being gay and Christian: Daring to Live, Daring to Move On, and Embracing Our Strength.

Daring to live

This is the first step. What gay and lesbian people have been offered by the Church is not life, but a long traumatic death. The kind of 'Christianity' we have received has killed many of us – literally – and almost killed the spirits of most of us. Not only have our external relationships been condemned but every hidden sexual thought, desire or fantasy has been denounced as utterly immoral, intrinsically wrong. This ruthless, internal and external oppression in the name of a loving God is an awesome evil. That any of us survived it is amazing. Yet somehow we have dared to live.

This choice was made the first time we risked imagining that our sexual feelings might just possibly not be so bad, that they might be okay. In that moment we began to trust our own inner sense of truth and life, and to undermine the authority of the religious institution. We began to break free. Little by little we started to trust our feelings more, praying about them, testing them, gradually coming to believe that this new-found ability to breathe freely, to enjoy feeling sexual and ultimately to embrace sexual expression was a gift of the God of love. What an astounding grace! From childhood we had been rigorously conditioned to become dedicated servants of a Church that dictated all truth – and here we were, beginning to enjoy life and desire and sex – and even trusting our hearts, and, yes, our bodies!

This is the most crucial step – to choose, and trust, Life. It is a coming out within.

Daring to move on

In this second phase we begin to break through more concretely from the institution and from our old patterns and regimented belief systems. There are no models for us, so we have to try things out for ourselves, experimenting, making mistakes, seeking out other gay and lesbian people, listening, reading, wondering, reviewing everything we have ever been taught about God and life and sexuality. We begin to build a real life for ourselves, with relationships and dreams based on the truth of who we are. We may maintain contact with the Church in various ways, but more on our own terms and often in the midst of much pain and anger. This will often express itself in rebellion, argument and the demand to be heard. There is a sense in which, even in this necessary process, we still define ourselves in terms of our 'parents' and our 'Church', rather like adolescents who are just trying their new-found strength. Interiorly, however, we are developing a radical freedom and there is an increasing sense of the impossibility of ever 'going back', despite our fears and uncertainties.

This period can also be a time of 'moving off'. In this phase people become intensely critical of the Church and often leave altogether, and perhaps that's as it should be. What matters is not the Church, but Life – and often people need to move right away in order to be free to build a future.

Coming out to family, friends and workmates is the clearest expression of this phase.

Embracing our strength

In this third phase we are coming to maturity and adulthood as lesbian and gay Christians, quietly confident of our own strength and truth. While there may still be real anger, it is mature anger at injustice and intransigence. We will challenge both society and Church but we do not define ourselves by either. This centred, inner freedom is threatening to many people and it is only attained at great personal cost. Coming out publicly, or taking a public stance, is often its first fruit.

In this third phase we are both realistic and hopeful. We know our own flaws as well as those of the Church, and we seek to work honestly with both. We become creative and daring in living out the Gospel, and we seek to share our joy and our gifts and to encourage others to share theirs.

What are these gifts? What do mature gay and lesbian Christians have to say?

Firstly, our experience of being marginalised has forced us to critique Christianity by the truth of our lives as gay people, to find out what is essential and life-giving about the Gospel. Simultaneously, our experience of being Christian has taught us to critique society and the gay community to find out what is essential and life giving there. This is our primary gift, however, we also have a good deal to teach the Church about the holiness of sexual pleasure, of earthy, embodied delight, of the goodness of human touch. We can speak about moral and ethical maturity, about taking core Christian principles and testing them in the crucible of experience. We can talk about the necessary messiness of human development, of our varied needs for different relationships and experiences as we seek healing and wholeness. We can talk about a trust in God that leads us out of our families and our Churches to build new patterns of community and of 'kin'. We can remind the Church that Jesus built a community based not on families or 'family values', but on equality, friendship, justice and loving service.

We can help the Church to let go of its rigidity and control, for we know that there is a holy chaos, and a sacred mystery only touched in darkness and surrender. We can bring to the Church's teaching on justice the experience of those oppressed in the name of the Christian God. We can gift the Church's rituals with our creativity, humour and sense of beauty. We can teach the Church to listen before it speaks. We can teach the Church to embrace rather than condemn, to serve instead of judge.

We are a gift to the Church – however hard it may be for the Church to receive us – but we must dare to embrace our strength, and we must dare to speak! There will be a cost to this, for the Church has rarely tolerated those who challenge her. However the struggle for wholeness, justice and freedom is not some hobby. It will ask everything of us. We must form communities of resistance and support, we must seek and live the depth of our own spiritual wisdom and we must honour our own heroes.

For there are, of course, those who have gone before us. I think of that most colourful of saints, Joan of Arc. Here was a young woman totally committed to her inner vision. She cross-dressed, challenged princes, defied bishops and led armies. She was condemned and burned as a witch by bishops of the same Church that would later canonise her. In his dramatisation of her trial George Bernard Shaw has St Joan say these words just before she dies: 'Christ's friendship will not fail me, nor His counsel, nor His love. In His strength I shall dare, and dare, and dare – until I die!'

Yes, it is possible to be gay or lesbian, Christian and healthy – but we are called to be much, much more. May we dare.

Campaign Magazine, Sydney, November 1999.

Francis of Assisi

a saint for troubled times

Who could resist a dancing saint? One day early in the thirteenth century, St Francis was invited to preach before Pope Honorius III and his cardinals. This was an important occasion for the fledgling Franciscan movement and so Francis's friend, Cardinal Ugolino, insisted that he memorise a long, theologically correct treatise, rather than following his usual custom of preparing to preach by praying through the night, then simply speaking from the heart. Francis humbly obeyed.

On the day, the papal court assembled in all its medieval splendour, adjusted its ermine, silk and cloth of gold, and muttered about this vagabond from Assisi who came preaching poverty and conversion of heart. Francis entered wearing his ragged brown habit. His eyes were downcast, his hands clasped, his bare feet scrubbed clean, but bleeding a little from old cracks in his calloused heels. Silence fell. Francis began quietly reciting the Latin text he had memorised. The papal court sighed, and settled back comfortably – nothing to worry about here.

Suddenly Francis paused – for effect, it seemed. The pause went on, and on, and on. The Pope cleared his throat a little too loudly, the cardinals exchanged glances from under their big red hats. Ugolino frowned. Francis had forgotten the sermon.

All at once laughter broke the silence. Francis was laughing at himself. As he laughed he began to pray, and as he prayed he began to praise God in earthy Italian, and as he praised he began to preach about God's love, and as he preached, he began to dance. He threw his arms in the air and turned and twirled and dipped and waltzed around the room as with all the fire and joy of his being he danced the sermon of his life. The Pope and his cardinals wept, pierced to the heart.

Most of us know St Francis through reciting his 'Peace Prayer', seeing his statue standing in bird baths, or pondering images of a gentle friar surrounded by doves. The real Francesco Bernadone, however, was a passionate, unpredictable character, a revolutionary in the most profound sense. One of the great miracles of religious history is the fact that the church found ways to cope with Francis. One of the great tragedies is the church's failure to embrace his joy, freedom and radical commitment to the Gospel. That challenge lies before us still.

Francis was born in 1182, the son of a successful merchant in Assisi, a walled city in central Italy. After a carefree, pampered and exuberant youth, he began to feel strangely drawn beyond the city and into the forests, the mountains and the silence of old, abandoned churches. Leaving the medieval city was dangerous; its walls marked the limits of civilisation, order and safety. Beyond the walls there were wild animals and social outcasts; yet it was here that the confused young Francis found his God and his destiny.

One day, on a lonely road, he met a leper. A chasm of choice opened. On the familiar side lay a life of measured generosity and comfortable faith. On the other stood the leper, raw, filthy, rotting from disease, aching from rejection, as broken as the crucified Christ. Francis could drop a bag of coins and run or he could cross over. After a moment of panic the young man stepped forward, took the leper in his arms and kissed him on the mouth.

Francis's life became the living out of that kiss. We see it in his embrace of the Gospel, as he discards shoes, staff, coat, money and conventional religious life and sets off barefoot and destitute to preach the love of God in the language of ordinary folk. We see it in his devotion to the peasants, the *minores* whose lives counted for nothing and who were exploited and oppressed by church and state. We see it in his daring love for women, as he helps the young St Clare escape the matrimonial scheming of her wealthy family, meeting her in the woods in the dead of night and initiating her into a life as poor and free as his own. We see it as he boards a ship full of crusaders, travels to the Holy Land and crosses battle lines to reach the very camp of the Sultan – not to attack him but to speak with him heart-to-heart. We see it in his embrace of Lady Poverty, the bride he wed at a time when Italy was exploring the excitement of commerce and the power of money, the lover he would keep faith with to the end, when he met 'Sister Death' lying naked on the naked earth.

Most of all, however, we see the kiss lived out in Francis's delight in Creation. When he speaks of 'Brother Sun, Sister Moon', 'Brother Fire, Sister Water,' he is not using poetic terms but naming reality as he sees it. Every creature was family to him, so he bent down to move tiny worms off busy roads, he preached to the birds and the fish, he danced with Sister Rain, he stroked the ears of fierce Brother Wolf, he tickled Sister Cicada and told her to sing to her Creator, he was always rescuing sister and brother lambs from slaughter and having them follow him around – and, if scores of eyewitness accounts are to be believed, wild animals, birds and even insects responded to him with trust and affection. They knew he was family, too.

Even in the darkest moment of his life, as he lay in agony in a rat-infested hut, he saw joy – not in some holy reflection, but in Creation itself. 'The Canticle of the Creatures', the first great Italian poem, was composed in that hut, a canticle so joyous and earthy that when Francis asked his brothers to sing it to him to ease his pain, he was reprimanded by a severe cleric who complained that this was no way for a dying saint to behave! Francis obeyed, but there is a story that God sent an angel at that moment and she played the violin for him all night long.

To kiss a leper is to become one with all 'lepers', it is to let love lead you beyond status and security, reason and religion, beyond your own life itself. In having nothing and being no-one, Francis was freed to embrace the poor, abandoned Christ, and he followed Christ with such passion and creativity that he inspired a spiritual revolution throughout all Christendom.

In his poverty he discovered that he was at home in the universe. In communion with all creatures he was free to celebrate life as pure gift, springing fresh in every moment from the heart of the One who dances and delights in all that is. It is here that we might find the seed and inspiration for the spiritual revolution we so desperately need today. For in our time it is creation itself, now as broken and bruised as any leper, that waits for our kiss.

Perhaps the dance of the poor man from Assisi can warm our modern hearts. Perhaps the song of his love for creation can rekindle in us a reverence for life, before it is too late. St Francis of Assisi, pray for us.

This essay was published in The Age *as a Faith column in October 1999.*

Kathy's story

why the Catholic church is in crisis

A few weeks ago I spent the day with the woman who was my colleague when I was a chaplain at a Catholic university in Northern California. Kathy and I were comrades in arms in our campus ministry team, both single lay people in our 30s, both qualified in theology and committed to developing a dynamic, inclusive faith community among our faculty and students. Now she is happily married to a former priest, coping with a bubbly two-year-old daughter and building a career in corporate America.

At the end of a long day full of lively chat I asked her, a little tentatively, how she was these days with faith, with the church, with the gospel we used to talk about so passionately. We lapsed into silence, then quietly she said, 'You know, it's a tragedy when someone like me can't find a home in the church'.

She spoke of how a bishop had vetoed her husband Dave's recent appointment as principal of a Catholic school because the Vatican wouldn't formally dispense him from his priestly vows. These days, she said, he is also cut off from the career path his religious order once offered him, even though he is the same man with the same faith – and even though the church is scrambling to find priests to fill the positions he was once offered.

Dave was a Jesuit for sixteen years. His broad experience in ministry was backed up by master's degrees in divinity and business administration. He is still a thoughtful and devoted Catholic. Kathy spent thirteen years in youth ministry and university chaplaincy. Her two master's degrees, both from Jesuit colleges, are in pastoral counselling and organisational development. What a pastoral team they could have been. Instead, Dave is trying to build a career as an accountant and Kathy is working for a company where her skills, and not her gender, will shape her career.

I asked her if she and Dave had at least found a parish where they felt at home. There was one, she said, but the friendly, talented pastor had just left. He had grown tired of the clerical closet, and had come out to the parish then left to marry the man he loved. 'His love and his honesty cost him his priesthood – just like Dave.'

As we shared our stories that night I felt as if we were comrades-in-arms again: she, a dynamic woman disempowered by the church because of her gender and because she married a priest; me, a publicly gay man whose seventeen-year career in the church had ended because I refused to be silent or invisible. Both of us felt wounded and excluded by a church we loved, but know too well.

Kathy's story is far from unique. All over the world, the church is in trouble. In Asia and Oceania, bishops have been pleading for married priests for thirty years. Some of their parishes only have mass once a year because of the shortage of celibate priests, but the Vatican refuses to budge.

In Africa, nuns and priests quietly distribute condoms to poor itinerant workers in an effort to stem the spread of AIDS. In so doing they defy the church's universal ban on safe-sex education and risk being disciplined by Rome.

In Austria, the Vatican imposed the arch-conservative Cardinal Groer on the diocese of Vienna, then vacillated for years after credible allegations emerged that he had a long history of sexually abusing people in his care. Even the Austrian bishops claimed that the affair was 'handled exceedingly clumsily' and had destroyed many people's trust in the church. In Ireland, the hierarchy has admitted that the sense of anger and betrayal among Catholics has soared, in the face of seemingly endless revelations of physical and sexual abuse by priests, brothers and nuns.

In Australia, the bishops' report *Woman and Man: One in Christ Jesus*, released in August, documented the pain and alienation of countless Catholic women. We read that many have left or are considering leaving the church; that the majority has 'difficulty' accepting the church's refusal to ordain women, while twenty-five per cent refuse to accept it at all; and that women remain 'the backbone of the church', even while the question of women's ordination is, as far as the hierarchy is concerned, closed.

The church in Australia faces a serious shortage of clergy. Statistics show that parish attendance is steadily falling, and morale among priests is 'at rock bottom', as three senior priests in Melbourne told me recently.

Morale was not helped when, late last year, the Vatican summarily suppressed the 'Third Rite of Reconciliation', a highly popular form of communal confession, provoking outcry among priests and parishioners across the country. Then, last month, the Vatican banned the Sisters of Charity from opening a safe injecting room for addicted drug users in Sydney, dismissing both the sisters' requests for dialogue and the reports of their theological and medical advisers.

Now it emerges that Father Bill Uren, president of the Catholic Moral Theologians Association of Australia, has been gagged by church authorities. Uren, a former provincial of the Jesuits, publicly criticised the Vatican's intervention in Sydney. In 1994, he was outspoken in his criticisms of a Vatican statement banning discussion of women's ordination, and clashed publicly with then Bishop George Pell.

This new move, which will effectively silence Uren, will cause widespread dismay, but he is only the latest in a long line of priests, nuns, theologians and even bishops who have been disciplined for refusing to toe the Vatican line.

Catholics all around the world are calling for change, but in the monarchical system of power that now dominates this church of one billion people, there is no process that compels the men at the top to listen. Pope John Paul II, despite his daring actions and profound words in support of human freedom, and despite the teaching of the Second Vatican Council calling for openness to the modern world, dialogue and collegial sharing of power, has centralised church power more than ever, stifled debate and forced the church into rigid stances on many pressing issues.

This has placed the church under immense strain. For this is the age of the most educated and articulate Catholic community in history, of democracy and civil rights, feminism and gay liberation, of astonishing developments in science and technology, of previously unimagined potential as well as deep social and environmental chaos.

An institution that responds to the times not with imagination but with dogma and control, that alienates its own most committed members, denies authority to women and silences critics, that refuses to face its own sin and sickness, that preaches love and justice while wielding power like a club, is surely in crisis.

It is said that times of crisis are also times of new and profound possibility. Perhaps, but it will not be the men of the Vatican who will seize the day that is already dawning upon the church. That will have to be done by Kathy and Dave, by that gay priest and his lover, by the Sisters of Charity, by all who believe in the gospel and in the vision of a community of love and justice that Jesus gave his life to bring into being.

This means that we will have to grow up spiritually – something our religious upbringing never taught us. It will mean refusing to be caught in the patterns of power and submission that have blighted Catholic life for centuries. It will mean speaking out, taking risks, casting off the mantle of the 'simple faithful' and claiming our dignity and freedom.

Above all, it will mean standing together, empowered by the motto of the Sisters of Charity: 'The Love of Christ Urges Us!'

Published in The Age *as a Faith column in November 1999.*

How a sorry church still destroys so many lives

No serious historian could deny that the Catholic Church's history of dealing with homosexual people has been bloody and brutal. It has also been bereft of the 'compassion, sensitivity and respect' that modern Catholic leaders claim to offer homosexuals. A formal apology, after many centuries of condemnation and persecution, would seem to be the least gay people could expect from today's more enlightened church.

And yet, as church leaders prepared the recent papal apology and looked back over twenty centuries of bigotry perpetrated in the name of Christ, they could not find it in their hearts to say sorry to gay folk. Why was this?

It is important to note that the papal apology was prepared in a climate of anxiety and conflict. It's no secret that many powerful cardinals and bishops were disturbed, even alarmed, by the whole idea. Their concern was that an apology might undermine church authority, give ammunition to the church's critics and call into question policies the church leadership has no intention of changing.

Despite all this, Pope John Paul II went ahead, determined to use repentance as a way to cleanse the church and prepare it for the third millennium. However, unless the church learns to admit and address its oppression of lesbian and gay people its apologies will be hollow and its future blighted by injustice.

Today the Catholic Church no longer advocates execution by fire for homosexuals. It no longer tortures or imprisons us, claims we are corrupted by demons, or condemns our love-making as more sinful then rape, incest, or murder. However, its oppression is real and it still destroys people's lives. What does this oppression look like today?

In 1986, the Vatican issued a crucial letter concerning homosexuality: *On the pastoral care of homosexual persons*. Despite incorporating some modern ideas and affirming the dignity of homosexual persons, this document declared the 'condition' to be an

'objective disorder' and an 'orientation to intrinsic evil'. It condemned gay relationships, no matter how committed or loving, and stated that when homosexuals seek a legal protection for 'behaviour to which no-one can have any conceivable right, then neither the State nor the church should be surprised when violent and irrational reactions increase'.

This document caused outrage throughout the Catholic world. Yet in Australia the gay question has only recently gained prominence within the church, perhaps because gay Catholics here have tended to accept the requirement of being silent and invisible – or they have simply given up on the church.

Most of the energy of our church leaders has been expended not on caring for gay folk or on listening to them, but on ensuring the church keeps the right to sack gay employees. The Catholic Church, which is Australia's largest private employer, has fought several expensive legal battles to ensure that it will never have to employ gay or lesbian people in any capacity – even as cleaners or truck drivers. The church's huge network of schools, hospitals, welfare agencies and community services, most of which are overwhelmingly funded by public money, are exempt from anti-discrimination legislation – so if a lesbian teacher or gay gardener comes out they can be sacked.

The real hypocrisy in all this is that the church leaders know they have plenty of gay employees who are doing good work. It's just that the secret needs to be maintained, the blanket condemnations need to be protected from the threat posed by honesty.

The same fear of honesty infects that clergy, which, as international studies repeatedly show, includes a disproportionately high number of closeted gay men. No church law officially prevents them from coming out, but church culture is rigidly opposed to such openness.

Church culture has also kept silent about the suffering of gay youth in Catholic schools. Every teacher knows that to tell young people who may be gay that they have a disordered orientation towards intrinsic evil, and they may never look forward to sexual and emotional intimacy is a recipe for despair. Teachers also know that it's hard to counteract homophobic bullying when church leaders seem to be standing with the bullies.

In Melbourne last year, for example, when the Rainbow Sash Movement sought to draw attention to the suffering of gay Catholic youth, our Archbishop responded by claiming that homosexual sex was a more grave health hazard than smoking. He also accused gay people of the 'recruitment' and 'seduction' of youth, and endorsed a group that encourages gay youth to seek conversion therapies so they can become heterosexuals.

For all this, however, it could be that the Catholic hierarchy's greatest crime against gay people in our age is its worldwide ban on education in using condoms for safer sex. The church's vast international networks are officially required to oppose condom use. Countless millions of lives may be lost to AIDS, but Catholic ideology is kept pure and intact.

The Pope and the bishops of the Catholic Church cannot and will not apologise to lesbian and gay people, because they are still actively engaged in our oppression. The Pope's Jubilee apology is a tragic, wasted opportunity for true conversion of heart among those who claim to follow the man who said, 'Whatever you do to the least of these my brethren, you do to me'.

May God forgive them.

This article was published on the Opinion page of The Age *in March 2000, a few days after the Ash Wednesday service of repentance, which was organised and led by Pope John Paul II in St Peter's Basilica, Rome, to mark the Millennium.*

Jesus gloried in a woman's touch

One quiet evening, just two days before the Passover, some of Jesus' friends gave a dinner for him in a town called Bethany. A woman Jesus loved came to him there, bringing with her an alabaster jar of precious ointment.

She knelt before Jesus, then broke open the jar, pouring out its entire contents and lavishly anointing his head and feet. The fragrance of the ointment filled the whole house. This woman then let down her hair – something a decent Jewish woman would never do in public – and with it she gently wiped his feet.

Jesus, reclining on a low couch in the customary way of his time, closed his eyes, breathed in the sweet perfume, surrendered his body to the tenderness of this woman's touch, and opened his heart to her intimate and extravagant devotion.

Some of those present were shocked. They reproached the woman, and complained that the ointment, which was worth some 300 days' wages, should have been sold and the money given to the poor.

'Do you really care so much for the poor?' said Jesus quietly. 'You have the poor with you always, and you can do good for them whenever you wish. You will not always have me.' He sat up and took the woman's fragrant hands in his. 'This woman has done a very beautiful thing to me. She has done all she could. She has anointed my body beforehand for burial. And truly I say to you, wherever throughout the whole world the Good News is preached, what she has done will be told also, in remembrance of her.'

Tomorrow most of the Christian world will begin Holy Week: eight days of solemn prayer and ritual commemorating the passion, death and resurrection of Jesus Christ. In the midst of all the ceremony, from the dried-out bits of cypress and palms that we will carry around on Palm Sunday, to the stripping of the altars on Good Friday, to the kindling of fire in the darkness of the Easter Vigil, the simple story of the woman who anointed Jesus' feet will be largely overlooked.

There will be no sacred ritual, no solemn commemoration, no hallowed way of fulfilling Jesus' command to remember her tender act of love. I think this is a tragic mistake. I also think it is telling and, perhaps, not entirely accidental.

The story that I have retold, and just slightly re-imagined, was clearly important to the Gospel writers and to the early Church. In differing forms, and with certain variations, this story appears in all four Gospels. This is itself highly significant, given that some of Christianity's best-loved stories –such as the journey of the Three Wise Men, the Prodigal Son and the Good Samaritan – only make it into one Gospel, let alone four. It is the two oldest accounts of the anointing, those of Mark and Matthew, that record Jesus' solemn command to forever remember and retell this story, a command which is almost unique in the Gospel tradition – paralleled only by his command that his followers share bread and wine 'in memory of me'. All of the evangelists obey Jesus, and tell this woman's story.

In three of the Gospels – Mark, Matthew and John – the story of the anointing is a crucial part of the narration of the passion and death of Jesus. The first two place it immediately before the account of the Last Supper, while John uses it as a prelude to the solemn entrance of the Messiah into Jerusalem, which begins Holy Week.

In other words, three out of four evangelists present this story as an essential part of the final, sacred climax of Jesus' life.

Unlike all the other events surrounding Jesus' death, however, the story of this anointing has long been ignored in Christian theology, spirituality and liturgy. Cloistered monks and nuns have sometimes been seen as pouring out their lives and their prayer, like precious ointment, over the feet of Jesus – but that's about it. Perhaps Martin Luther, in his meditations on the Gospels, offers us an insight into this studied neglect.

Speaking of the anointing which, by any reckoning, must have been intensely pleasurable and sensually rich, he writes: 'The Lord suffered it. He took no pleasure in the perfume for his heart was full of heaviness and thoughts of death. He who knows certainly that he will die on a particular day will take no delight in gold, pearl necklaces and clothes, for his spirit is in deep anguish, because he must shed his blood. But Christ permitted it. He was wrestling with death and took no delight in this of itself.'

Luther's comments tell us little about Jesus, but a great deal about the Church. Preoccupied with death, often obsessed with suffering and the mortification of the flesh, deeply suspicious of pleasure, the Church has never known what to make of this sensuous, even erotic moment in Jesus' life.

Christianity has found it easier to adore the broken, lacerated body of Christ Crucified than to celebrate the living, sweaty, vibrant, sexual body of Jesus – or of anyone else.

The origins of this ancient spiritual neurosis are complex, though they may date, in part, from the religion's birth in the midst of blood and persecution. The effects, however, have been all too clear.

They include centuries of denigrating women, condemning sexual pleasure, approving slavery, persecuting homosexuals, and justifying coercion, and even violence, in pursuit of Christian 'truth'. Small wonder, then, that there has been no place for that woman with her sensual touch and her jar of fragrant oil.

Jesus, by contrast, publicly honoured this woman, embraced her gift and delighted in her touch. He also commanded that her story be told. It is as if he were saying to those scandalised dinner guests, and to the Church itself down through the ages: 'Yes, there is poverty. There is suffering. There is death. These must be faced, accepted and even embraced if you would follow me.

'However, there is also *this*!

'There is the delight of the senses and the erotic joy of the body. There is bliss, intimacy, tenderness and pleasure.

'There is the generous and gracious outpouring of an open heart. There is touch, and there is love. These are grace and blessing.

'It is the memory of this woman's touch that will sustain me through death and even into the tomb itself, and when you tell the story of my death and proclaim the Good News of my Resurrection, you must tell also the story of her love. For I will go forward into death, but her love will go with me, and will rise with me. For love is all there is.'

Perhaps this week, as the Church blesses its palms, remembers the Last Supper, follows the Way of the Cross and awaits the Resurrection, this woman's love can inspire us anew. Perhaps she can teach us to open our hearts and our bodies to the seduction of grace. Perhaps we can learn, at last, to revere the human body, in all the beauty and sensuality of our living and our loving, in the harsh reality of our suffering and dying, in the wonder of our rising to new life. For here, surely, we find the mystery of Easter.

This essay was published in The Age *as an Easter Feature in April 2000.*

End this evil teaching

Today, Premier Steve Bracks and Archbishop George Pell will open the new campus of Australian Catholic University in East Melbourne. This multi-million-dollar development will house several Catholic institutes, and it is a real coup for George Pell.

Literally a stone's throw from his new offices in Victoria Parade, the campus will radically centralise this archdiocese's resources for education in theology, teaching, nursing, counselling and family welfare, putting everything under his watchful eye. There is no doubt this will greatly facilitate his continuing project of imposing his brand of conservative Catholicism on the future of the Melbourne church.

And so, when our Catholic Premier and our Catholic Archbishop meet to cut ribbons and sprinkle holy water, I must confess that I, as a Catholic gay man, will feel rather uneasy.

Last week, ABC and SBS television screened documentaries examining violence and abuse directed at homosexual people. The bashings, the murders, the endless abuse and the threats were brutal, commonplace and shocking. Almost equally disturbing, however, was the way so many of the abusers, both in Australia and the United States, relied on Christian teachings to justify their disgust with homosexuals.

'I am a Catholic!' proclaimed one young Townsville man, as if this obviously explained his next statement: 'It's meant to be a woman with a man, not a man with a man. That's sick. That's hitting material.'

Most church leaders would rush to dissociate themselves and their religion from all forms of gay bashing. However, their actual teaching deserves closer scrutiny.

The Townsville man's claim that 'It's meant to be a woman and a man, not a man and a man' could have been proclaimed from any pulpit in the country. This is what all mainstream churches teach as the will of God and the order of nature, readily dismissing all the evidence of modern biology, psychology and anthropology. Our man in Queensland learned this lesson well.

His second statement, 'That's sick', expresses succinctly what most churches continue to teach. Consider Catholic doctrine, which calls homosexuality 'disordered' and an 'orientation to intrinsic evil', claims that all homosexual lovemaking is 'grave depravity' and says gay relationships undermine the family and threaten the fabric of society. In simply saying 'that's sick', our man neatly summarises lesson two.

It is true that most churches condemn physical violence against homosexuals, at least overtly. Yet in 1986 the Vatican issued an official letter saying when homosexuals seek legal protection 'for behavior to which no-one can have any conceivable right', then 'neither society nor the church should be surprised when violent and irrational reactions increase'. In less-elevated terms, 'that's hitting material'. Lesson number three.

These three lessons and their violent results are inextricably connected. You cannot repeatedly, and in the name of God, present a group of people as unnatural, disordered, oriented towards evil, depraved and a danger to society and family, and not expect that violence will break out against them sooner or later. Church leaders must have the moral courage to face the destructive results of teachings they claim are the Word of God. They must also examine their own words.

On this page last year, for example, Archbishop George Pell repeatedly claimed that gay adults engage in the 'recruitment' and 'seduction' of youth. This is one of the most dangerously inflammatory of all anti-gay slurs. Pell spent only four words condemning homophobia, in a long article that gave voice to some of its ugliest claims.

This man is archbishop of a city where 84 per cent of gay people recently reported experiencing physical or verbal abuse in public places, and where more than 90 per cent of gay-identified youth report being abused and harassed, mainly at school.

When Steve Bracks and George Pell meet to open this new campus that will shape the future of the Melbourne church, I will be wondering what place gay youth will have in that future. Who will care for them?

Some things can, and must, be done.

First, Catholic school principals, religious orders, teacher unions, welfare agencies, hospitals and individual priests, teachers and church employees must commit themselves, whether privately or publicly, to never teaching or promoting official Catholic doctrine on homosexuality. Mahatma Gandhi said that not cooperating with evil is a moral imperative, and this teaching is evil. It must not be given space to do its work.

Second, federal and state governments – including that of Bracks – must show vision and backbone. They should require, as a condition of funding, that all schools, whether state, Catholic or independent, give students age-appropriate and continuing instruction about homosexuality that is objective, scientifically and psychologically sound, free of ideology and based in understanding and appreciation of diversity. (Many religious schools may insist on teaching their traditional doctrines as well, and the resulting discussions should be all to the good.)

Our schools, right across the board, have raised too many homophobic young adults, too many potential gay-bashers. The lives and wellbeing of thousands of gay youth continue to be at risk, and our society must demand that they be cared for.

Finally, those of us who claim to be Christians must educate and challenge our leaders. We have been sheep for too long, listening passively to prejudice and fear masquerading as Absolute Truth. It's time we found a passion for justice, and stopped the abuse.

This article was published on the Opinion page of The Age, *July 2000.*

Christmas letter to Archbishop Pell

Dear Archbishop Pell,

I am writing to inform you that I plan to attend Midnight Mass on 24 December in St Patrick's Cathedral, wearing the Rainbow Sash.

It is possible that there may be a small number of other people wearing the sash with me, and as always we will participate in the Eucharist with reverence and respect. This attendance will be low-key, and we plan no media involvement.

Over the past few days it has been reported that you have written to the members of our State Parliament claiming that plans to recognise same-sex partnerships, no matter how committed, stable and loving, would cause 'irreparable harm'. You went on to characterise these relationships as concerned mainly for the security, economic advancement and entertainment of the couple.

It seems we cannot win.

If we engage in casual affairs you will say we are irresponsible and promiscuous. If we seek to form stable loving relationships then we are living in sin. If we seek to have our relationships supported and affirmed by society then we are causing irreparable harm and undermining the family. If we seek to adopt children, foster them, or parent them through artificial insemination or in vitro fertilisation then we are making children into 'commodities' for our own pleasure and damaging them by bringing them up without a traditional family. If we seek to live happy lives without children, in partnerships that are mutually fulfilling, then we are basically self-centred and concerned only for our own economic welfare and entertainment.

I will be at Midnight Mass, celebrating with you, and with our Church in Melbourne, the birth of the child who is love incarnate. I will be standing up for the love incarnate in gay and lesbian people, honouring our loving, our embodied joy, our delight at being created in the image of God.

I will also be witnessing to the heroic love and sacred devotion shown by the many thousands of gay men who have cared for their dying partners and friends over the past two decades. I cannot believe that you fail to recognise that the selfless love shown by such men, love often grounded in intimate spousal commitments, is holy, graced, filled with the Spirit of God and a gift to our society and our church. If we – you in your life and I in mine – can learn to love as generously, as humbly, as tenaciously, day by day, whether for better for worse, for richer for poorer, in sickness or in health, as these homosexual brothers of ours have done, then we shall be blessed indeed.

So, I will be at Midnight Mass. I ask you to open your heart to gay and lesbian people in new ways this Christmas. You have said so many hard things about us over the past few years – whether the words were orthodox or not, they were often hard and bruising to the spirit. Could you find a way over the next few weeks, especially if the rumours are true and you will be moving to a new role, to speak words that will build up gay and lesbian people – words that affirm our struggles to build lives for ourselves in the midst of misunderstanding and hostility; words that affirm our loving and our generosity and our creativity – even if you cannot affirm our sexual expression; words that will help build understanding and tolerance and welcome for we who are still so often bashed and abused; words that express the tender, gentle, embracing, healing love of Jesus – and not simply the strict rules of sexual morality?

The Word was made flesh and dwelt amongst us.

Gay and lesbian people are words of God made flesh – even within the church.

May you hear these words, spoken in love, in new ways this Christmas, and may your heart rejoice.

I can wish you no greater Christmas joy.

Sincerely,

Michael B Kelly

This letter was faxed to Archbishop Pell's office on 22 December 2000. There was no reply to the letter itself or to the requests made within it. At midnight Mass on 24 December, I was refused Communion by George Pell. In early 2001 he was appointed Archbishop of Sydney.

Could Jesus have been gay?

Apparently, the question is provocative. Comments and letters in the media this week indicate that even asking it is blasphemy, a vilification of Christianity, and a mockery of people's deepest beliefs. The Priests Anti-Defamation League is on alert, the Australian Family Association is outraged, George Pell is being 'kept informed', and even Muslims are appalled – and all because of a play, *Corpus Christi*, that imagines Jesus as a tender, thoughtful and gutsy young gay man in modern-day Texas. Why all the fuss?

Some years ago I taught a religious education course called 'Jesus: Man, Myth, or Magic?' Each year I would tell my Year 12 students about the church's teaching that Jesus was 'truly man', and we would then list some of his human characteristics. The students were fine with the dark eyes and long hair and beard, but things got tricky discussing Jesus' digestive system or male reproductive organs. Some students were embarrassed, some shocked, and a few flatly refused to accept that Jesus was built like a normal man. Something in Christian culture and piety had instilled in these twentieth century teenagers a revulsion at the idea of Jesus Christ, True God and True Man, having to go to the toilet or cope with sexual arousal like any other man.

These students were not the first to feel this way. Some early theologians speculated that Jesus would have perfectly regulated his intake of food and drink so that he satisfied his nutritional requirements without ever needing to urinate or defecate. Some of the desert monks tried this themselves, with sadly predictable results. Even more common was the claim that Jesus had 'perfect' control over his sexual responses, so that he would never, for example, have had to cope with an inconvenient erection.

Most modern Christians would chuckle at these ideas, yet the smell of a pious, shame-based, anti-physical moralism has lingered long in Christianity. I suspect that beneath this week's outrage at the suggestion that we might imagine Jesus as gay is a persistent horror at the idea of him being truly human at all: sensual, emotional, sexual, physical. The same outrage erupts when a film maker, Martin Scorsese, depicts Jesus' love for Mary Magdalen, or a theologian, Bishop John Spong, questions the virginity of Christ's Mother, or when openly gay Catholics line up to receive Holy Communion. The sacred and the sexual, spirituality and sensuality, must never be merged or celebrated together.

Yet this is precisely what happened when the divine became human in Jesus.

The gospels show Jesus as a man who understood and treasured the sensuality of life. Literally and figuratively, he brought the fine 'new wine' of celebration. He loved parties, dinners and weddings, and was accused of being a 'drunkard and a glutton' and of partying with 'prostitutes and sinners'. He responded by saying that the Kingdom of God would be one great feast where the poor, the prostitutes and the ritually unclean would have pride of place. He healed with spit, clay, touch and breath. He cuddled children, hugged lepers and delighted in a tender foot massage offered him by a woman of ill-repute. He taught using images of earth, weather, animals, flowers, birds and house-building. He revealed the secret of his identity to a woman from a despised religious sect who had been married five times and was 'living in sin'. He left bread and wine –those essential elements of dinner parties ancient and modern – as living symbols of his abiding presence. He referred to himself as the 'bridegroom' and called everyone to an eternal banquet of love.

Given all this, could Jesus have been gay? The gospels tell us nothing about Jesus' 'sexual orientation'. They are equally silent about whether he was ever married or ever had sex. What they do show is a man who loved fearlessly and without regard for cultural norms or religious rules. The love he shared with Mary Magdalen was clearly intimate and committed. The people he made his 'family of choice' were three unmarried adults – Martha, Mary and Lazarus – and if Jesus too was unmarried they must have been viewed as a somewhat shocking little community in a culture strictly regulated by 'traditional family values'. In fact, Jesus was always telling people to leave their families, homes and properties to form a new community of equality, love and justice.

Jesus was also comfortable sharing intimate love with men. Two were especially close. John, 'the disciple Jesus loved', would lay his head on Jesus' chest at that final dinner and, alone of all the apostles, stand by him during his crucifixion. And Lazarus was referred to by Jesus' friends, when speaking to Jesus, as 'the man you love'. Jesus wept openly at his tomb and performed for him his most astounding miracle.

A rarely explored gospel story also might reveal Jesus' attitude towards homosexuality. One day a Roman centurion asked him to heal his dying servant. Scholars of both scripture and ancient history tell us that Roman centurions, who were not allowed to marry while in service, regularly chose a favourite male slave to be their personal assistant and sexual servant.

Such liaisons were common in the Graeco-Roman world and it was not unusual for them to deepen into loving partnerships. This particular centurion was well known in the Jewish community, so when he humbled himself and pleaded with Jesus to heal his *entimos pais*, his 'beloved boy', everyone would have known exactly what he meant.

Jesus offered to go to the servant, but the centurion asked him to speak a word of healing, since he was not worthy to welcome this itinerant Jewish teacher under his roof. Jesus responded by healing the servant and proclaiming that even in Israel he had never found faith like this. So, in the one gospel story where Jesus encountered people sharing what we would call a 'gay relationship', we see him simply concerned about – and deeply moved by – their faith and love.

(The history of this story contains a deep irony, noted by Father John McNeill, a gay theologian expelled from the Jesuits on Vatican orders. The words of the centurion, 'Lord, I am not worthy that you should enter under my roof. Say but the word and my servant shall be healed' form the basis of the prayer said by Catholics over many centuries just before they receive Holy Communion. They come from the lips of a man we would call gay.)

So, to return to our original question, could Jesus have been gay?

I believe the answer is yes, but ultimately I don't think it matters. What matters is Jesus' revelation that tenderness, passion, generosity and overwhelming love are the very heart of God. What matters is that lesbian and gay people claim the grace of seeing, in the face of Christ, our own true face reflecting the image of God. What matters is that our heterosexual sisters and brothers learn to see shining in our eyes, no less than in theirs, the light and love of the God we all worship.

Each of us must be able to say to the other, in the words that open *Corpus Christi*: 'I bless you and honour your divinity as a human being.'

This essay was published as a Faith column in The Age *in January 2001. It was later re-published in* Courage to Love, *an anthology edited by Geoffrey Duncan, Darton Longman and Todd, London, 2002.*

Father, I am troubled

the hidden lives of gay priests

One cold Thursday in May I had a surprising conversation on the Internet. I had clicked into a local gay chatroom and was soon swapping messages with 'Bill'. He was keen to meet. I declined, and was just about to sign off when 'Bill' told me he had an unusual job.

'Look, I'm a priest.'

(I took a breath. How do I handle this?)

'Catholic?'

'Yep.'

'Resigned or still in ministry?'

'Still in.'

(I need to go gently here – this man could be making himself very vulnerable.)

'Must be tough at times … so, how do you handle all the teachings and rules?'

'I knew you'd ask that!!! Actually, I'm a traditional Catholic. I believe and teach what the Church believes and teaches.'

'So, how come you're in this chatroom?'

'Well, I've been celibate for 17 years – I'm starting to explore a bit.'

'Fair enough.'

(Now I find myself caught between irritation and compassion – but I have counselled gay priests and I know what they can go through. Maybe I can help this guy a bit.)

'So, how do you cope with your desires? 17 years is a long time.'

'Don't know … go to Confession??? Still working it out.'

'Fair enough … I understand.'

'But I don't try to rationalise what I may do.'

'You just do it and then condemn yourself for it?'

(Damn. Too strong. Lost him.)

* 'Bill' has left private chat *

This story is true, and 'Bill' is far from unique. Gay priests exist. They minister in every country and at every level in the Church. Some of them live in total celibacy. Some have occasional affairs. Some have a committed lover. Some frequent sex clubs and beats and hope they won't get caught. Some of them, like 'Bill', reach out for sexual intimacy through Internet chatrooms. Some of them love solemn ceremonies in cathedrals, and some work in rough parishes, helping homeless kids and getting up in the middle of the night to calm family rows and patch up shaky marriages. All of them have traditionally been united by one thing – silence. That silence is finally being broken.

In *The Age* last year Paul Rogers, a former Melbourne priest who is now married, spoke openly of gay priests, many from conservative circles, who regularly 'get their rocks off' at a certain sex club, then support the refusal of Communion to gay Catholics who openly affirm their sexuality. In a recent ABC *Compass* program a former Sydney seminarian spoke about having his first sexual experience with a fellow seminarian – a story common amongst gay priests. The recent 'Spice Girls' controversy made public a situation long discussed amongst Melbourne clergy, who coined the term to describe priests in the 'inner circle' around George Pell, who are perceived by their colleagues as being closeted homosexuals and who, in the words of one of Pell's friends, Mary Helen Woods, 'love their incense and their dressing up' and are rather 'girlie'. Some of the priests most critical of such clerical camp are themselves gay, but live it out very differently, committing themselves to grass-roots pastoral work.

Some of that takes place in gay bars. I personally know priests who have heard confessions and counselled young gay men in smoke-filled venues in Collingwood. I know priests who have a committed lover, others who live celibately, others who use their day off to visit a certain sex club where, as one prominent priest told me recently, 'you could practically have a senate of priests meeting some Monday nights'.

Stories like these are simply the local version of a worldwide and age-old phenomenon that is finally being discussed.

In 1999 a book called *The Changing face of the Priesthood* rocked the Catholic Church in the United States. Written by Father Donald Cozzens, a highly respected seminary rector and professor of pastoral theology, it was an incisive study of the crises facing the Catholic priesthood today, from paedophilia, to aging, to resentment at the Vatican's abuse of power. It was Cozzens' chapter on sexual orientation, however, that fanned into flame a long-smoldering controversy.

For more than ten years researchers had been reporting that a substantial number of priests were homosexual. However, Cozzens' experience and status as the 'ultimate Catholic insider', as one Catholic journal put it, gave his statements a power that could not be ignored by the Church establishment.

Cozzens quotes studies that found 'from 23 per cent to 58 per cent of priests' and '48.5 per cent of priests and 55.1 per cent of seminarians' are gay. These figures are similar to estimates made by Richard Sipe, the most respected researcher in this field, who was a monk for twenty years then became a psychiatric specialist in the field of clerical sexual habits. In 1990, after counselling priests for twenty years, Sipe estimated that 30 per cent of priests were gay and said that without these men 'the church as we know it would cease to exist'. He went on to predict that by 2010 more than half of America's priests would be gay. Many researchers say that figure has already been reached, and most of them agree the percentage of gay seminarians is higher still.

On the basis of several decades of working closely with priests and bishops, Cozzens says that in addition to figures like 50 per cent, it must be recognised that the percentages are even higher in Religious Orders, and that there are also 'priests who remain confused about their sexual orientation and men who have so successfully denied their orientation that in spite of predominantly same-sex fantasies, they insist they are heterosexual'.

With admirable frankness he moves the discussion forward: 'At issue at the beginning of the twenty-first century is the growing perception – one seldom contested by those who know the priesthood well – that the priesthood is or is becoming a gay profession.'

Not surprisingly, Cozzens has his critics, yet even they concede that a 'significant percentage' or a 'substantial minority' or a 'disproportionate number' of priests and seminarians are indeed gay.

Many of them are also sexually active. Over the past three decades, as tens of thousands of priests have left to marry, the percentage of gay priests has risen and the observance of total celibacy, amongst both straight and gay clergy, has dropped. These were the years of Vatican II, the 60s, the pill, feminism, gay liberation, and the collapse of many of the certainties of the past. Only those caught in a vision of the Catholic priest formed by Bing Crosby and *The Bells of St Mary's* could be surprised that the priesthood, too, has changed. Men who joined 'minor seminaries' in their late teens and made vows of permanent celibacy in their early twenties have found that, in a more liberal era, their repressed sexual urges, chronic loneliness, and the mixed wisdom and cynicism of middle-age have combined to force them to confront human intimacy in ways they thought they had escaped.

Many priests have left, often to marry, and among those who remain there are many who live double lives. Richard Sipe reports that 'roughly 50 per cent of homosexually oriented priests are celibate just as are the heterosexually oriented'.

Here in Australia there have been no statistical studies of gay priests or of sexually active priests, though in 1999 Janiene Wilson, a psychotherapist working in a Sydney seminary, told journalist David Marr that Sipe's US findings are relevant to the Australian context. Extensive anecdotes and 'guesstimates' from Australian priests tend to confirm this observation. This is not surprising, given the similar cultural and ethnic composition of these two Catholic communities.

Information concerning both homosexuality and sexual activity amongst the clergy are extremely difficult for researchers to gather. However, in January 2000, a newspaper called the *Kansas City Star* published a series of articles that showed that in the United States there are at least 400 known deaths of priests from AIDS, and that probably twice that number has occurred – ranging from four to eight times the rate in the general population. In a confidential poll of 800 priests, two thirds said they knew of at least one priest who had died from AIDS, and one third said they knew at least one priest who was living with HIV.

When one considers that many priests with HIV keep their status secret, and that men with HIV are just one segment of a much larger population of sexually active men, it becomes clear that many priests are having sex.

How do such priests reconcile their sex lives with their vow of celibacy? Some think the vow is a just a formal requirement that will inevitably change. Some re-interpret it as an inner commitment to the Gospel. Others see it as simply a promise to remain unmarried. Many of them believe that facing their desires has made them more integrated men and better priests. As a gay priest wrote to me recently, 'some of these men pour upon their communities a warmth and compassion they have learned in occasional life-giving encounters or in the arms of their committed lover'.

Inevitably, some people will be shocked by such comments. Right-wing Catholic groups are already starting to claim that 'sodomites' have perverted the City of God and they should be shunted out of the priesthood and holy order restored. Even some more responsible commentators talk as if gay priests present an obvious and grave problem for the Church simply because they are gay.

Fr Donald Cozzens, honest, heterosexual celibate that he is, says calmly, 'throughout the Church's history many priests, popes, and saints were homosexual in orientation... without question, gay priests minister creatively and effectively at every level of pastoral leadership.' He says that gay priests tend to be 'nurturing, intelligent, talented and sensitive' – echoing psychologists and anthropologists who suggest gay men have always offered their communities particular gifts of spiritual leadership. Cozzens adds dryly that those who complain there are too many gay priests never seem bothered that they are criticising God, who is the source of their vocations.

Homosexuality itself is not the problem. Nor, I would suggest, is sexual activity. The real problem is secrecy.

Historians like Mark Jordan of Emory University and the late John Boswell of Yale have established that 'men who love men' have always been attracted to priesthood and religious life. Such men have traditionally accepted the imposition of silence and secrecy as the price of maintaining a congenial haven during hostile times. We should remember that for many centuries both Church and State punished 'sodomites' with exile, torture and death by fire. Even in Australia in the late 1970s men caught having sex with men were still being dragged before the courts and having their reputations, careers and lives destroyed.

In such climates, sensitive, spiritual young men who felt no particular desire to marry readily saw priesthood as a natural and holy option. Having been one such young man myself, I know that most candidates for priesthood sincerely seek to devote their lives to prayer and service. Most accept the Church's teaching that homosexuality is 'unnatural' and that sex must be restricted to marriage, and most believe the love of God will be enough to sustain a lifetime of celibacy. Some of these men are very young. I was seventeen.

In time one discovers how urgent sexual desire can be, how persistent the longing for intimacy, how subtle the love of God. One either leaves or begins to look around for strategies of survival.

One soon discovers that individual priests live with a 'zone of privacy' around them. Everyone gets along by never becoming too close or knowing too much. As long as sacred protocols are observed and certain beliefs officially promoted, what one thinks or does privately is politely, deliberately ignored.

When one lives for years in a rigid but very rewarding system, as priests do, this arrangement can come to seem sensible. However, over the centuries this wedding of institutional inflexibility with private license has created an entire culture of secrecy, duplicity and fear that has ended up punishing those who tell the truth and rewarding those who defend the teachings, structures and deceits that keep the system together.

This is the world of the clerical closet, where the left hand refuses to know what the right hand is doing, where bishops who vigorously condemn homosexuality are privately known to be gay themselves, where no-one is really surprised when a conservative parish priest dies of a heart attack in a gay sex club – as happened in Melbourne a few years ago. In this world many clerics play covert and complicated games for 'the good of the Church', often doing emotional violence to themselves and to others as they publicly condemn what they cannot integrate in their own hearts.

Mark Jordan warns against imagining the clerical closet as 'a suite of inner rooms sheltering all the gay clergy. There are no well-established rituals or sweeping histories or even enduring networks of support. There is no inside. The varieties of sexual lives in the clergy are too complicated and too compartmentalised'. For every high camp 'lavender rectory' (a term coined by priest-sociologist Andrew Greeley) there is an isolated priest looking for occasional sex at a beat, and another conscientiously striving to sublimate his desires through prayer and service.

The pervasive power of secrecy ensures that homosexuality amongst the clergy is almost impossible to discuss openly and calmly. Those who try are usually accused of sensationalism. Official silence, public denials and repeated condemnations of homosexuality are the standard strategies used by the hierarchy to stop the discussion in its tracks.

In 1995 a dozen American bishops jointly complained that their own National Bishops' Conference was refusing to discuss 'rumours of a higher percentage of homosexual men in seminaries and the priesthood'. Jordan comments that here we have 'bishops complaining to bishops that it is impossible to talk openly even about *rumours* of homosexuality'.

So what has been the hierarchy's response to the work of Fr Donald Cozzens?

After much initial outrage, many bishops are grudgingly admitting that there is an issue worth discussing here. The Vatican is said to be looking at policies to remove homosexual candidates from seminaries – though this could mean the end of the priesthood. By contrast, some Church leaders are claiming that the only issue is sexual activity, since 'celibacy makes equals of us all' and sexual orientation in itself is 'totally irrelevant'.

This has been the approach taken by seminary officials in London after a recent Channel 4 documentary *Queer and Catholic* interviewed Donald Cozzens, along with seminary officials in Rome and England and former seminarians. Faced with an issue that can no longer be denied, the Church claims it doesn't really matter anyway.

Even Archbishop George Pell has taken to claiming that sexual orientation in itself is 'morally indifferent'. This will come as news to former seminarians like my friend Laurie who was told to leave the Jesuit Novitiate simply because he was gay. It will be news to former priests like Julian Ahern, who was refused Communion then marginalised by Melbourne's hierarchy because he came out as gay.

Most of all this would be news to Cardinal Ratzinger, who polices Catholic doctrine on behalf of the Pope. In 1986 he wrote an official letter, authorised by the Pope, explicitly designed to refute those who claim that the homosexual orientation in itself is 'neutral or even good'. It is, he stated, an 'objective disorder' because it consists of a 'tendency to intrinsic moral evil'. On this basis the Church has sacked gay teachers who come out, kept gay priests firmly in the closet, demanded exemptions from anti-discrimination laws, and opposed extending civil rights for gay people.

The 'celibacy makes equals of us all' approach also avoids the fact that many priests, both straight and gay, are sexually active. Indeed, throughout Church history celibacy has been largely 'honoured in the breach'. When the respected Cardinal Seper told the 1971 synod of bishops in Rome, 'I am not at all optimistic that celibacy is being observed', he was stating what bishops from Africa, Europe, Asia, the Americas and Oceania – and certainly Church historians – already knew. It is time this was talked about openly.

The Church is clearly entering an era of confusion and public contradiction in its approach to homosexuality. The hierarchy can see discussions about gay priests as a public relations nightmare, or they can see this as an opportunity to invite the entire Catholic community to re-examine the Church's whole approach to sexuality, chastity, pleasure and power. Whatever they do, the issues won't go away. Modern phenomena such as a free press and an educated laity will see to that.

And here we touch on the fear that underlies much of the hierarchy's handling of sexual issues. The whole structure of doctrines and rules is like a house of cards. The more shaky it starts to look the more fiercely the place of each card must be defended. Permit married couples to use contraception, or allow lesbian teachers in schools, or admit there are sexually active gay priests who are good pastors, and the whole edifice of sexual teaching – which many theologians say has no sound basis anyway – could collapse. The Vatican and its most loyal bishops fear that with it could go claims of sacred authority, infallibility and 'Absolute Truth'.

The Catholic Church is the last great institution in the West that still campaigns against homosexuality. The discussion about homosexuality amongst its own clergy is just beginning. Things could get heated and messy as the sacred closet becomes unstable, and as ordinary Catholics start to feel they have been deceived. There may be accusations and condemnations from within and without the Church.

In the midst of it, I will remember my Internet chat partner, 'Bill'.

I will think of this man who has ministered for years in an average suburb, working long hours with little support and poor pay, keeping his vows despite his loneliness and his horniness – and all because he believes 'what the Church believes and teaches'. I will think of his seventeen-year struggle with ordinary human desires which have been branded disordered and evil. I will think of his tentative search for intimacy. Most of all, I will think of the power of grace, which no ecclesiastical pronouncement, however hallowed, can limit or stop. I will pray for Bill, and I will pray also for myself, that I will see in Bill not an opponent or a sinner, but a trapped brother.

This essay was published by the Sydney Morning Herald *as a cover story in its Spectrum section on Saturday, 18 September 2001. In Melbourne* The Age *published an edited version on the front page of its Insight section. George Pell, the Catholic Archbishop of Sydney, responded by writing a public letter accusing me of 'slanders', 'smears' and 'unctuous vilification' of Catholic priests. He had this letter distributed after Mass in all Sydney parishes on Sunday, 19 September.*

Fire, stone and living faith:

the mystery of transformation

It's late afternoon on a wild, cold day in June. I sit looking out over the stormy bay, watching the night closing in more swiftly and surely as the Winter Solstice approaches, and I find myself thinking about the dark times of life.

In many ways these past few years have been a long struggle for me. I have often felt as if in a dark passageway, with no signposts, no map, and no end in sight. In the midst of uncertainty and exhaustion my old choices have been coming back to haunt me, old drives and desires have been rising within me, and even if I could have exercised an iron will and forced them into neat shapes, I have sensed the effort would be foolish and doomed.

I think of the beginning of Dante's *Inferno*:

In the middle of our life's road
I found myself in a dark wood
The straight way ahead lost.

Over these years I have learned, gradually and painfully, how to sit still and let the uncertainty spin around me in its way, how to balance fragile symbols of meaning on my empty hands before holding them up to the dark and asking, 'is this it?'

Of all the symbols I have played with throughout my life, it is 'transformation' that helps me now.

A few months back I visited my friend Dave. He is a sculptor who works with iron and fire, and he showed me one of his recent pieces. It was a large cube made of intersecting bars of solid iron. At the top of the structure Dave had used intense heat to break open and push outwards the middle of the bars, leaving them to cool into iron flames. It looked as if a fiery force had broken through from the middle of the metal cube, leaving only these twisted, blasted shards to mark its passage to freedom. Dave calls the piece *Transformation*.

It is an appealing image. Who wouldn't want to burst through life's iron bars and explode into fiery freedom?

I remember seeing another image of fiery transformation when I hitchhiked around the Big Island of Hawaii some years ago. Most of the island is made up of the immense mound of the volcano Mauna Loa. Its huge, gentle slopes are covered with rainforests and lush grasses, all teeming with life, all moist and fertile and seductive in the Hawaiian way.

On one shoulder of Mauna Loa, however, the caldera of Kilauea has been erupting continuously for two decades. Years of massive lava flows have added hundreds of hectares of land to the island, however the volcano now forces its lava through underground vents that burst through at the new coastline. You can trek over kilometres of cold hard lava and watch the fresh, brilliant, orange streams surging out of the black crust and pouring directly into the ocean. The sight is breathtaking, mesmerising. Here is transformation in its most fiery, most exhilarating form.

If you think to turn and look behind you, however, you see a very different face of transformation. The whole landscape on which you stand is desolate, hard and bleak beyond belief. You can see huge black solidified rivers of lava that have poured down from high green ridges, spreading out and destroying everything in their path.

Rainforests, roads, townships, wildlife, temples – all have been annihilated as the lava surged towards the ocean. The new land on which you stand is forbidding and impregnable. Here, stretching as far as the eye can see, is the vast and awesome wake of a devastating energy that moves forward without counting the cost.

Transformation can be exciting, liberating and joyous as it frees us from the past and opens us to unimagined possibilities. It can also annihilate the self we knew, devastate the life we had been struggling to build, and leave us bewildered and alone in a strange, bleak life-scape that looks empty and without promise. As unlikely as it may seem, it is only here, after the fire and the glow of change have cooled and died, that the real work of transformation can begin.

In my own life, the process of opening to transformation has demanded relentless patience and mundane endurance, and has brought the deepening realisation that surrender and trust are the only way forward. The empty, unknown land on which I stand, this land that is my future and myself, belongs not to me but to the hidden force of creativity that brings forth both the fire and the stone, the irrepressible, loving force that alone can coax life out of death.

I think of that land of cold, hard lava. Over aeons the persistent, irresistible work of salty ocean winds, tropical rains, microbes, insects, birds and animals will penetrate, split, erode, crumble and eventually fertilise this implacable new ground. The fire and the stone are both, in fact, the foundation of a new rainforest, the seed of a whole new community of life, creativity and diversity – but only imagination can see it, and only nature's blind, patient hoeing of the hard ground can permit its promise.

This is the most crucial part of the process of transformation. It comes without fire or fury, and it is tough, thankless work. How do we live with it? How do we do its work – or better, how do we allow the ground that is ourselves to be cooled, penetrated, broken open and seeded with unknown life as transformation has its way with us?

The old writers say that in the mature spiritual life it is a kind of dark receptivity, an 'active passivity' that opens us to Divine Life. We must let go of all we could have called a life or a self, and face the mystery with empty hands. This can feel like the greatest folly – like we are dying, like life itself is being annihilated in us, like despair and failure are all that is left for us. Yet it is only when we surrender our restless striving that the *gift can be given.*

I remember going to a ritual on St Kilda beach a few years ago. It was a night in early summer and all kinds of symbolic actions were planned in memory of people who had died from AIDS. This being Melbourne, the night was cold, and a rough wind was blowing across the bay and whipping up the waves and the sand around us. All along the beach scores of people were trying to place lighted candles in the sand. Huddled together, we dug trenches, scooped out little caves, piled up sand and shared tips on keeping our flames alight. We re-lit each other's candles, shielded them with blankets to beat the wind, chuckled and cursed and cajoled our flickering flames, trying everything imaginable to keep them alight on that blustery night.

I remember standing up and looking around, and seeing all these people sharing a ritual far more profound than anyone could have planned.

Today I see something else too.

There comes a time to let the flame go out. The wind, the rain, the salt, and the dark night are not enemies we must defend ourselves against. The little flame I see may have its own beauty, but there will come a time for it to sputter and die so that something new may be born.

There comes a time to let the flame go out, to turn my gaze to the bleak new land around me, to sit and to simply wait. 'I said to my soul, be still, and wait without hope. For hope would be hope for the wrong thing.' TS Eliot was right: 'The faith and the love and the hope are all in the waiting.' To wait – without images or hopes – and yet to wait.

This is how to live with the splitting apart, the breaking open, the subtle, relentless crumbling of the self I thought was mine and the life I had been working to build. To wait – like a cold iron bar, like a land of hard lava, like a winter's afternoon, like a man in the middle of his life.

I think of those good people on St Kilda beach that night, struggling to keep their little flames alight. All the while beneath them, unseen, without their effort or intention, the huge Earth was moving through the darkness, inevitably, inexorably, bringing the Dawn.

This essay was published as a Faith column in The Age *in June 2002.*

Silence, shame and shadows

the ugly truth about gay bashing

Who takes 'poofter-bashing' seriously?

The director of the Australian Institute of Criminology said yesterday that gay homicides in Australia are often committed 'as sport'. Apparently this sport is not only alive and well, but young men who excel at it can expect to be treated somewhat leniently by our courts.

In February this year a group of five young men deliberately set out to bash and rob some 'poofters'. The attacks were coolly pre-meditated and vicious. One young man was quietly riding his bike through Alma Park in East St Kilda when he was surrounded, punched, kicked, stripped, robbed, and humiliated before being struck on the head with a machete. 'Let me chop him, bro', let me kill him,' chanted one of his attackers. Two other men at Point Ormond in Elwood were threatened with the machete, severely bashed and robbed. The attacks took place in secluded areas often frequented by gay men – the group knew where to look for victims for their sport.

Two of the attackers were sentenced earlier this week. The one who wielded the machete could be paroled within two years. His mate could be out in eighteen months.

The young man cut up in Alma Park, by contrast, is suffering acute post-traumatic stress syndrome, has lost three teeth and needs extensive dental surgery, has had to move house because his attackers, who took his wallet, found out where he lived; and he was 'outed' to family and workmates by publicity surrounding the attack. He will take years to recover.

Gay people following stories like these – and there have been plenty of them over the years – experience, like the victims themselves, a double assault. First, there is the horror of realising that we are still identified targets for the bloody Aussie sport of poofter-bashing. There are still young men out there who want to batter us and even kill us, just for the violent fun of it, just to prove they are men. There are places we know, places some of us know well, where our lives can be in grave danger just because we are gay. 'Have you heard about Alma Park?' 'Do you know what happened at Point Ormond?' – mutterings like these go around in the community and we shake our heads and fall silent and wonder how it can still be going on. We might remember the last time we walked along the beach near Point Ormond, and reflect that it could easily have happened to us. We start saying 'Be careful' to one another more often, and with a bit more of an edge.

Then we wait for the case to come to court – and so often we feel battered again when we hear the court's sentence. One of the favourite defences used by gay-bashers, and even more so by those whose victim is dead and so unable to contradict them, is the claim that they panicked after their victim made a sexual advance. This was part of the defence used by the two men who beat young Matthew Shephard to death on a freezing Wyoming prairie several years ago, but the principle is also enshrined in the history of Australian law – and therefore can be invoked in certain cases.

In the case of *Malcolm Thomas Green v. The Queen*, finally settled after a High Court appeal in 1997, the defendant explained himself thus, after admitting to police that he had killed thirty-six year old Don Gilles: 'Yeah, I killed him, but he did worse to me.' When asked why he had done it he said, 'Because he tried to root me'. Gilles had apparently made some unwanted advances to his straight friend, Malcolm Green; but there was no question of force. Green smashed in his skull and stabbed and beat him to death with a pair of chicken shears. Police said they had never seen such a battered corpse, a comment which reflects something the Director of the Institute of Criminology, Adam Graycar also said yesterday –that murders of gay men usually involve extreme brutality and unusual violence.

Green's case was long and complicated because of this 'gay panic' defence – but finally the High Court voted three to two to allow the argument that his brutal response to a light touch on the groin could, possibly, be seen as an understandable reaction from an ordinary Australian. This opened the way for him to be convicted, as he was in late 1997, of manslaughter rather than murder. It also endorsed the 'homosexual advance defence' – which can now be invoked whenever a gay man is bashed or murdered in this country.

This tactic is regularly used, as David Buchanan SC, of the NSW Government's Homosexual Advance Defence Monitoring Committee said yesterday. He also commented that if women reacted in similar ways to unwanted sexual advances, 'the streets would be littered with corpses'.

In the case of these bashings in Elwood and St Kilda, however, there is no question of any unwanted sexual advance. There were also no arguments, no pub fights, no family trouble, no road rage. These men simply set out to bash poofters with fists and machetes, and in about eighteen months to two years they will be free to do it again. It is hard for a gay man in Victoria, reading the news stories and driving past Alma Park, not to feel that despite all the 'trendiness' of being gay, despite all our legal advances, we are still not safe on our streets, and our lives are still not held as equal to those of straight men.

Young men in Australia are still growing up in a culture that produces 'poofter-bashing'. The roots and the reasons for this are complex and sinister, but one thing is clear – our courts are not responding with the outrage, the strategies, and the penalties these crimes demand. And so the killing sport goes on.

Published on the Opinion page of The Age *in August 2002.*

September 11

facing the sacred centre of violence

As he walked to the pulpit the Cardinal's robes, red as blood, looked startling against the sombre grey, black and navy worn by a government in mourning. The tone of the televised prayer service in Washington's National Cathedral had been solemn and grandly, soothingly, predictable. Amid the pageantry, the hymns, the prayers for victims and the gratitude for heroes, the scent of sacred vengeance had hung in the air like incense – understated, undeniable, and utterly expected. America, the shining city on the hill, would answer the call of history, defend freedom, uphold civilisation, enforce justice and protect its own way of life – all of which were synonymous. And so the nation's leaders had gathered in this sacred place to receive the blessing of that God in whom America trusts.

Then the Cardinal spoke.

Blessed are the poor in spirit, theirs is the kingdom of heaven.
Blessed are the gentle, they shall inherit the earth.
Blessed are those who mourn, they shall be comforted.
Blessed are those who hunger and thirst for what is right, they shall be satisfied.
Blessed are the merciful, they shall receive mercy.
Blessed are the pure in heart, they shall see God.
Blessed are the peacemakers, they shall be called children of God.
Blessed are those who suffer in the cause of right, theirs is the kingdom of heaven.
Blessed are you when they persecute you and accuse you falsely on my account. Rejoice, for your reward will be great in heaven.

Without comment, the Cardinal sat down. In the brief silence, the shock of these words from the Sermon on the Mount was palpable.

Had he continued, the Cardinal would have read, 'I say to you: Love your enemies! Do good to those who hate you!' As it was, after a polite pause President Bush took the pulpit and, in reverential tones, got on with the business of preparing his nation for waging war.

If it is true that September 11 put religion at centre stage in world politics, we need to become very conscious of the different meanings 'religion' can have, and the different ways religious fervour can be used.

British theologian, James Alison, has written that on September 11 we all felt as if summoned to participate in something awesome, transforming, transcendent – something 'religious'. All around the world people who had no actual link to the real human tragedies unfolding in New York, found themselves mesmerised, magically drawn into an immense vortex of grief, fear, awe, horror, excitement and sanctioned voyeurism. Suddenly our mundane lives, with their petty dilemmas and moral ambivalence, seemed transcended, and we felt secretly glad to be swept up into something huge, something almost holy, something that 'really mattered': an epoch-making, life-changing event that 'stopped the world'. At the core of this irresistible spectacle was a violent sacrificial centre that drew us all towards it, binding us together in sacred unanimity. 'We are all Americans now' they said that day – and who would have dared to disagree?

Alison, however, dared to name this whole process 'satanic': something full of apparent meaning and transcendence, but something that is, in fact, an empty show and a dangerous illusion that 'leaves us all prey to violence and revenge, our judgements clouded by satanic righteousness'.

For a time, he says, this 'sacred centre' holds, and we seem unable to break the spell by questioning sentiments that seem so noble and unifying. However, the seduction inevitably reveals itself, as 'unanimity and grief harden into the militant goodness of those who have a transcendent object to their lives'. Suddenly, it seems, there are those 'like us' who 'love freedom', and 'others' – 'faceless cowards' – who 'hate us and our freedoms'. Dissent begins to be suppressed, civil rights curtailed, the media self-censored, and political analysts accused of treason – even as people flock into churches and wave flags.

Politicians, often with the benefit of clergy, adopt High Priestly tones and proclaim that we are 'called into a crusade' of 'infinite justice' against 'evil-doers', 'enemies of freedom', and the 'axis of evil'.

As the religious rhetoric builds it becomes inevitable that someone, somewhere, is going to be sacrificed – preferably someone 'faceless', whose ordinary, common humanity remains invisible, so the sacred lie is not undone by plain compassion. (Amongst all the images screened this past week did anyone see footage of even one Afghan family torn apart by American bombs?)

Although September 11 offered a profound example of communal fascination leading towards righteous violence, this phenomenon is far from being uniquely American. The roots of sacralised violence go deep into all human culture and religion, for group identity, security, righteousness and continuity have long been grounded in exclusion and victimisation as we shore up 'us' by rejecting 'them'. Here in Australia we have had our own recent version of the 'sacred lie' as our government promoted falsehoods about asylum seekers who were 'not like us', and officials banned humanising photographs of refugees, so they could be demonised more convincingly.

One of the crucial things about 'sacred unanimity' or 'satanic transcendence', however, is that it does not last. It is fake. It fails to grip us completely or to endure. Questions start being asked, critical discussion emerges, people get bored and feel manipulated and start wondering who these 'evil-doers' actually are. In time we discover it is simple acts of human kindness that still move us, not the grand show of 'the day the world stopped' – and we suspect no-one has a monopoly on kindness, the one force more powerful than the sacred lie.

Ultimately, the voice of a young widow at Ground Zero who said she opposed the bombing of Afghanistan because she did not want others to suffer like her, has more enduring power than Presidential talk of crusades.

This brings us right back to the Sermon on the Mount, to the command to love our enemies; and to the murder of a young Jew who challenged the powerful and righteous of his time with a love that would allow no victims, no outsiders, no faceless others on whose suffering culture or religion could be built. To suggest we need to follow his way may seem outrageous in the aftermath of September 11.

Certainly, it may mean risking his fate – which simply means falling through death into the hands of God, but not a God who sanctions wars, not a God of Christians ,or of Muslims, not a God who has anything to do with violence. The God of Jesus is simply the One who is revealed in the plain, ordinary love of people learning to build a new 'us', a new human community without victims, without exclusion, without end.

This essay was published as a Faith column in The Age *in September 2002. I am indebted to Dr James Alison for his reflections on the nature of 'sacred violence', and especially for his essay on September 11, 'Contemplation in a World of Violence', which has been reprinted in his book,* On Being Liked, *Darton Longman and Todd, London, 2002.*

Loaves and fishes in the dust of Nicaragua

It was 7am on a steamy morning in Managua.

Six of us crowded into the back of a rusty old ute and headed out through crazy traffic and comfortable suburbs towards the slums – or *barrios* – that sprawled on the city's edge. Gradually the roads became rougher, the houses poorer, the air more ripe with the smell of open drains, refuse and human living.

Eventually we turned off the sealed road and onto a dirt track that meandered through hundreds of shanties. These huts were typically about four metres square and made of strips of old corrugated iron, broken boards and cardboard daubed with pitch. Each housed an entire family. We learned later that there was no sanitation – except for open pit latrines on the edge of the *barrio*, no running water – except for the occasional tap that serviced scores of families, and no electricity – except for some illegal lines hooked up to nearby power poles.

Children playing in the dirt laughed and waved as we bumped our way into the heart of the *barrio*. We stopped at a little house made of cement blocks. This was the home of a community of Franciscan sisters, and we had been invited for breakfast.

There were six adults in our group, and we were visiting Nicaragua as representatives of a parish community in California. You could say that we were part of a movement that began in the 1970s, as Christians from North America began travelling to Latin America to support justice movements among the poor, and also to learn firsthand about a new way of living out the Gospel which was loosely called 'Liberation Theology'. This particular day would teach us affluent Christians a lesson we didn't expect.

We were to share breakfast with the sisters – and also with eight teenagers from the *barrio*. Ranging in age from twelve to eighteen, they bustled around the kitchen looking excited and all scrubbed up. Over plates of beans and rice we chatted about life in Nicaragua, then prayed together and discussed the journey planned for that day.

With our guide Ellen interpreting, we learned that a couple of weeks earlier a large volcano had begun erupting near the city of Leon, about three hours north of Managua. All the people had to be frantically evacuated as hot ash and dust poured down on the town. Thousands were now living in tent cities with no facilities, no possessions and little food. The teenagers from the *barrio* had spent the past week collecting clothing, food and money to take to these desperate people. The sisters had organised a minibus, which pulled up as we were talking.

I remember asking one young man what response they had as they went from door to door. He replied that in the *barrio* itself every family, without exception, had given something – a bag of rice, a few cents, a piece of worn but freshly washed clothing. In the more comfortable suburbs nearby, however, they were often refused. Doors were sometimes slammed. I asked how he would explain this. He replied, 'Poor people know what it means to be poor. They feel it in their hearts. When they see someone else with nothing they give whatever they have. For the rich it is easier to close the door because they don't understand.' 'Or perhaps because they don't want to understand,' I added. He smiled – or winced – and looked at the floor.

I pushed the discussion further. 'So, now you have these plastic bags full of clothes and food – and some money too'. They all nodded, looking shy but pleased with themselves. 'We have just driven through your *barrio*, and we see that your families too are poor. Will it be hard for you to give this stuff away when you are in need yourselves?' There was a long pause. Finally the young man said, 'That is a hard question' – and everyone laughed.

A young woman named Anna took up the issue. 'Yes, it is hard. But the Gospel says we must treat others as we would like to be treated ourselves. These people from Leon have lost their homes. We don't have much but we still have our homes, so we are happy to give whatever we can.' As the young people murmured agreement, we visitors glanced at one another and thought of what 'home' meant to these kids who lived in the shanties around the convent. I could see that Arlene, a middle-aged mother from a wealthy enclave near San Francisco, was holding back her tears.

Later that day we watched our group of teenagers preparing to make their presentation to the youth of the city of Leon. They were standing on the back of an empty semi-trailer on the edge of a tent city a couple of hours' drive north. Behind the truck hundreds of rows of old army tents stretched across dusty fields, and the humid afternoon air was heavy with the smell from hastily dug sewage trenches. The Red Cross and Doctors without Borders were there, and someone had rigged up a microphone on the back of the truck. Little kids crowded around curiously and their parents moved in to listen.

Our teenagers sang some songs about the Gospel and solidarity, songs well known in Christian communities across Nicaragua, songs that emerged during the long struggle against the brutal US-backed dictator Somoza. Then Miguel, the young man I had questioned earlier, read a story from the Gospel. He read in Spanish but, using my high school Latin and Italian, I was able to recognise the passage. It was the one about Jesus feeding the five thousand. He came to the part where the little boy offers his five barley loaves and two fish and the apostles say to Jesus, 'What is this amongst so many?' I thought of how the boy gave all he had, of how Jesus blessed his gift and used it to feed the hungry multitude, and I started to cry. I noticed that Dan, the blonde, pony-tailed hippy in our group, had squatted on his heels and covered his face with his hands.

Ellen, the young American woman who was both guide and inspiration to our group, came and took my arm. She translated as Anna took the microphone. 'We come from a poor part of Managua. We have collected these bags of food and clothing – and a bit of money – from all the people in our *barrio*. It is not much among so many people, but we hope you will accept it as the gift of poor people who want to be in solidarity with you. These gifts are small but the care in our hearts is great. Please accept what we have to give and let us pray that Jesus will bless it and bless us all and make new miracles of love happen.' The gifts were presented, everyone clapped – and I wiped my eyes.

Ellen nudged me and said, 'Come on. Let's put up the *pinata*!' So we found a tree and strung up the huge, coloured papier-mache star, its middle stuffed with candies, that Latin American kids love to spin and whack and eventually break open to squealing delight.

And so the day ended, with songs sung, gifts given, hearts softened – and children made sticky with lollies. When we farewelled the teenagers back in the *barrio* I thought I would never forget that day.

I was wrong. The passage of nearly ten years, and my own cares, crowded it out. I suddenly remembered it all and dug out my notes a week or two ago. At the time I was thinking about those refugees at

Woomera, our government's 'tough stance' on 'border protection', and the 70 per cent of Australians – many of them Christians – who so vigorously endorse it. I have no answers to the refugee crisis, anymore than those teenagers had solutions to the problems of the citizens of Leon. However, those young people from a Nicaraguan slum knew something that most Australians have yet to face. The people we turn away, the children we keep behind razor wire, are our sisters and brothers, bone of our bone, flesh of our flesh – our family and kin.

We can defend our borders, secure our lifestyle and wall up our hearts, but it is love itself – and Christ himself – that we are shutting out. And I find myself wondering whether God can forgive us – for we know precisely what we do.

This essay was accepted for publication by The Age in 2002, but was subsequently omitted for editorial reasons. In the early 1990s, while living in California, I was involved in fostering a 'sister-church' relationship between a Lutheran parish in Danville in the San Francisco Bay area, and San Francisco Libre, a Catholic parish in an impoverished rural area of Nicaragua. This included leading a delegation of parishioners to Nicaragua, and engaging in the challenging prayer and communal reflection that are at the heart of the movement known as Liberation Theology.

Live without illusions, love without reasons

Across Australia over the past two weeks thousands of people have attended worship services. Religious leaders have attempted to say something about the tragedy in Bali, something of comfort, something of hope. Candles have been lit, wreaths laid, prayers offered, rituals performed. There have been some moving sermons, tender thoughts, and beautiful gestures. Have all these words and gestures, however, had any real, enduring meaning? Has faith had anything authentic to offer in the face of this horror?

A theologian once wrote, 'So much religion seems like a bad cosmetic job on the ravaged face of human existence'. Cosmetics can have their place, of course – as can soothing rituals. They help us to get by and go on, to hide the horror a bit, to bear what we feel cannot be borne. Eventually, however, the ravages break through, and we face times when the suffering hidden in the heart of living is ripped open.

Without our consent or comprehension, life's random agony, unpredictable brutality and impossible pain tear away our securities and illusions, leaving us bewildered and vulnerable.

It is just at this point, when individual suffering could deepen into real confrontation with the agonising, wondrous mystery of living itself, when personal pain could shock us into a new kind of awareness and compassion, that religion tends to soothe us with slogans and platitudes.

One of Michael Leunig's prayers says that in the end there are only two forces in life: love and fear. For all its comforting sights and sounds, much 'religion' is based on and colludes with our fear: fear of suffering, of the unknown, of our helplessness and loneliness, of death. We sprinkle holy water and whistle hymns in the dark, and talk of hope and resurrection before the corpse is cold or the tears shed. It all helps for a while – but when faced with overwhelming grief, appalling carnage, mindless slaughter, and the incineration of the innocent, much traditional religious talk is exposed as achingly hollow.

What then of love? What does love have to offer in the face of horror?

A friend of mine once put this question to an elderly nun who had spent several decades working with destitute women in the slums of an African city. My friend was a priest, overwhelmed by his own work for Africans with AIDS, and feeling increasingly desperate. 'What does it mean to live the Gospel and talk of faith, hope and love amid the chaos and devastation of Africa?' he asked. She replied, 'It means facing the horror and not running away'.

For many Australians, the horror and injustice that saturate our world suddenly became real this month. For some it was a profound shock to realise that we are not insulated from the pain and death that accompany life at every point and in every person. We are just ordinary humans – searching, fearful, loving and vulnerable; and we will never grow up, never learn justice and compassion, and never understand spirituality, unless we face the reality of suffering. Instead of replacing false securities with fake religion, instead of setting out, with grim determination, to make sure this atrocity does not alter our 'carefree Aussie lifestyle', can we learn to love one another enough, and love life enough, to sit together and face the horror without running away?

This kind of love defies rational explanations and religious formulas, and faces life as it is. Simone Weil wrote, 'The mind comes slap up against physical suffering, affliction, like a fly against a pane of glass'. For all our reasoning or our piety, our work for justice or our medical progress, our secure borders or our wars against terrorism, life remains full of suffering. In every life, in all life, there comes a time when, like Job in the Bible, all we can do is cry out to God – even against God – suffer life's agony and face God's silence. Weil says, 'It is when from the innermost depths of our being we need a sound that means something – when we cry out for an answer and it is not granted to us – it is then we touch the silence of God'.

Religion must not betray that silence. If it tries to put words where silence belongs it ends up in idolatry or triviality. Let pain be pain, let silence be silence, and let religion do its real job of binding us together, holding us as we suffer, weaning us off cheap comforts, and releasing in our guts the cry of Christ, 'My God, my God, why have you abandoned me?' This is the cry of every creature, and of all humanity, as we face the darkness and pain of existence itself.

If there is any faith, any hope, any life after death and despair, it lies within, through and beyond the deepest emptiness humans can bear. Sometimes through ecstasy, mostly through pain, life shatters us and seduces us into this void. Here, religion must fall silent and fall apart, once it has taught us to live without illusions, to love without reasons, to let go of our securities, to trust the emptiness, the mystery, that draws the cosmos out of silence – and life out of death.

This essay was published as a Faith column in The Age *in October, 2002, two weeks after the terrorist bombing of tourist venues on the Indonesian island of Bali, which claimed the lives of over 200 people, including 88 Australians.*

Coming to the Christmas crib with new eyes

One December weekend, when I was about thirteen years old, I made a Christmas crib.

It was an elaborate affair made of broken fence palings, chicken wire and papier-mache, all moulded together on a workbench in our backyard. Following the warps in the wire, I shaped a cave-like stable surrounded by bumpy hills and fields, and then populated the scene with a fine set of nativity figures bought on sale from a local shop. My final masterstroke was setting tiny battery-operated torches within the papier-mache. Then, while playing a musical version of the Christmas story sung by Mario Lanza, Bing Crosby and the Choir of Kings College, I could stage my very own Christmas pageant.

Looking back, it seems an unusual holiday project for an Australian lad, but I was proud of it and, frankly, it sure beat playing cricket.

Many years later I spent Christmas Day visiting the churches of Rome with their extravagant Nativity scenes – featuring flying angels and travelling kings – and discovered that my own crib was part of a hallowed Catholic tradition.

The first Christmas Crib was set up by St Francis of Assisi in the Italian village of Greccio around 1223. Francis wanted to show the local peasants just how poor and human the birth of Jesus really was, and so he set up the whole scene in a stable – with real animals and a young couple dressed as Joseph and Mary. The legend says that people miraculously saw Francis cradling a tiny infant as he preached at midnight Mass.

This re-presentation of the Nativity, with concrete images that could be seen and touched as they silently drew the faithful into the ancient story of Jesus' birth, was an act of spiritual genius. Eight centuries later, in parishes, cities, schools and villages all around the world, millions of people see that story played out – an enchanting story of angels and shepherds, exotic wise men, a wondrous star, a lowly stable and a poor young couple with their little baby. There is something so simple, so right, about actually seeing it all set out before us year by year.

The Incarnation, the mystery of Divine Love becoming human in Jesus, is not some abstract theological concept. It is bodily, ordinary, sweaty, sensual – as physical as childbirth and as earthy as animals. The 'sign' which the shepherds were told to find was not some awesome sound and light show – but a little baby lying in a food trough among the animals. You can't get much more physical than that. This same familiar, embodied grace is at work each Christmas as grandparents take little children up to the manger to 'see the Baby Jesus'. It's all very human, homey and physical. Yet within that 'seeing' lie depths it takes a lifetime to plumb. The child and the grandparent 'see' the same Crib, but there is a journey between them that only the mature, weathered heart can know.

St Paul once famously wrote, 'When I was a child I thought like a child and reasoned like a child – but now that I am an adult I have put away childish things'.

The first stage of faith is rather like the way a child sees the Crib.

For all its wonder and beauty, everything is very literal, historical and specific. When I made my backyard Crib I immersed myself in the Christmas Story with real creativity and devotion, and every aspect had to be presented and venerated. At this stage reflection on one's faith can be as literal as a child wondering if the sheep licked the baby Jesus, or as profound as a preacher inspiring his people to emulate the courage of the three wise men – but it is always based in historical 'certainties'.

The next stage of faith, which involves 'putting away childish things' can be profoundly disconcerting. In my early twenties I studied the 'Infancy Narratives' in the gospels of Matthew and Luke. I discovered that our familiar 'Christmas Story' is not found in any one gospel. Rather, while Matthew gave us three wise men, the star and the flight into Egypt, Luke gave us the journey to Bethlehem, the angels and shepherds, and the stable. My beloved Crib was actually a collage made from two somewhat contradictory accounts of Christ's birth.

I then discovered that each of these accounts was itself a collage composed of images from the Hebrew Scriptures and key spiritual themes from the particular Gospel it introduced. Matthew and Luke each offer a kind of 'overture' to the major 'opera' of their gospels, weaving in ancient, sacred motifs to make their accounts familiar and inspiring to their first century communities.

All this made me appreciate the literary skill of the evangelists, but it was hard to see the Christmas Story emptied out by modern biblical scholarship – however sound and impressive it was. I felt a bit like a boy standing before the scholars and saying 'What! No Star?' There was a real sense of loss.

I soon found, however, that the stories shaped by Matthew and Luke carry meaning and beauty as rich as any historical fact. In the three wise men from the East, for example, we see the revelation of Christ offered not just to Israel but to the whole of humanity, and all the nations come rejoicing, just as the scriptures prophesied. In Luke's story of the angels and shepherds we see Christ's 'good news of great joy!' proclaimed to the most despised members of society. Shepherds were not just poor – they were outcasts, 'ritually unclean', since their lifestyle made it impossible for them to observe the rigid religious 'purity laws' of the time. Yet it is to them that the angels come. This theme – that in Christ the love of God is revealed most vibrantly among the outcast – is central to Luke's whole gospel.

And so, with study and reflection, I was gradually led to decode the whole rich tapestry of symbols that make up the Christmas crib. This more mature way of 'seeing', this second stage of faith which St Paul described as 'becoming an adult', has deepened as the Christmases have passed, and I have found that for all I lost in surrendering my literal, historical 'certainties', I have received back a hundredfold in spiritual depth and radical challenge.

In the Crib this depth and challenge is focused most poignantly, of course, in the central figures of Joseph and Mary and the baby. The whole Christmas tableau is just a cute fairy tale unless we truly 'see' them, and in this deeper seeing we find layers of meaning that draw us into the very heart of life, if only we are willing.

A young child might see the tender image of the holy baby Jesus sleeping in the hay, the lambs bleating softly to honour him. An adult might see the homeless family seeking asylum, the filth of the stable, the exhausted parents sheltering their new-born in desperate circumstances. A believer might see the staggering claim that it is among the helpless and driven of the earth that Divine Love takes flesh and the face of God is seen. A contemplative, and a wise old woman or man, will sit in silence before this child, before every child, seeing and pondering the mystery, ever ancient ever new, of God becoming human so that humanity might become divine.

In this last stage of faith, beyond both child and adult, we are led back to the Crib with new vision. Here, after all our growing up, our deconstructing and disenchantment, our theologising and sophistication, our striving for justice and our struggles with living, we return – like the grandparent and the child – to see the Baby Jesus, to smile quietly at that Love whose depth always exceeds our grasp, yet who is given, age after age, into our hands.

And so I will set up a simple crib again this Christmas. On each of twelve nights I will light a candle and sit a while in silence. I will ask for the grace of receiving, as simply as a child, the gift that longs to be given – the gift of joy, the gift of life, the Son of God, love's pure light.

Published in The Age *as a special Christmas Faith column in December 2002.*

Ash Wednesday

In just over two weeks' time churches around Australia will celebrate Ash Wednesday. I suggest that this year ashes should be gathered from charred buildings at Woomera Detention Centre and sent to every church – or at least every cathedral – in the country. Then, when the ashen cross is traced on the foreheads of those Australians who call themselves Christians, we just might realise that we have something to repent of.

Ash Wednesday marks the beginning of the Christian penitential season of Lent. It is meant to be a sombre, soul-searching day when we face our personal and communal failure to live out Jesus' teachings, and humbly open our hearts to conversion, charity, penance and reconciliation. These themes will ring hollow this year unless the churches face the fact that a majority of Australians – most of them Christians – support a government that is running a concentration camp on our soil and in our name.

Ash Wednesday is also meant to be a day of fasting, an ancient spiritual practice that is strongly recommended throughout Lent's forty days. Heeding the Church's call for fasting this year will feel like a pious farce, unless we fast in solidarity with scores of desperate people who sit and starve behind government-issued razor wire, their lips sewn together in a gruesome, perhaps unintended parody of the silence of so many Australians, including many of our religious leaders.

Ash Wednesday is often said to be the first step of a long journey with Jesus, as he walks towards the Cross. We are invited to reflect on his suffering, his courage and his selfless love as he stands vulnerably yet resolutely before the forces of domination, intimidation and sanctioned violence that will crucify him. How will our hearts and our consciences bear the burden of this story this year as our own society, through our recently re-elected officials, vilifies and crucifies some of the most powerless people in the world?

It is not necessary to have a detailed solution to the world's refugee crisis, nor a settled view of what Australia's role in it should be, to know that what our government is doing to asylum seekers is profoundly immoral, unjust and, frankly, evil. It is also undeniably unchristian – if the word 'Christian' has anything at all to do with the Gospel of Jesus Christ, who said, 'Whatever you do to even the least of these brethren of mine, you do to me'. Yet, as the *Canberra Times* noted recently, 'The government believes it can continue with this abhorrent policy because it is popular' – which means it must be popular with plenty of good Christians around Australia.

Where, then, are the Churches and Church leaders – those guardians of the moral fibre of our nation; where are those who decry the spiritual bankruptcy of our society and claim we have lost the 'sense of sin'; where are the powerful religious lobbyists who storm Canberra whenever an issue of Church exemptions or sexual ethics is raised in the public forum? Where are the pastoral letters, the nation-wide prayer vigils, the bishops protesting in front of detention centres, the ministers risking arrest through civil disobedience, the excommunications of those who support, administer or mandate what the Convenor of Pax Christi, Fr Claude Mostowick MSC has publicly called 'a crime against humanity'?

More importantly, perhaps, where are the sermons and campaigns of education in parishes right around the country – networks where the churches have unparalleled access to the hearts and minds of ordinary Australians, places where this 'popular policy' might be made unpopular as it is critiqued by the Gospel and the clear social teaching of the Church? Or are the Churches and their leaders to offer a challenge that is too little and too late, as they did in Germany in the 1930s, thereby allowing 'onlookers to become desensitised to evil, bit by bit', as Professor Tony Kevin of ANU recently put it?

So far the official response of the churches has been, for the most part, weak and ambivalent. It has been limited to occasional press releases or isolated statements. I am informed that repeated calls for strong public action, made by church peace activists to powerful Episcopal figures, have been ignored. Individual Christians are left feeling at a loss, isolated in the face of an evil that is 'popular' in this nation that still begins parliamentary sessions with the Lord's Prayer.

What then of Ash Wednesday? What then of this coming season of Lent?

There are times in life when all the holy words you have read, all the ideals you have espoused, all the prayers you have said, all the beliefs you have founded your life upon come into clear and simple focus, and call you to act. I suggest this Lent is such a time for Australian Christians.

We could begin by making the Ash Wednesday service a public event – holding inter-faith services in civic spaces, inviting all and calling all to repent of the selfishness, fear and apathy that is allowing asylum seekers to be demonised, imprisoned and denied basic human rights. We could mark out large crosses in ash in front of our parliaments, our local members' offices, our cathedrals. We could hold candlelight vigils every Friday before immigration offices. Some of us – and especially our religious leaders – could travel to detention centres, leading prayer rallies and then performing civil disobedience by attempting to enter the centres to offer support to those imprisoned there.

In parishes and schools we could learn the basics of peaceful non-violent resistance; we could organise letter writing campaigns to challenge politicians – but also to support individual refugees. We could educate ourselves about refugee issues, so we can challenge the secrecy and the lies of this government, and the prejudice and fear in our communities and amongst our friends. We could study the church's social teaching, the biblical demand that we welcome strangers, and the duties of citizens in societies where human rights are violated. We could also prepare for Palm Sunday.

During the early 1980s many Christians and other people of good will became involved in the annual 'Peace March' through some of Australia's capital cities. In their heyday some sixty or seventy thousand people could be seen marching down Collins Street – for 'Peace'. In their way these gatherings were exhilarating and empowering, but there was always a lurking sense that 'Peace Issues' ultimately depended on the two superpowers of the day. As Australians, many of us felt impotent in the face of nuclear threats and international politics.

Perhaps this Lent we might revive the old 'Peace March' – but this time focus it on this very Australian crisis of faith. In parishes throughout the country we could prepare for a very public challenge and witness, bringing the message of the Gospel to bear on this issue that is tearing apart the very soul of our nation. Palm Sunday would be a good day to hold such a march – as the churches prepare to commemorate the judicial murder of a reviled criminal and troublemaker named Jesus, and as most Australians look forward to a relaxing Easter break. It would be a powerful way to show our government that we do not support its treatment of refugees, to challenge our fellow citizens, and to express public solidarity with all who are exiled, reviled and persecuted.

However, whether we make crosses in ash on the steps of Parliament House, write personal letters to newspapers, bishops and politicians, or organise nation-wide vigils and marches, come Ash Wednesday the time is past when we could call ourselves Christians and remain silent. As Christ himself said: 'Why do you call me 'Lord! Lord!' and not do what I say? What I command you is to love one another.'

This essay was published in The Age *as a Faith column in February 2003, shortly before Ash Wednesday. Partly inspired by this article, a group of seminary students from the Uniting Church, working with Church officials and other groups, helped organise a Palm Sunday March through the city of Melbourne. The march focused on the plight of asylum seekers in Australia. Tens of thousands of people took part.*

Flawed saint or wounded hero

the legacy of Fr Mychal Judge

A paper given at Union Theological Seminary, New York City, at an evening of discussion and reflection in honour of Fr Mychal Judge OFM, 8 May, 2003.

It is an honour to be with you this evening, and to reflect with you on the life, death and legacy of Fr Mychal Judge.

I come from that part of the Church, and that part of the world, that is not American. I also come here tonight as a very openly gay Catholic man, whose public challenge to the Church – and the road that led me to make that challenge – has cost me my Franciscan vocation, my potential priesthood, and my career as a religious educator. Therefore, I come here with some very particular concerns – and questions.

First, I wonder whether Mychal Judge, in his life and his death, is a gift and a treasure for the Universal Church and for the whole human family. Does his life and death have deep resonance and relevance for the entire Body of Christ, and for the world as a whole as we face the twenty-first century, or is he simply a holy New Yorker?

Second, I wonder what issues and questions arise from the fact that Mychal Judge was a gay man and a gay priest who, whilst offering great support to many gay people over many years, never actually came out publicly himself?

Third, I wonder whether anything in Mychal Judge's life and death helps give birth to the 'New Church' that he often talked about and longed to see?

These are the questions I would like to reflect upon with you this evening.

Is Mychal Judge a gift and a treasure for the Universal Church and for the human family?

I believe the answer is – unquestionably – yes.

Let us consider how many 'saints' and 'heroes' actually come to prominence.

There are countless good and courageous people, holy people – saints, if you will – all around us, living lives of dedication and generosity in all sorts of ways and contexts. Most of them will never be canonised or celebrated beyond, perhaps, intimate eulogies and treasured personal memories. Their holiness is real, but 'local', so to speak. And there is nothing surprising in this. This is one of the reasons, of course, why we celebrate 'All Saints Day' every November – to recognise and honour all the unknown saints and unsung heroes. No doubt we have all known such people – there may well be some of them here tonight.

Few of these saints will ever emerge as having a kind of universal significance, an almost archetypal depth or a symbolic greatness – but some will, some do. Mychal Judge is, I suggest, one of those ordinary, real, loving Christians, whom God, or life, or an accident of history, has thrust into extraordinary prominence, giving him a significance beyond anyone's imagining – certainly beyond his! – and making his life and death a gift of enduring worth and profound sacramental depth.

On that dark cataclysmic day, the date of which is burned into the consciousness of our age, during that defining, devastating moment at the birth of a new century, in the midst of anguish and terror and despair and violence, it is as if we were given a gift. In all the madness and horror of September 11, 2001, in an overpowering tragedy that was spawned by, and that would spawn, anger, fear, injustice and hatred, there was this man – this Mychal. In an extraordinary way, his image – silent in death but potent in love – became a gift, a light that was literally beamed around the world even as the towers fell. And, amid all the chaos and destruction, this image, this icon, spoke not of fear or violence or despair, but of self-sacrificing love, of compassion, of grace, of faith, of hope. In that terrible time, this man, this priest who laid down his life, became an image of all that is finest and most precious in those who follow Jesus of Nazareth – indeed, of all that is finest in the human heart itself.

Please note, it's not that there weren't hundreds of others who also laid down their lives in service. Many people were heroic, even saintly, both on that day and in the weeks to come. Yet somehow this man, this gift, this light was thrust up onto the 'Lamp-stand' for all the world to see, and began to shine with radiance and power that continues to touch millions of people. In this he is already, without doubt, a gift and a grace to the universal Church and to the human family – and this happened at a speed and with a reach unheard of in the annals of more conventional saints. We need to claim this, to honour this, to celebrate and give thanks for this – how much we have needed this light, this gift, this image of love in the midst of violence and despair!

We also need to 'unwrap' this gift that has been given us, and look honestly at the nature of this 'light' that has been lifted up for us – and this is where some people have faltered. Many in the Church, including many leaders, rushed to claim and honour Mychal – some with more than a hint of concern, I suspect, for ecclesiastical PR. And then – as the actual man who was this gift, this light, began to emerge from the 'wrapping' – they panicked, decided they weren't sure they wanted this particular gift after all, and tried to wrap it up again and 'return to sender'. They tried to put the light back under the bushel. Of course, it doesn't work – and we must resist the attempt to hide or distort or forget Mychal Judge. We must lead the way in unwrapping this extraordinary gift, and let this light shine – God knows we will need this witness, this image, this icon of love in the dark times this century has already faced, and may well continue to endure.

As this unwrapping proceeds, as we discover who this gift of God really was and is, we are also learning some profound lessons. I will mention just one core lesson tonight, and that concerns the true nature of holiness.

In Michael Ford's recent book called *Father Mychal Judge* someone who knew him makes the observation that Mychal was certainly a 'hero', but, well, not really a 'saint'. I wonder what we expect our 'saints' to be like? Here was a man whose heroism was totally grounded in, fuelled by and directed towards his commitment to the Gospel of Jesus, and who lived that Gospel somewhat idiosyncratically to be sure, but also with unwavering dedication. What more do we want of our saints?

There is no question that Mychal repeatedly, persistently, almost obsessively put himself at the centre of situations of profound human suffering, anguish and brokenness – and into them he brought simple, deep faith, hope and love. I guess we are fine with that, impressed by that.

Then we find that he, too, was suffering, anguished and broken, struggling with addictions, struggling to integrate his sexuality, struggling to accept and love himself, struggling to open himself to faith, hope and love in his own messy, complex, real, unresolved human journey – and we get unsettled. Do we still want our saints to be utterly peaceful, serene, balanced, integrated, composed, somehow above it all – and somehow safely above us? Real saints would be the first to say they are none of these. It is their utter honesty, their realness, their total trust in God that makes them saints, not some cold, flawless 'perfection'. They are just themselves.

Two of my favourite sayings about holiness spring to mind when I think about Mychal Judge. One modern writer on spirituality says that saints have an unusual freedom that sometimes unsettles people, since 'God has not fashioned a wimp, a weasel or a robot'. Mychal Judge was certainly none of these, but he was deeply free and real in ways that liberated and affirmed marginalised people – and that also disturbed the powerful. An ancient writer, St Symeon the New Theologian, says that 'Christ makes us utterly real'. Mychal was certainly, perhaps remarkably, real – remarkably himself.

A great deal more needs to be said about what Mychal Judge reveals to us concerning the nature of holiness. We are close enough to him to hear all the anecdotes and jokes, to taste the shocking honesty and mischievousness which others both loved and feared, to record in unflinching detail the fact that this man was no plaster saint, no safe, saintly cleric. His holiness is the kind of holiness that modern people need to know about – for he gives us the hope, and presents us with the challenge, that we too can become 'holy'; we can become – and are called by God to be –truly human, profoundly ourselves.

Mychal Judge was a gay man and a gay priest.

I have to confess to having some ambivalence about the fact that Mychal never came out publicly. This decision, weighed and tested, I am sure, over many years, does not sit easily with me.

However, I recognise and respect the fact that this was truly a decision made honestly and conscientiously by Mychal. He was not running away from the struggle and the challenge, he was not ducking the question or pretending there was no 'issue' here that needed facing. Although he remained 'semi-closeted' he was no cowering sacristy queen, no tastefully, discreetly gay academic theologian, no quiet, conforming, closeted pastor who kept his sexuality a secret, except at camp clerical dinner parties. On the contrary!

Here was a gay priest who took risks, who dared to challenge the ecclesiastical status quo on all kinds of issues, who was subversive and radical, and who used to the absolute hilt the access, the money, the resources, the status, the priesthood and even the Franciscan habit that his role afforded him. Whether financially supporting organisations such as P-Flag (Parents and Friends of Lesbians and Gay Men), leading the inclusive St Patrick's Day Parade in Queens, or quietly sharing the truth of his gayness in order to encourage a troubled gay adolescent, Mychal was inexhaustibly committed to supporting his gay sisters and brothers. He used his priesthood, even as he maintained his cover, to passionately affirm, encourage, embrace and empower gay people so that they might live with the freedom, the dignity, the joy and the intimacy that he struggled to embrace in his own life.

What a compelling role model Mychal Judge offers for all the gay priests, bishops, religious, theologians and church workers who remain in the system and who benefit from it. Surely the only way to remain in the ecclesiastical system with integrity is to use it in every way possible to empower and support gay people! This too is Mychal's legacy to the Church – and this is a gay priest that I can live with!

I also find that I can live with this gay priest because he offers a challenge to the Gay Community as well as to the Church. Mychal teaches us that, in itself, coming out is not everything, and certainly not the one thing necessary. Mychal's life was devoted to solidarity with the poor, the disenfranchised, the homeless, refugees, people with HIV/AIDS – to concrete, grass-roots ministry wherever people were in need. His obsessive, heartfelt generosity, his love and care for all kinds of people that others would not touch or welcome, teaches all of us 'openly, proudly' gay people that our own liberation must not become simply a licence to set up a comfortable, consumerist lifestyle for ourselves. Rather, our coming out needs to deepen into a call to radical spiritual solidarity with all who suffer injustice. Even though he maintained his ecclesiastical 'cover', Mychal was indeed a model and inspiration for this profound dimension of gay holiness.

It is important to recognise that much still remained unresolved in Mychal around his sexuality – he was very much still 'in process' here. However, his struggle to find integration and wholeness as a gay man very much shaped him as a man, a minister of the Gospel, a Franciscan, and a saint. He did not just 'happen to be gay', as he happened to have blue eyes. No. This journey into his own incarnate, sexual reality, his embodied truth before the God he loved, was the journey of opening to grace itself. The honesty, vulnerability, earthiness, freedom, compassion, humour and integrity that people so loved about Mychal were forged very powerfully in his journey towards finding himself as whole and loved and graced by God as a gay man. In the same way, the journey to be who we truly are shapes and makes each one of us. In Mychal we see that opening to gay sexuality as a gift of God is integral to his path to holiness. Here is another profound lesson about holiness – and about gay sexuality. Let those who have ears, hear!

It is important here to recognise that much of this grace came into Mychal's life from the gay community, and from specific gay people in his life.

Mychal lived for many years in New York City – a place where, over several decades, countless gay and lesbian people had laid down their lives and loves for the sake of liberation, dignity and justice for gay people. He knew of their example, their exploration, their writings, their courage, their successes and failures. He also knew them personally, and he gained enormously from the experience. Sure, he daringly supported openly gay priests like Fr Bernard Lynch and Fr John McNeill when they were under fire from the Church – but they also inspired and challenged him at new personal depths. Sure, he supported and affirmed the gay Catholic group Dignity, but his friends there also offered him an example and a safe space in his own struggle to be gay and Catholic. Sure, he encouraged and blessed his friends Tom Moulton and Brendan Fay in their deepening love and commitment – but they also challenged him to wonder about intimacy, love and embodiment in his own life as a gay man. This was no one-way exchange – and Mychal Judge would have been the first to acknowledge that.

Here, in this exchange, in this openness to mutual vulnerability and enrichment, we find a model of how life in the Church should be lived. Yes, we need the official Church – with its scriptures, history, wisdom, spiritual traditions, sacraments, social justice teachings, saints and heroes – and maybe even its structures, to an extent. However, the Church also needs us. In our time, the Church desperately needs the living witness and challenge of lesbian, bisexual, gay, transgender, intersex people – of all those whose lives as sexual beings have been marginalised and silenced. We need to open up the doors and windows of all these dusty church structures, unwrap and defrost all those rigid sexual proscriptions, and let in the unsettling, fresh air of real warm, sweaty human experience. If it is ever to become what it is called to be – the BODY of Christ – then the Church needs us!

Mychal Judge, this most modern of saints, not only knew this intellectually, he lived it.

I have just called Mychal Judge a 'modern saint'. I wonder whether in his life or death we can see the birth of the 'New Church' that his friends tell me he longed to see – and that so many of us long to see too.

In many ways Mychal was a very traditional priest. As I have read and listened and pondered his life, I have often thought that he seemed like a really wonderful 1950s pastor – a brilliant example of the best of that breed. Clearly, he loved being a priest – being a sacramental presence in people's lives, offering consolation, forgiveness and reconciliation, anointing the sick, blessing everything that moved and plenty of things that didn't, wearing his habit around Manhattan, bringing Eucharist and healing wherever he could. He did this all so well, so generously, with such joy and tenderness and panache. However, beautiful and inspiring as all this is, I believe this model of priesthood is dying.

Whatever ministry will look like in the future, it will not be lived according to the model that Mychal Judge knew and loved. Can his life or death help us as we shape the 'new church' and the 'new priesthood'. I believe so.

Mychal may have lived as a traditional Catholic priest, but in his dying I believe we can see an amazing, profound model of the ministry of the new church. Let me explain.

I have a habit, when something extraordinary happens in my life, of asking myself: 'What would this symbolise if it were a dream?' In this way I try to draw out the deeper, enriching significance of events, wondering what the Spirit might be saying to me through them. As Mychal Judge died, an extraordinary scene was played out, both historically and symbolically.

The scene I will describe is entirely factual – but I invite us to consider it as profoundly sacramental.

Just after he was killed, Mychal Judge's body was carried from the rubble. He was laid on the ground – like St Francis, who was laid on the bare earth just after he died. One of the police officers who carried his body, and who was a Catholic, was screaming 'Can somebody get this man a priest! Can somebody get a priest!' Another young officer, also a Catholic, saw and heard all this, learned that the dead man was a priest, and he ran into the nearest Church shouting, 'Is there a priest in here? We need a priest!' There was no priest in the Church – but there was a woman. She was ripping up linen to give to people as masks, so that they could breathe in all the dust. The officer says she was ripping up sheets – but churches don't have sheets. I wonder if she was ripping up those old, long, starched, white altar cloths, tearing up the old sacred cloths, the old sacred forms, and making of them something to help people breathe?

The woman tells the officer that there is no priest, but then she says to the young man, 'Are you a Catholic?' He says that he is. She then tells him that he can give the last rites – so he should go and do it! He is surprised, as well he should be. The woman was wrong – canonically – but she was right on every other level on that devastating day. She effectively said: 'You are looking for a priest. There is no priest here, but I say this to you: claim your baptism and your priesthood! You are a member of the Body of Christ. Go and do what needs to be done!'

The young officer also gets it right that day. He is not sure about what the woman has told him – but he goes and does what she says. He tells the other officer that this woman in the church had said that he, as a Catholic, could give the last rites. He too is surprised – but they both do what she has told them to do. They kneel by the dead body of Fr Mychal. They touch him with respect and reverence, laying their hands on his head and on his heart. And there, in the midst of all the madness and chaos, they pray for him. They get it right. They say the Lord's prayer, the prayer that unites all Christ's family, the prayer in which there are no hierarchies, no roles – only sisters and brothers, children of 'Our Father'. They say the 'Glory be to the Father' – again they get it right. They give praise for the 'Glory' – before time began, here in this actual moment of death as they give thanks for Mychal's life, and at the end of time. Glory.

Then, the two cops stand up and hug – they find communion together there, and a bond that will stay with them. The young cop says: 'In all that madness – people running and crying – there was just the three of us, the lieutenant and me and the father'. I heard this and thought 'Where two or three are gathered in my name, there am I in the midst of them!' Right there, of all places, in all that tragedy and chaos, two or three were gathered – and that is all it takes. That is all it ever takes.

These two men then left Mychal's body, and went back to lay down their lives as he had done.

It seems to me, as I reflect on this story, that here in Mychal Judge's dying we have a stunning enactment of the birth of the new church, the new priesthood, the new community of faith and love where all will claim their baptism, even in the midst of chaos and devastation, and do for one another what needs to be done. Thank God for that woman, ripping up the old sacred cloths so that people could breathe, and ordering her fellow Christians to claim their baptism. Thank God for those two cops, who hadn't learned enough theology to disagree with her, but who knew enough Christianity to pray and bless and hug and lay down their lives. Thank God for Mychal Judge, who even in dying left us a sacrament of priesthood, communion and new birth, right there on the streets of the New York he loved so much.

As St Francis lay dying he said to his friends: 'I have done what was mine to do. May God show you what is yours.' Perhaps these words should accompany this final scene from Mychal Judge's life. They send us into the future, to rebuild the Church he served so well as a priest, but which he longed so deeply to see transformed. He has done what was his to do. May God show us what is ours.

I am indebted to Brendan Fay and Tom Moulton, both close friends of Mychal Judge, for sharing their memories and insights with me. The video produced by Brendan, Fr Mychal Judge: A Month's Mind, *has been an invaluable resource, as has Michael Ford's book,* Fr Mychal Judge, an authentic American hero, *Crossroads, NY, 2002.*

In Christ's name

the marriage of Brendan and Tom

One rainy Spring day in New York City, my friend Brendan married his sweetheart.

On that cool Saturday morning I caught the subway from the Upper West Side, and arrived at the lovely old church in Brooklyn in good time for a strong coffee at a nearby diner. If I knew Brendan, I reasoned, this ceremony would be prayerful, beautiful, moving – and long.

Inside the church all was candlelight, dusty grandeur, flowers and smiles. Musicians were tuning up, and the soprano was polishing her pronunciation of *A Thiarna dean trocaire. A Chriost dean trocaire* – which is Gaelic for 'Lord have mercy. Christ have mercy'. This wedding was to be both very Catholic and very Irish – not just because Brendan is Irish, but because love blossomed between himself and his partner, Tom, as they organised events for the Gay Irish Alliance, 'Lavender and Green'. Today the couple looked stunning in their deep green, navy and lavender kilts.

The wedding was to be Catholic because both men are deeply committed to their faith, which forms the basis of their shared life. They come from different worlds – Brendan from County Louth, north of Dublin, with a background in theology, education and activism, and Tom from rural Illinois, with a career in paediatric haematology and oncology. They first met one evening in St John's Church in Greenwich Village. Brendan had rushed in, late as always, for Mass with the Gay Catholic group 'Dignity', and the only seat available was next to tall, handsome Dr Tom Moulton. Eight years later they are a committed couple – committed not just to one another, but to supporting the homeless, working for social justice and caring for sick children and their families. Today they had come to church to seal their commitment and their love during another celebration of the Mass.

Gradually the bustle of preparation died down. The priest, a Franciscan named Fr Raymond, took his place in front of the altar. The organist began 'Jesu, Joy of Man's Desiring', and some five hundred people turned to smile as Tom, escorted by his frail, eighty-year-old mother, then Brendan, with a teary Irish sister on each arm, walked down the aisle. Together we sang, 'Let us build a house where love can dwell, and all can safely live; a place where saints and children tell how hearts learn to forgive. Built of hopes and dreams and visions, rock of faith and vault of grace. Here the love of God shall end divisions – all are welcome, all are welcome in this place!'

After the readings, the hymns and the Gospel proclamation, Fr Raymond called Brendan and Tom forward. As they stood before the altar he bound their joined hands with his priest's stole and solemnly questioned them. Did they believe God had called them together in love? Would they give themselves to each other wholeheartedly and without reserve? Would they do all in their power to make their life together a witness to the love of God in the world? Would they share their wholeness and brokenness, their joys and sorrows, their health and sickness, their riches and poverty, their successes and failures? They said they would.

Tom and Brendan faced one another and, in clear, gentle tones, pronounced their vows: 'In the Mystery of Divine Love, you have been given to me. And, in my own free will and destiny I embrace you, choosing and being chosen. And with and in that Love, I promise to be for you, and for your well-being forever, to honour you as a dwelling place of God, and to be loyal to you, and full of faith in you, our life-day long.'

As everyone smiled and dried their eyes, Tom's little nephew and niece came forward with the rings, which were blessed with Lourdes water and exchanged 'in the name of God the Creator, Redeemer, and Sanctifier'. Then the whole congregation crowded round these loving men as they stood silently in the sanctuary, and we laid hands on them and blessed them as Fr Raymond prayed over them the Solemn Blessing of the Rite of Christian Marriage.

He prayed that God, the giver of all grace, would look with favour upon Tom and Brendan, giving them 'wisdom and devotion in their common life together, that each may be the other's strength in need, comfort in sorrow, and a companion in joy. Grant that they may grow in love and peace with you and with each other all the days of their life. Give them grace when they hurt each other, to recognise and acknowledge their faults, and to seek forgiveness from each other. May their life together be a sign – a sacrament – of Christ's love to this broken and sinful world. May their home be a place of blessing and peace. Bless them in their work and in their companionship, in their waking and in their sleeping, in their life and in their death. We ask this through Jesus Christ, our Lord!'

We pronounced a soft, hearty 'Amen', then all the solemnity melted into hugs, tears and gentle laughter.

Later in the Mass, I remember sitting in my pew and watching the streams of family members, friends and supporters lining up to share Holy Communion with these men they loved. I noticed Ernie, an elderly homeless man who was all scrubbed and dressed up for the occasion, colleagues and co-workers from Tom's hospital in the Bronx, folks from the 'Catholic Worker' who serve the destitute in Manhattan, gay priests and radical nuns, people with AIDS and refugees from Latin America, politicians, journalists and activists – people young and old and rich and poor – and I knew that Tom and Brendan were already a living sign of God's love in our broken and lonely world.

These two men had lived through intense personal struggles, through society's prejudice and the Church's condemnation, through scorn and shame and oppression, and together they were building a house where love could dwell. This was as much a miracle, as real a marriage, as true a sacrament, as anything I have ever witnessed.

As the Mass ended and married life began for Brendan and Tom, we sang, 'Come! Live in the Light! Shine with the joy and the love of the Lord! We are called to act with justice. We are called to love tenderly. We are called to serve one another, to walk humbly with God!'

Brendan and Tom are answering that call, and their love, in gentle and courageous ways, is changing the world.

This essay was published in The Age *as a feature article in August 2003. Brendan Fay and Thomas Moulton celebrated the sacrament of marriage in St Anne and the Holy Trinity Episcopal Church in Brooklyn Heights, New York, on 24 May 2003. On 27 July 2003, they were legally married in Toronto, Canada.*

Sex with soul, body and spirit

a personal experience of 'celebrating the body erotic' and the Body Electric Movement.

I first encountered the 'Body Electric' movement through its founder Joseph Kramer. At the time, I was about to come out publicly as gay and lose my career as a religious educator. I was at a turning point – and at a bit of a loss. I knew that I needed not simply a new career, but a whole new experience of life and energy, a new way to heal and play, a new vision of the rich layers of human living that had been denied me by my church and my culture. Experience had taught me that therapeutic talk –however helpful – would never engage my body, and that most recreational sex – however plentiful – would not inspire my soul. Where to turn?

As I drove to a meeting one evening in Berkeley, California, where I was living at the time, I mused about the way forward. 'Nothing is drawing my heart!' I said out loud as I pulled into the church parking lot. By the end of the evening, that would have changed.

Joe Kramer was the speaker that night, and the audience was mainly younger gay men who were looking for ways to integrate their sexuality and spirituality. Kramer was clear and challenging. He spoke of how, after eleven years as a Jesuit, he had gone to live in New York and spent countless hours in sex clubs, not just having sex but soaking up the atmosphere – 'vibrating the deadness out of my body'. I knew what he meant. He also characterised most sex in modern societies as 'mutual necrophilia: dead bodies having sex with dead bodies'. He explained how, over several years, he had shaped a system of bodywork that used erotic massage, breath-work and focused awareness to lead men into profound states of physical pleasure and spiritual openness. He talked about transformation, full-body orgasms, inner healing and discovering sex as 'non-addictive, non-shaming and non-stop'. Frankly, it sounded too good to be true.

However, something about Kramer also sounded authentic. This man had been on a long inner journey, and he was now free enough to speak about genital massage, sex play and divine presence – all in the one sentence, and all interwoven in creative, if slightly shocking, ways. I wasn't totally convinced, but I wanted to hear more.

Two weeks later, on a cool Spring morning, I turned up at a plain brown door on Berkeley's famous Telegraph Avenue. A young, curly-headed man in track pants welcomed me with a smile: 'Are you ready to Celebrate the Body Erotic?' 'I guess I could give it a go', I quipped, and headed up the stairs.

Inside I met Collin Brown, the man who now headed the 'Body Electric School' that Kramer had founded. It was Brown who had invited me to 'Come and see' after several phone conversations following my meeting with Joe. I had been impressed by the frankness and clarity of both men, and, despite the misgivings of some friends who thought the whole business amounted to 'a back-rub and a circle jerk', I had decided to invest a couple of days in the school's introductory weekend program.

In the upstairs room there were about twenty men, and we stood around looking nervous and making small talk. I was struck by the age range of the group – from mid twenties to mid-sixties, with the full spectrum of sizes and shapes. Almost without thinking, I found myself sorting out which guys I might like to massage – then I chuckled and checked the impulse.

We began by warming up with simple body movements – clothes on – then being led into gentle one-to-one and communal interactions. This 'weaving' of the group energy was skilled and respectful, and gave people plenty of space to get comfortable with one another, and to face their feelings of awkwardness or uncertainty. This was just as well – since we would soon be 'massaging' each other's clothes off, and learning to feel at ease with our common nakedness. I remember the way the facilitators dealt with that inevitable male concern – 'at Body Electric erections are welcome but not necessary' – and I appreciated the directness and relaxed humour.

Breathing is a core aspect of Body Electric's work, and after being taught a simple technique that brought more oxygen and aliveness into the body, we were led into our first experience of a kind of 'breath orgasm', using music, the pulse of the drum, and varying patterns of breathing. The effect was extraordinary. I remember lying on the floor, breathing with the drum and the surge of music, and feeling waves of energy, grief and release sweep through me.

As one man said when we broke for a late lunch: 'And we're not even halfway through!'

Ahead of us, over the next day and a half, lay hours of learning and sharing genital massage, of breathing that would become increasingly deep and freeing, of laughter and tears, of profound conversations in which men would share their euphoria, their visions, their grief and joy, their sense of opening bodily to the transcendent as never before. All this would come through simple, skilled practices of breathing, touching, and releasing in the company of supportive brothers.

I remember looking around our circle at the end of the two days – looking at these naked, glowing, open men – and feeling that human community should always be like this. Certainly I felt grateful that, at last, I had found that gay community could be like this, that male community could be like this, and I wanted to be part of it. Something was drawing my heart.

Over the next couple of years I was able to deepen my involvement with Body Electric, and I found that the two day workshop was only the introduction to a whole program of workshops and retreats, and to a widening community of people who were committed to exploring the deepest capacities of erotic energy for bringing healing, freedom and spiritual awakening.

In time, I also found that the Body Electric movement, like all human communities and projects, had its flaws, its gaps, its personalities and its issues – but for me that has only served to make it all the more real. When people ask me, as they sometimes do, where they can find places to heal from deep sexual wounding, or where they can begin to integrate sexuality with spirituality in truly embodied ways, or where they can discover sex, touch and sensuality as joyous and holy, I think of Body Electric. It is not perfect – but it is real.

After years of gay activism in Australia, after the dry-as-dust struggle against right wing Catholic bishops in their campaign against sexual pleasure and erotic freedom, I visited my friends at Body Electric again in June. It was like coming home. I did another introductory 'Celebrating the Body Erotic' workshop and watched once more as nervous men relaxed, released and breathed, and their bodies began smiling again. I visited 'Wildwood' retreat centre in the redwoods north of San Francisco, and touched, laughed and meditated with men trained by Body Electric who are on a deep spiritual journey – but one that does not require you to check your body, or your genitals, at the door.

I also joined in a Body Electric workshop taught by Rob Anderson, a trim, sandy-headed Australian who was visiting California the same time I was. Rob is developing the work in Brisbane, Sydney and Melbourne, and while I liked his approach I found myself chuckling at his efforts to translate Aussie slang into Californian. At the end of the weekend, in our final circle, Collin Brown made a point of welcoming me back, especially at this 'Aussie led' weekend. 'It feels like a little miracle that you are here this weekend', he said. I couldn't help but agree.

This essay was published in the Sydney Star Observer *in February 2003.*

Can a gay man be a saint?

As I stand looking eastwards from the corner of Church and Vesey Streets, everything in lower Manhattan looks normal.

The traffic on Church Street is heavy and aggressive. The subway entrance is grimy and crowded. The old trees in front of Trinity Church are rustling in the afternoon wind, and vendors are hawking trinkets to foot-sore tourists. A rabbi and a few boys wearing yarmulkes stop to buy sodas from a street-stand.

When I turn and look West, however, a chasm yawns and there is a strange sense of light and space. On the ground there are trucks and red flags, acres of green netting, makeshift traffic barriers and men in hard-hats. One tall building is shrouded in black netting. On the side of another there is an enormous mural of a heart-shaped American flag, above the words 'The human spirit is not measured by the size of the act, but by the size of the heart'. Suddenly I find myself blinking back tears, here on this sunny afternoon on the edge of Ground Zero.

I have come to New York to honour the man whose death certificate, 'Number 00001', marks him as the first registered victim of the attacks on the World Trade Centre on September 11, 2001, and I am standing on the spot where they laid his body.

Father Mychal Judge, Catholic chaplain to the New York City Fire Department, died in the lobby of the North Tower after being hit by falling debris. Some say he had taken off his helmet as he gave the Last Rites to a fallen fire-fighter. His body was carried out by a group of fire-fighters and police and laid on the corner of Church and Vesey Streets. One of the policemen, a Catholic, was crying out 'Can somebody get this man a priest!' A young officer was running south towards the Towers as hundreds of people surged north. He heard the cry and ran into nearby St Peter's Church calling out for a priest. Inside there was a woman who was ripping up church linens to use as masks so that people could breathe in all the dust and devastation. She told him there was no priest there, then said, 'Are you a Catholic?' When he said he was, she told him that in an emergency he could give the Last Rites, so he should go and do it. He went back to the other officer and told him what the woman had said.

And so, in the midst of all the chaos and horror, the two cops knelt down in the street. As people ran screaming all around them, they laid hands on the dead priest's body, said the Lord's prayer and paused for a moment of silence. They then stood, hugged each other, and ran back into the burning buildings to keep pulling people to freedom.

Those who knew Mychal Judge say that he died the way he had lived. He had been a Franciscan priest for forty years and his life had been filled with grass-roots ministry to the homeless, refugees, alcoholics, people with AIDS, and New York City's fire-fighters and their families. He was, perhaps, the city's most recognised and beloved Catholic priest, with an unwavering dedication to putting himself at the centre of human anguish – and an uncanny knack for ending up in the limelight. For years he had walked the streets of Manhattan in his brown Franciscan habit, blessing everything that moved and bringing compassion, faith and earthy humour into situations of desperation and brokenness. He was loved by the homeless people outside the Friary on 31st Street, respected by the city's powerbrokers, and tolerated by the local Church bureaucracy who had learned to live with his maverick ways.

On 15 September some three thousand people packed St Francis of Assisi Church for his funeral, while crowds in the street outside watched on television screens. Inside, former President Bill Clinton remembered how Fr Judge 'lit up the White House' at a prayer breakfast, New York's new Archbishop, Cardinal Egan, proclaimed him 'a saint', and his fellow Franciscan, Fr Michael Duffy said, 'Mychal Judge has always been my friend. And now he is my hero'. Thousands felt the same. One of the fire-fighters who had come to the church still covered in grime from Ground Zero simply said, 'I just think God wanted somebody to lead the guys to heaven'.

In the months following Father Judge's death accolades continued to pile up around him. He received honorary doctorates, religious prizes, an international award for 'Moral Courage', and had streets, ferries and scholarships named after him. New York's fire fighters solemnly presented his helmet to the Pope in St Peter's Basilica, France gave him its 'Legion of Honour', and Ireland named him its 'Man of the Year'. Across the world churches began to invoke him as an inspiration for young people, a model of the Christian hero and an image of the ideal priest. Websites sprang up dedicated to 'Saint Mychal'.

This outpouring of esteem, this sudden elevation of Mychal Judge to 'saint' and 'hero', says as much, perhaps, about our common need to find hope and meaning in the midst of overwhelming violence as it does about the man himself. Somehow a symbol of moral courage and self-sacrificing love had to be drawn out of the rubble of September 11, and Father Judge provided not simply a symbol – he was the real thing. It seemed that official canonisation would only be a matter of time.

Mychal Judge, however, was not just the real thing – he was a real man. Inevitably attention turned to the actual life, personality and spirituality of the man who died so heroically in lower Manhattan on that dark day. What was found was both inspiring and unsettling.

In many ways Mychal Judge seemed the model of the good priest. 'He was the ultimate servant of God and people', said writer Malachy McCourt. 'He embodied the ideal blend of spirituality and public service', said Mayor Rudy Giuliani. 'If we are looking for saintly people in New York City, he would fit the bill', said Senator Tom Duane. Without question, Judge was passionately committed to pastoral ministry and his generosity and compassion made people flock to him, especially in times of need. It was common for him to return to his room late at night and find forty messages on his answering machine. He would sit, exhausted, and answer them all. One Franciscan remembers an evening when Mychal took him on a long trek across the Brooklyn Bridge, then returned home to news that a fireman's father had died. It was midnight, but Judge drove more than an hour north to be with the man's family. This was typical of him.

However, some suggest there was something obsessive about Judge's commitment to ministry. Underneath his genuine warmth, humour and dedication he was a driven man who struggled with issues of self-worth and addiction. He was an alcoholic who had been sober since 1978, and he relied upon regular meetings of Alcoholics Anonymous to maintain focus and inner peace. He took the spirituality of AA's 'Twelve Steps' deeply into his soul, and he learned self-acceptance and perseverance in the company of people who were struggling just like him. He had no illusions about himself, and it was his direct, transparent humanness that drew all kinds of people to him.

People also turned to him when the Church had failed them. He was always ready to bend the rules, offer a hug and a blessing and show people what the love of God was really like. In the early days of the

AIDS epidemic, when nurses were frightened to touch people with AIDS and priests were refusing to bury them, Mychal Judge would often turn up at a hospital room unannounced. He would quietly turn back the covers on the bed of an AIDS patient and gently massage his feet. One man remembers that when his partner was dying Fr Judge came to give him Holy Communion. After the ritual the dying man anxiously whispered, 'Do you think God is angry with me?' Mychal responded by taking the man in his arms, cuddling him, rocking him against his chest, then kissing him.

Father Judge's commitment to being close to people in their brokenness, and his astonishing tenderness, were forged in a heart weathered by his own struggle to believe he was embraced and blessed by God. Mychal Judge, you see, was gay.

A week or so after the attack on the World Trade Centre I received an email from an Irish friend, a priest, who had known Mychal for more than a decade. It read, 'What has not yet come out is that Mychal was gay. He was also not fully 'out'. Sometimes when we visited gay clubs in the Village he would joke that he had his clerical collar in his pocket, so that if a fire-truck passed him on the street he could slip it on and say he was on a pastoral visit'.

As a gay Catholic myself, I read this email with conflicted emotions. I wanted the world to look at this man the Vatican would have labelled an 'objectively disordered homosexual' and see the saint and hero. I felt almost cheated that Judge had never fully come out as gay. However, I also knew that public knowledge of his sexuality could stall any canonisation process. 'How do we tell the world about this?' I emailed my friend.

I need not have worried. Mychal Judge was no cowering, closeted cleric. His fellow Franciscans, senior fire-fighters, people in AA, and countless Catholics in New York knew he was gay, and knew he was committed to using his priesthood, his resources and his energies to support and empower gay people in spiritual, practical and even financial ways. He did this even as he maintained his 'cover' within the institutional church, taking extraordinary risks and making the system serve justice. After years of struggle and uncertainty, Mychal had learned to accept his sexuality as a gift of God, and when gay newspapers in Manhattan broke the story of the 'gay saint' and printed his picture on their front pages – instead of the usual brooding hunk – friends agreed that he would have laughed and been delighted.

Church officials, however, were not so pleased. Cardinal Egan of New York literally fled from journalists who questioned him about the homosexual he had proclaimed a 'saint'. Some of Judge's friends received angry phone calls from conservative clerics after speaking to the gay press. Judge's image started disappearing from church websites and newspapers, and talk of canonisation died. It seemed Catholic leaders had no idea how to handle this holy gay man. Perhaps this was not surprising, since just at that time senior bishops were starting to make gay priests into scapegoats for the Church's sex abuse crisis, and the Vatican was working on a document to ban homosexuals from entering seminaries. A gay saint was not on their agenda.

Among ordinary people, however, Judge's name continued being venerated, his image passed around, his story told. Then in May this year the oldest Protestant seminary in New York, Union Theological Seminary, held a seminar to reflect on the legacy of Father Judge. I was one of those invited to speak, and to help move the phenomenon of Mychal Judge from storytelling to theological refection.

I remember sitting in a cafe on Christopher Street and wondering what to make of this heroic, alcoholic, obsessive, semi-closeted gay priest. What could he have to teach the church and the world at the start of the twenty-first century? Was this a man who embodied that most elusive of qualities –holiness?

Sometimes God, or life, or an accident of history thrusts an individual into prominence at a time of great need. This was true of Mychal Judge. In a time of devastation and violence that was spawned by, and that would spawn, hate, anger and injustice, this priest gave his life in service and emerged as an icon of courage and love. It is as if we were given a gift to bring us hope in this dark time.

When we unwrap that gift, however, we find a man whose life teaches us that holiness is not about being perfect but about being real. As a great saint once said, 'Christ makes us utterly real'. The journey into God is a journey into our deepest selves, and along the way we have to confront all our demons and illusions, surrender our comforting pieties and learn naked trust. Mychal Judge, I believe, was holy because he learned to embrace the truth of who he was, and because he was not afraid to face his emptiness, pain and need and go on loving.

At the core of this journey was the truth of his gay sexuality – the part of his being that he had been taught could not be of God. Embracing this dimension of himself meant trusting God so deeply that he could risk being wrong, risk exploring his own embodied truth, risk facing down the secure and self-righteous condemnations of the Church he loved and served. In that risking he found, again and again, that he was loved and held, and so he was able to love others and free them to go on their own journeys into life and faith.

This also meant that he was able to be in the Church with unusual inner freedom. He chose not to come out publicly as gay, but even in that he offered a model for all the thousands of gay clerics who remain within Church structures. His life shows that the only way to remain 'in' is to use all that the Church is and has to empower and support people in their own search for love, freedom and grace. Encouraging each other in that search is, perhaps, all we can really do for one another, and all we can ask our saints to do for us.

The day before I left New York I went down to the corner of Church and Vesey Streets. I thought about those two cops as they knelt and prayed over the body of Mychal Judge. I bent down, touched the asphalt and concrete and paused for a moment. I thought of the final words of St Francis as he lay dying on the bare earth: 'I have done what was mine to do. May God show you what is yours.'

I stood and looked back towards the open space, towards the place where Mychal had poured out his spirit. I prayed that he would show us what is ours to do, as this troubled century begins. Then I turned into the wind, and walked north on Church Street.

This essay was published as a feature article in the Review section of The Age in December 2003. It has since been reprinted on websites around the world, including a human rights website in Latin America. See also the notes for my talk at Union Theological Seminary, 'Flawed saint or wounded hero: the legacy of Fr Mychal Judge', earlier in this book.

Sing a rainbow

the challenge of being gay and Catholic

The following text is an extended version of a talk given at Melbourne Town Hall, at the invitation of the Cultural Affairs Officer of the City of Melbourne, on 30 January 2004.

In many ways this is a historic night. It is, almost certainly, the first time a gay man has been invited by the City of Melbourne to talk publicly about his experience of being 'Gay and Catholic'. I want to mark this moment, to celebrate it, to make sure it does not pass without reflection and informed comment. That this night can be happening at all, let alone in a climate of respect and affirmation, shows how far we, as gay people, and we, as a society, have come in just a few decades.

For me, personally, as a Melbourne boy, this is also an historic night. I grew up in the suburbs of this city. It was here that I was educated, that I developed a sense of what it means to be part of society, that I learned, as all children must, both the stated and the unstated values and codes that govern human interactions. That boy, growing up in this city, could never have imagined this evening – and neither could the people around him.

I remember covertly browsing through my father's copy of that venerable Melbourne tabloid, *Truth*. I am sure plenty of people here tonight have had a passing acquaintance with it in years past. Dad, of course, only read it for the Racing Form guide – or so he said. Even those who didn't read it, however, could hardly have missed its lurid headlines at newsagents and newsstands. Throughout my boyhood years, *Truth* often had shocking stories of men caught doing scandalous things with other men, often in public toilets. It followed the subsequent demise of these men, reporting their names, their convictions, the destruction of their careers and families and lives. All the institutions of society, from the Supreme Court to the salivating reporters from *Truth*, joined in the condemnation of homosexuals.

It was in this climate that I, and all gay men over about forty, grew up. To be homosexual was sick and shameful. To act on it was not only disgusting, it was criminal. This social dogma was regularly, and often ruthlessly reinforced.

And so, for me, to stand here tonight as a publicly, self-affirming adult gay man, and to be offered a welcome and a platform in this city, and by this city, is cause for celebration.

Of course, I not only grew up as a Melburnian, I grew up as a Catholic. The Church has not yet grown, as the city has, into a mature, honest and liberating understanding of gay people. Despite my seventeen years as a Catholic teacher and religious educator I am denied a career, a platform – and even Holy Communion – by the Church in which I grew up and which I served, and for one reason: I am openly, publicly both gay and Catholic, and I will not bow to the condemnations.

Those condemnations are still active. They still crush the spirits and blight the lives of queer people in this city and around the world. They still destroy the hope of the young. In my speaking tonight I want to remember that with issues like 'being gay and Catholic' we are not just talking theology or dogma – we are dealing with real people, with actual lives.

A few years ago I was invited to a meeting with the directors of one of the most respected Catholic social welfare networks in Melbourne. This organisation does real grassroots work with prisoners, drug addicts, homeless kids, street workers, refugees. They represent the church at its best, and they are the kind of people who make you feel the Catholic Church is worth supporting and worth belonging to.

In this discussion these two men, one of them a priest, said their workers had identified the fact that a large proportion of homeless youth were gay or lesbian. Many of these kids had been forced out of their homes or been harassed at school, and they had ended up on the streets and become involved in prostitution and drug use. They were at particular risk of both disease and suicide. The directors had called this meeting to get some input about how their resources and funds could best address this endemic and growing problem. How could they specifically target and help these gay and lesbian youth?

Well, we had a long and fruitful discussion, but at the end of it I had to address the unnamed 'elephant' that had been in the room all along. I turned to the priest, a man I respect enormously, and said, 'Have you given any thought to how your organisation might begin addressing the problem at its source? How about changing the attitudes of people in homes and schools and parish churches and rural communities so that these kids don't end up on the streets in the first place? As a church organisation, you need to be addressing the root problem of entrenched, sanctified homophobia, both among ordinary Christians and among religious leaders who claim to speak in the name of Christ'. He knew exactly what I was talking about, but with a sad, wry smile he said, 'As you can imagine, we don't have the resources or the backing for that kind of work. We do what we can'. He might well have added that if they had tried to address the real source of homelessness, alienation, self-hatred and despair among gay and lesbian youth by working at the educational level, the familial level, the ecclesial level, and the doctrinal level, many of their philanthropic supporters would have taken their funds elsewhere, and the church authorities may well have closed them down.

As a gay adult man who has suffered at the hands of this same church system, as an educator and as a citizen, I find myself outraged at the refusal of Church leaders to face the human cost of their attitudes and teachings. I find myself appalled at the subtle but entrenched homophobia and prejudice that permeate Church politics, institutions and culture. I find myself shocked that the 'godless secular city' – so condemned in Vatican rhetoric – can listen respectfully to the experience and insights of a gay man like me, while the Church, the 'mystical Body of Christ', wants to silence, sack, condemn and exclude me. I find myself stunned by the mendacity of church leaders who know that their own theologians and scholars reject much of the current teaching around homosexuality, who know that many of their best priests are gay, who know that the church's traditional sexual doctrine is founded on flawed biology and ancient misogyny, yet who persist in defending the ecclesiastical status quo with variations on the oldest, most morally bankrupt defence of all: 'I am just following orders.'

I need to ask, then, how I, as a gay man, can remain a Catholic. In many ways it would be easier for people like me to walk away from the institutional churches, shaking the dust from our feet as we go. I must say that for many gay and lesbian people, at least in certain phases of their life journey, they may well need to do precisely this. We are called to life, freedom, love and delight; called to know in our bones, flesh and blood that we are beloved children – not deviant, disordered, defective, depraved dangers to family, society and all that is holy. We may well need to reject not only such destructive language, but also the hierarchs and the institution that use and promote it. However, for various reasons, not all gay and lesbian people leave the Church, and there can be very profound reasons for that.

It is also worth noting that in the past few years the struggle within the churches around homosexuality has emerged into the public spotlight worldwide. This is an issue that is beginning to look like a watershed, defining concern for Christianity in the twenty-first century. Increasingly, the conservative, evangelical, fundamentalist strains within the churches look as if they are fighting a rearguard action – at least, this is how they see things. Certainly, there is a new kind of openness, a new depth of affirmation for gay people, a new level of scholarship and self-critical reflection developing in mainstream Christianity – and the proof of this is shown, paradoxically, in the bitterness of the furore over the ordination of a gay bishop in the USA and the harsh, almost hysterical condemnation of gay unions issued by the Vatican last year. Things are changing. A new spirit of openness is abroad. This is a painful, but an exciting time to be a gay Christian and a gay Catholic.

I would like to reflect with you on this experience of being gay and Catholic today – and because the topic is huge and time is short I am going to be using some very broad brush-strokes. I would like to approach the topic under four headings: Length, Breadth, Depth, Height.

Length

Being a gay Catholic today, dealing honestly with the 'gay issue' and trying to maintain some sense of equanimity and hope, means holding oneself open to the enormous length of the Church's story – past, present and future. It means seeing oneself as living one moment within the sweep of a very long and complex story – a moment that only makes sense within the context of the whole, but a moment, nonetheless, that can make a real, even a vital contribution to the ongoing, unfolding drama. If I am to make any sense of the struggles and joys that make up my life as a gay Catholic today, not to mention having a sense of what I am called to, I need to know something about where we, as a Church and as a People, have come from and where, on earth, we might be going.

First, I need a sense of the past. The current attitudes to homosexuality within the Church are founded on an approach to sexuality, the body, pleasure, eroticism, procreation, women and marriage on the one hand, and holiness, purity, resurrection and the nature of salvation on the other, which developed very early in our history. The story of this development is complex and the reasons for it are much discussed by scholars, but what is undeniable is that within the first few centuries Christians developed a very deep negativity towards sex, body, and erotic pleasure. This was expressed in the exaltation of virginity, public sexual renunciation and life-long abstinence and in the denigration of sexual desire, women and even marriage. Groups of permanent virgins developed early within Christian circles. They were seen as embodying the triumph of the resurrection over flesh and as a symbol of the 'end times' in that they brought to an end the cycles of birth, marriage, procreation and death. Such permanent virginity was actually used in those early centuries to develop some credibility for the new religion among Roman philosophers. The reasons for it, however, are more complex than that, and they also involve something of a quagmire of ancient misogyny, ritual 'purity codes', biological misunderstandings and the spiritualisation of martyrdom and physical suffering.

In addition to this cult of permanent virginity, in the fourth century individuals and small groups of devout Christians began moving to the desert and embracing solitude, asceticism and deprivation in attempts to subdue the flesh and find perfect union with Spirit. This whole 'desert' movement has had an enormous impact on the development of Christian spirituality. At the time, however, it served to strengthen the already existing sense that true holiness necessitated rejection of sex, body and pleasure.

In those early centuries the developing Church faced intense struggles between the reality of marriage, 'house-holding', procreation and the need for stable, structured forms of human community, and the radical 'spiritual' renunciation of time-bound, earthly, fleshly lifestyles. By the end of the Patristic period around the end of the fifth century, a kind of 'deal' had been struck – a fateful deal, I would suggest. In short, the Church embraced the idea that permanent virginity, celibacy and total sexual renunciation were always to be preferred as a higher, more perfect form of Christian life. However, marriage, sexual activity and procreation were to be allowed within specific norms. Sex was to be permitted within marriage, though solely for the purposes of procreation, which 'justified' it. Married couples were exhorted to take as little pleasure in sex as possible, never to indulge in sex simply for the sake of pleasure, and never to even contemplate having sex without intending procreation.

So, what we had developing here were not just two approved lifestyles for Christians, but two classes. Virgins, monks and committed celibates formed the higher class of Christian. Married people formed a lower class. Not surprisingly, then, total sexual abstinence gradually came to be demanded of the clergy – though this took centuries to implement. I have no doubt that any Catholic here tonight over the age of, say, forty, would be very familiar with this structure of two lifestyles and two classes within the Church. The 'deal' was amazingly successful and resilient. We live with it still. Now, imagine for a moment all the structures, arguments, legislation, theology, disciplines, spirituality, practices, education, condemnations, exhortations, and indoctrination that have been built up around this 'deal' –and around the ideas underpinning it – over the past 1500 years.

In some ways, the 'deal' has been so successful because it is very 'neat' – the messiness of human sexuality, relationships and even holiness (which can be pretty unsettling, unpredictable and messy) are neatly classified and categorised. In any case, the deal held until the twentieth century when the Church began to talk about sex within marriage having *two* purposes – and equal purposes, at that: procreation *and* the loving union of the couple. The ancient deal was further compromised by increasing acceptance within the Church of marriages, and sexual activity, between people who were infertile. Then, with Paul VI's encyclical, *Humanae Vitae*, we find married couples encouraged to make use of the woman's infertile periods to deliberately plan to have sex without procreating. Sex can be justified, even be holy, without procreation (though only within heterosexual marriage). Such an idea would have been shocking, anathema, to most of the thinkers and leaders within the Church over the past 1500 years.

In some ways most of us have missed the enormity of this change in Church teaching because the context for sexual activity 'looks' the same: heterosexual marriage. However, when we come to the 'gay issue' things are different – perhaps because things 'look' different. In reality, the whole mentality, not to mention the biology, that used to underpin the 'deal' around sexuality, has collapsed. Modern people, including modern Christians, do not accept that life-long virginity is a more perfect way of life than living in a committed loving sexual relationship. They do not believe it is wrong to enjoy sex simply for the delight and intimacy it offers the couple. They do not believe couples must always intend to procreate in order to justify sex. They increasingly *do* believe that it is the quality of interpersonal relating that makes sexual activity healthy, life-giving and holy. Moreover, rather than focusing on so-called 'objective acts', both ordinary Christians and moral theologians are today concerned with the humans who do the 'acting' – with their inner motivations, the meanings they bring to their lives through their 'acts' and the interpersonal relationships between the people who 'act'. For all their protestations and equivocations, Church leaders themselves are increasingly speaking this sort of language too.

Of course, it is not a big step from here to suggest that same-sex couples can be committed, loving, generous and responsible in their sexual activity –and so they can be. When they come forward in the Church, however, and seek honest acceptance, support and blessing, then the collapse of the ancient 'deal', the old mentality around sex, body, pleasure and holiness comes into sharp focus.

This is one of the key reasons why gay relationships are becoming a watershed issue in the church. They make it clear that the structures, theology, legislation, and spirituality built up around the ancient 'deal' regarding sexuality are falling apart. They call for honest change – or, rather, they call for change to be faced honestly. Today we have an Anglican bishop openly hugging his same-sex partner, openly admitting that they enjoy loving sexual relating, and in a context where procreation is not possible. What will the Church do?

So, the 'gay issue' calls for a deeper, more expansive, more honest understanding of human relationships and demands a more profound basis for moral discernment. Underpinning all of this, however, is a very simple, bedrock question that Christianity has still not resolved. In the realities of gay desire, expression and relationships the Church is being forced to ask: Is it good to be embodied? Can bodily, sexual pleasure be good, holy, life-giving – or does it need to be 'justified'? Could 'sex' be good – a human good that can be distorted (like eating or drinking), but that is, in itself, good? What is the meaning of the 'Incarnation' – the core Christian teaching that in Christ God became fully, truly, physically, sexually human?

When I, as a gay Catholic, seek to engage with the institutional Church I need to be aware that I am at the centre of a maelstrom. I also need to see that the long and complex history I have so briefly sketched will continue to unfold, and that my life, faith and experience are a crucial part of that. The 'story' is far from over, far from resolved. I also need to have a sense of the future.

This future is uncertain and unclear. The 'sexual issue' and the 'gay issue' are part of another profound dilemma that will shape this future. How is the Catholic Church going to relate to the modern world? Can the Church survive, thrive and contribute to modern society? Can this 2000-year-old faith, and structure, engage meaningfully with modern, Western, developed, pluralist democracies and with the educated, autonomous adults who live in them? Can the Church engage with modern cosmology, science, biology, anthropology, sociology, psychology, evolutionary theory, cultural diversity, the free press, individual human rights, and articulated human experience itself? And can it do this on the terms of these disciplines and experiences themselves, not on terms set by the Church hierarchy (where some insights from psychology, for example, are deemed worthy by Vatican officials and others are rejected on purely ideological grounds)?

Within the Church itself we also see coalescing around the 'gay issue' a range of intense struggles around the way scripture is used, the way authority is structured and wielded, the place of human experience in the development of doctrine, the various crises faced by celibate clerical culture, the lack of structures to allow lay people to have an active voice in the Church, the absence of processes for discerning the living *sensus fidelium*, and, of course, issues of accountability, transparency, and integrity. Will the Catholic Church be able to reform itself from within, engage creatively with the faith of its own people, and engage wisely and openly with the modern world?

Frankly, I think the jury is still out on these questions. I note, for example, the tendency of conservative Catholic leaders to trumpet the numbers of seminarians in, say, Africa, or the numbers of Churchgoers in parts of Latin America as evidence that 'traditional' Catholicism is alive and well – unlike the situation in the 'decadent' West. Well, I find this sad and delusional. As Africa and Latin America become more developed, their populations more educated, their societies more secular and democratic, the Church will face exactly the same questions it faces now in Europe, the United States, Australia etc. (It is ominous but instructive, for example, that at the United Nations the Vatican has made regular alliances with some of the most repressive and theocratic nations in the world in its attempts to thwart contraceptive education, AIDS initiatives, women's rights and gay rights around the world).

Meanwhile, in the decadent West, whole populations, which include millions of Catholics, are already engaging with the modern world and with modern thought and research, and are welcoming new understandings of the rights of women, the dignity and equality of gay and lesbian people, the importance of environmental care, the need for responsible population planning, the importance of free media, democratic government and pluralism and diversity. The Catholic hierarchy, spurred on by Vatican officials, are running around frantically trying to stamp out these developments – or at least keep them in Vatican dictated 'check'. It won't work, of course, but in the process the vast, profound, messy, wondrous, deeply human blessing that is Catholicism could be turned into a right-wing sect.

The Australian Church historian, Paul Collins, has said that being faithful to 'Tradition' – a term much prized by the Vatican – does not mean slavishly, mindlessly repeating formulas from the past. It means, rather, that I, as a person of living faith, am called to embody in my time and place and actual experience, the faith of the People of God, and to live it out, to *transform* it in and through my living, and to hand it on to a new generation that they might do the same. The only way the 'faith' is alive today is through you and me – and it is only through us that it will be passed on as a living experience, not as a fossilised curiosity from ages past.

So, I stand here today as a gay Catholic, part of this long and unfolding story, and I am called to play my part in shaping the future.

Breadth

In playing my part, I also need to have a sense of the 'Breadth' of the Church, especially in a time when it is looking more and more narrow.

The Catholic Church is an enormously vast, complex and influential phenomenon. Underlying my comments in this section is the question often put to gay Catholics: why do you stay involved?

Many Australians, and certainly many queer Australians, like to imagine that the churches in general, and the Catholic Church in particular, are a spent force, an irrelevant relic, a fading refuge for the old and the weak. This idea might seem credible on a balmy Saturday night in a trendy inner city location, but it is basically a delusion. Let's consider some statistics. The Catholic Church currently has just over a billion members worldwide. It is the oldest and largest and most highly organised multi-national organisation on earth. A quarter of all citizens in the world's biggest superpower – the USA – are Catholics. Australia's largest employer is the Catholic Church, and its huge network of schools, hospitals and welfare agencies is almost totally funded by public money. The Catholic Church educates almost a third of all Australian youth. This same organisation demands, and gets, exemption from all anti-discrimination legislation. Politically, as David Marr has written, 'the churches are the most powerful, influential, best funded, least scrutinised lobby group in Australia'. From phone calls between Popes and Presidents, to what a teacher can say in class in South Melbourne next Monday morning, or to what Catholic parents will tell their teenage children about masturbation, the Catholic Church remains enormously influential on global and local levels.

Consider, for example, the recent document from the Vatican which condemned, in the harshest terms, any legislation to give civil rights to gay couples. In the Latin American country of Colombia the parliament had been moving ahead strongly with legislation for just such civil rights. Furious lobbying, based on this document, has put a sudden stop to that. The proposals have been abandoned. Meanwhile, in Australia, no Catholic teacher can stand up in class next week and say, simply, 'There is nothing wrong with gay relationships'. If she said that her job would be in jeopardy, and no Australian law would protect her.

An organisation that has this sort of power, and this breadth of reach, must be engaged from within and without. Tragically, unjustly, this same organisation has absolutely no structures or processes for allowing challenge or questioning from its members. Indeed, its hierarchy very actively stamps out any challenge or question they deem inappropriate –and they are not slow to discipline the questioner. This makes it all the more crucial that Catholic people who have any conscience, any integrity at all, find ways to challenge the status quo, to make their voices heard, to face down the silencing and structured, sanctified oppression. In Australia one potent example of Catholic people doing just this, and using the free press to make their voices heard, is the Rainbow Sash Movement, a movement which I am privileged to represent.

Another dimension of the 'Breadth' of the Church is more hopeful and empowering. With more than one billion members, the Catholic Church is a vast, rich and diverse 'communion of communities' whose members live enormously varied lives filled with prayer, faith, scholarship, work for justice, service to the poor and marginalised, music, art, ritual, activism and quiet heroism. I think of a gay priest I know who runs AIDS clinics in the slums of an African city, of elderly nuns sentenced to jail for challenging the US military schools that train assassins for repressive regimes in Latin America. I think of networks of nuns and ordinary Catholics in Melbourne who support asylum seekers and their families, of experienced married couples in parishes who volunteer their time to prepare young people for marriage. I think of church workers who care for homeless gay kids on the streets, of monks who live out the decades of their lives in simple work on the land and in silent prayer. The Catholic community is vast. It is filled with people of all cultures and backgrounds who share a love for the Gospel of Jesus and a rich, profound, radical and beautiful heritage of spirituality and justice. Our society desperately needs to be engaged with, and challenged by this community, these people and this heritage – it needs the depth, wisdom, vision and challenge of Catholic people. Catholicism is not owned by any pope or any bishop, and we must not cede it to them.

And so, as a gay Catholic, I claim this broad and rich heritage, and embrace this diverse, quirky, complex, flawed, saintly community.

Even more simply, this is my family, this is the language I speak, the culture I know. I take my stand for justice here.

Depth

At the same time, staying in this community is far from easy, especially for a gay person. The only way to stay, in any creative or life-giving way, is to go 'deep'.

As a Catholic, I have to deal not only with societal prejudice, but with homophobia that has been sanctified and mandated in the name of God and Christ, and that is built into the fabric of Church structures and doctrines. I have to deal with it in other Catholics and I have to deal with it in myself – I have imbibed it just as deeply as they.

So, I find I have to dig deep. I have to go to the very core of faith, hope and love, to the roots of the Gospel, to the heart of the liberation in love promised in Jesus. I have to go just as deep into the truth of my own experience, an experience that has been denied me, that I have been taught to condemn, to flee from, to confess as sin. The first time a gay person begins to just barely suspect that his feelings, his spontaneous attractions and innocent desires might just be – well – 'okay' – he has taken a mighty step on the road to freedom, towards being true to life as he, or she, experiences it as a loved child of God. The day when we can honestly face the delight and inner wellbeing, indeed, the holy peace and joy we feel in the arms of a lover or an intimate friend, we are truly on the way to wholeness and freedom. This freedom is not lightly won, of course, and to discuss this inner journey would take a lifetime – or, at least, another talk.

Put it this way – to go deep into being gay and Catholic means to discover that the liberation in love promised by Christ is not meant to be simply some 'spiritual' reality you experience at Mass, or when you die, after uniting your life-long sufferings with the Lord's Cross – as the Pope puts it. Nor is it simply meant to be political or social or legal freedom. Rather, this kind of freedom is meant to be experienced at every level of body and personality, at the most profound and intimate depths of who you are as human and embodied. It is meant to be experienced sensually, sexually, erotically, as freedom to play, to explore, to delight, to make mistakes, to love and touch and to be loved and be touched.

To be gay and to live honestly and freely within the Catholic tradition means that you must take your life – your real, actual, sexual, embodied life – in your hands, come into the presence of the God who is love, and, with daring and deep trust, decide to risk discovering and living out a story never told in the Church before: the story of God's beloved gay sons and lesbian daughters, the queer story within Christ's mystical Body.

It means creating a voice where there was only the silence of condemnation and the secret of spiritual abuse. It means bringing into the Church, for the first time in history, the spiritual and sexual and relational revelation that God is becoming flesh in gay and lesbian people.

And so, the gay Catholic is called to discover and to create a spirituality that is more truly personal and inter-personal, more adult and honest, more daring and humble, more passionate and physical, more open-hearted and tender, more critical of the status quo, more tenacious and realistic, more forgiving and hopeful, more experimental and playful, more questioning and more radically visionary. The Divine invitation to embrace being a gay Catholic today is a painful, astonishing, frustrating, wondrous, surprising, risky, delightful, uncertain, and prophetic call to walk a path into full, vulnerable, graced humanness. It is a true pathway into wholeness and holiness. It is a gift and grace and blessing for the Church – all the more needed and precious because it is being rejected.

The Body of Christ is sick. It is diseased with abusive patterns of power, with misogyny, homophobia, hypocrisy, hatred of the erotic, and fear of the Incarnation itself. If this Body is ever to be healed, gay and lesbian people will be one of the most potent and profound sources and sacraments of that healing. And so we must live with Depth.

Height

Christ says, 'I came that they may have life in all its fullness'. The Church teaches that 'the Glory of God is the human person fully alive'. If gay Catholics are not merely to survive but to fully, gloriously LIVE, we must lift our sights, we must have a sense of vision that opens us to vistas, hopes and horizons beyond the struggles we face with the institutional Church. We must dare to believe in the coming of the

Reign of God, the kingdom of justice and peace, the liberation of all people in dignity and joy.

We need to have a vision of the liberation promised in Christ spreading out into and through the world, transforming structures, releasing the oppressed, undermining the sanctified status quo and subverting all social forms that rely on exclusion and victimisation. The Reign of God is not about church or piety or simply saving one's 'individual soul' – the Gospel is meant for the world, for the liberation of all people and especially all the marginalised and oppressed, all those whose lives are counted as worthless, all those whose voices are silenced.

So, we need to look up – to seek new vision. As gay people in Australia today we need to look up and see that the Holy Spirit of freedom and justice is binding up the broken-hearted and setting the captives free, as Christ promised – even in the face of the protestations of Church officials! Society is opening to the Spirit in ways the Church still flees from. Society is seeing the intrinsic goodness, the life-giving love, the creative contributions, the earthy humanness, the plain, ordinary, unspectacular dignity of its gay and lesbian citizens. More and more strongly our society is saying to the Church: we will not endorse, or kow-tow to, your condemnation and demonisation of these sisters and brothers. We affirm them as citizens equal in rights and dignity to other Australians. Maybe one day soon our society will go further and refuse to allow the Church itself to discriminate against gay people, but even now we can see a stunning example of how society – secular, democratic, pluralist, free – is evangelising the Church. We need to lift our sights!

We also need to look up and see that gay and lesbian people are already rising, with some style, from the ashes of condemnation and spiritual abuse, and claiming the right to dignity, to life, to love, both as individuals and as communities. We need to see these miracles of grace and courage all around us. How is it that someone with my history as a gay Catholic can stand in this Town Hall tonight and speak what was for so long deemed, literally, 'unspeakable'? How is it that you can feel free to listen –and, I hope, even feel freed *in* your listening? Grace and freedom are breaking in upon us, and within us, here, in Melbourne, tonight. This is no spiritual fantasy. This is the

Word becoming flesh. This is what it means. We need to open our eyes and look up.

I wonder whether the leaders of our Church will ever 'look up' in this way. Perhaps one day, centuries hence, another Pope will light a candle in Rome on Ash Wednesday and ask forgiveness for the Church's sins and crimes against God's gay and lesbian people. Perhaps.

Tonight, instead, we call *this* Pope, *this* hierarchy, *this* Church to embrace, celebrate and learn from gay and lesbian people who stand within the People of God with faith, hope and love, and who have words of grace to offer that are desperately needed if the Church is to be faithful to the Gospel in the modern world.

However, whether they embrace us or condemn us, the Spirit of God calls us, and we need to look up and listen. We have lives to live – with fullness and freedom. We have love to share – with generosity and passion. We have spirituality to embody – with joyfulness and depth. And we have creativity and daring, with which to renew the face of the earth.

May I conclude with words from an old Catholic prayer I learned as a boy – and I pray this for all gay and lesbian people here tonight:

Come, Holy Spirit! Fill the hearts of your people.
Kindle in us the fire of your love.
Come Holy Spirit, and we shall be recreated
And you will renew the face of the earth!

This talk was given as part of the Forum series of public conversations on important social issues, hosted by the City of Melbourne in the summer of 2003-2004. This extended version has been accepted as a chapter in the forthcoming anthology: The Burning Pillow: spirituality in the lives of queer Australians, *edited by Rev Rod Pattenden.*

Ass. Arse. Butt. Bum. Backside

I have a friend in San Francisco who has been dubbed, by many grateful men, the 'Avatar of Ass'. These days his hair may have greyed and his belly relaxed, but his passion for the anus is undiminished.

Chester Mainard first honed his skills in a Master of Science degree, then taught the 'art and science of male pelvic exams' to medical students at the University of Wisconsin for some fourteen years. He combined this work with private practice in massage and psychotherapy. In the mid-eighties he moved to California and began to teach at the Body Electric School of Massage, merging his expertise in the anal area with Joseph Kramer's 'Taoist Erotic Massage' – which focuses on breath, genital massage and full-body orgasm. This deepened and enriched Body Electric's healing and transformative work, and anal work soon became a crucial part of the movement's more advanced courses.

I remember a summer evening during one of Body Electric's extended retreats. It was a balmy night in the mountainous area north of San Francisco, and about forty gay men were listening with rapt attention to Chester give a talk that all of us had needed for years, but that none of us had ever heard. (Apart from information about safe-sex and prostate exams, who has ever seriously talked, in depth, to gay men about our anuses?) Chester's presentation was frank, witty, respectful and so transparently honest that any embarrassment or awkwardness we felt was gently dissipated, leaving us free to really listen and learn.

As gay men, most of us had stumbled into discovering that our anal area could be a locus of pleasure, but that discovery was often accompanied by shame, tension, pain, ignorance, and the kind of secret, smutty guilt fostered by a culture that coined the term 'the abominable crime of buggery' to describe some of the most intimate, intense pleasure male humans can experience.

The anus, Chester informed us, has as many nerve endings as the tip of the tongue, the eye, or the glans of the penis, and so it is an area of exquisite sensitivity and responsiveness. For the same reason, this place of pleasure can also be a place of pain, a place where our bodies and psyches quickly shut down if physical or emotional abuse is experienced or sensed. From an early age, he pointed out, all of us had been taught to react to our anus as being dirty, smelly, unclean and disgusting – the one part of our bodies that was truly 'untouchable'. Not surprisingly, much of the unhealed, unacknowledged, shame-filled, rejected parts of our emotional, psychological, spiritual selves had come to be associated with, pushed down towards and 'held' in this anal area. The good news was that release, healing and ecstatic pleasure were possible, but only through dealing honestly and creatively with our assholes – or arseholes, as we Aussies would put it.

Over the next couple of days Chester and his team led us into an extraordinary exploration of anal pleasure. The preparation was gentle, thorough and sensitive on both physical and emotional levels. Clear and careful protocols were established so that, with hygiene responsibly taken care of, we could relax into the process and open ourselves – both figuratively and literally – at new depths. Just as importantly, there was time for reflection, group process and personal support, so that our emotional needs and boundaries could be honoured.

What became clear was that for many men the whole anal area carries a sense of deep vulnerability. It is that part of our body-selves that we cannot see, and that we rarely allow others to see. We have learned to regard it with disdain, to keep it 'private' and to hide it from 'polite' company. Paradoxically, the kind of lusty anal play that many gay men enjoy can be a way of by-passing the more revealing, vulnerable kind of seeing and touching that truly conscious anal work demands. For some men it can be easier to be fucked than to be truly seen, easier to be rimmed than to be tenderly exposed and opened, easier to be roughly fingered than to surrender to intimate, delicate pleasure in this most vulnerable part of themselves.

Over those few days on that mountaintop, many of us discovered that when we allowed ourselves to fully receive this kind of conscious anal touch, all kinds of emotions, memories and yearnings rose into awareness. Along with new levels of profound pleasure, new levels of self-knowledge and healing became possible. All this was done with a lightness of touch, a gentle sense of humour and a respect for the plain, earthy realities of being human. At the very least, we all became aware of our arseholes in more realistic, honest ways, and developed a simple, healthy acceptance of this much derided, much neglected dimension of ourselves. That experience, in itself, is remarkable in our culture.

For myself, the whole experience was deeply affirming and healing, especially given my religious background, where 'incarnation' was spoken of in reverent tones that in reality hid unacknowledged fear of the body and sanctified the rejection of the messiness of ordinary humanity. If the 'Glory of God is the human person fully alive' – as the Churches love to say – then that human person has an arsehole; and until this plain reality is integrated with reverence and delight, the Glory of God cannot be manifested and I cannot be the person God intended me to be. The path to emotional, psychological and spiritual healing and wholeness lies in and through our arseholes – with all the blessing, anguish, joy and learning they hold for us.

For all that, one of my favourite memories of this journey into anal pleasure, led by the 'Avatar of Ass', came towards the end of the retreat. Chester was making the point that we could no longer refer to difficult people as 'assholes', since we now knew our assholes were sacred places of delight. What to do? After various suggestions, we hit upon 'haemorrhoids' as the appropriate word – painful and pointless irritations that get in the way of anal pleasure. I know a few – I suspect you do too – and the best way to deal with them is to have a healthy, holy, happy anus.

This essay was published in the Sydney Star Observer *in February 2004.*

Tasting the wine

the nun, the filmmaker and the risk of freedom

Wearing her sensible shoes and carrying her oversized handbag, Sister Jeannine Gramick walks along the grand colonnade that frames St Peter's Square. Her dark skirt and check jacket stand out against the pale old marble of the huge pillars. The viewer's eye is drawn to her, this small figure moving amid all the immense immobility.

Sister Jeannine stops to talk to a Swiss guard then turns left and walks to the front door of the Holy Office, the headquarters of the Inquisition. She has come with a gift for the Grand Inquisitor. It is her little book, newly translated into Italian as *Anime Gay*.[1]

Sister Jeannine's gift giving is daring and symbolic. For more than twenty years her ministry to lesbian and gay Catholics has been under investigation by officials from this office. She has been scrutinised, criticised, silenced and condemned. She has borne it all with grace and gentle resolution, and quietly found ways to continue her work.

Finally, in May 2000, in an attempt to silence her permanently, she was banned from ever speaking about the procedures used in the Vatican investigation. Gramick responded in an unforgettable statement: 'I choose not to collaborate in my own oppression.'[2]

It was this statement that first drew the attention of New York journalist and filmmaker, Barbara Rick. As part of her freelance work at ABC news, Rick was poring over the *New York Times* when she discovered this nun 'standing alone, standing on principle and standing up to the Vatican. I knew I had to make a film about this woman'[3]

Four years later Rick's film, *In Good Conscience: Sister Jeannine Gramick's Journey of Faith* [4], is receiving standing ovations in festivals as far afield as Milan, Toronto, New York and Dublin. It had its Australian premiere in Sydney in September.

---

1 J Gramick and R Nugent, *Building Bridges: Gay and Lesbian Reality and the Catholic Church*, Twenty-third Publications, Mystic River CT, 1992. Translated into Italian as *Anime Gay* by Editori Riuniti in 2004.
2 Quoted in the film, *In Good Conscience: Sister Jeannine Gramick's journey of faith*, Out of the Blue Films, New York, 2004.
3 This, and all other unreferenced quotes are from personal conversations the author of this essay held with Barbara Rick and Jeannine Gramick in New York City in May 2004.

I met Barbara Rick and Jeannine Gramick on a windy afternoon in Manhattan. The warmth between them, the good humour and the mutual respect were striking. The sixty-one year old nun, with her smiling eyes and soft pastels, and the feisty forty-five year old New York filmmaker in her basic black, seemed like sisters as they argued and chuckled about the church and the world.

Barbara Rick's office is filled with awards. Three gleaming Emmys hold pride of place and the walls are covered with commendations from institutions across the US, including the prestigious Peabody Award. There are also framed clippings and photographs from her years working with legendary television journalist, Gabe Pressman, who spotted her talent while she was still in college and hired her as his assistant and later as his producer. Success came early to Rick. For more than a decade she threw herself into the world of television journalism and she was rewarded with professional respect and material prosperity. She tells me she enjoyed the gracious lakefront home, three boats and light aircraft that she shared with her first husband.

As she shows me around her office it becomes clear that she takes pride in her achievements. I decide to probe a little. 'Do awards matter to you?' 'Yes, they do', she says. 'It's great to have your work acknowledged. Of course, a BMW convertible and a house in the Hamptons would also be nice!' 'Didn't you already go on that trip?' I protest. She laughs and leaves me to take a phone call. I scan the panoply of awards and wonder how an ambitious, heterosexual Manhattan journalist came to make a film about a demure Catholic nun silenced for her ministry to gay people. Clearly, there was more to this woman than success and prosperity.

Barbara Rick grew up in New Jersey, the eldest of six children in a devout Catholic family. She imbibed three quintessential Catholic qualities: a sense of the spiritual, a concern for the oppressed, and a gnawing shame around sexuality. As we talk, she hunches her shoulders and lets her dark hair fall forward, mimicking her own adolescent attempt to hide her developing breasts, to cover the shame of being sexual, being female. There is still a quiet fury in her at the Church's treatment of women and at the burden of embodied guilt that so many Catholics carry. She tells me she cannot endure the hypocrisy in the Church, the aggressive patriarchy, the abuse of power.

'How can anyone remain in an institution that treats you as inferior and unworthy, that refuses to let you speak?'

I think of the twenty-one year old woman in those framed photographs, surrounded by political and media heavyweights – most of them male. She looks vulnerable and naive. Yet her talent and passion drove her to succeed in one of the toughest professions of all. Was she proving something to herself, I wonder – or perhaps to the hierarchies of power that would have kept her in her place?

Either way, she chose a very particular proving ground. The documentaries that earned her so many awards focused on issues such as: *Homelessness: the shame of a city*[4]; *Asylum in the streets* [5]; *The politics of cancer* [6]; *The hungry* [7]; and *To bear witness*[8] – which chronicled the first world-wide meeting of Holocaust survivors in 1981. Rick likes to be on the cutting edge – but it seems to be the edge where the disenfranchised gather, not simply the edge where the glittering prizes are found. Her journalism in those years shows a person who, almost in spite of her drive for success, is passionate about the rights of the underdog.

In 1993 Rick left her job at WNBC-TV. She says it was because the network had been sold to corporate America and it no longer championed the serious journalism to which she was committed. However, I cannot but wonder whether, having moved beyond the need to prove herself, she was ready for a more radical life challenge. Around the same time she had also left her troubled first marriage and her luxurious but unhappy home. When she speaks of this period, Rick uses terms like 'my life's turning point', or 'having my shackles removed'. She began to turn regularly to meditation, seeking guidance for her new and uncertain path. In time, inspiration came in the form of four short statements that Rick has embraced as her mantras for living: Be humble. Walk erect. Enjoy everything possible. Seek God always and in every situation. In 1998 Rick founded her own independent film company and brought together into a new synthesis

---

4 Homelessness: the shame of a city, WNBC-TV News Productions, produced by Barbara Rick, 1981.
5 Asylum in the streets, WNBC-TV News Productions, produced by Barbara Rick, 1983.
6 The politics of cancer, WNBC-TV News Productions, produced by Barbara Rick, 1985.
7 The hungry, WNBC-TV News Productions, produced by Barbara Rick, 1982.
8 To bear witness, WNBC-TV News Productions, produced by Barbara Rick, 1981.

her skills, passion and deepening spirituality. Her company, Out of The Blue Films, Inc. operates out of an office on East 11th Street. Its mission statement reads like the climax of Rick's personal journey and a blueprint for her future: 'To serenely, enthusiastically and profitably create critically and commercially successful documentary and feature films that explore, articulate and celebrate humanity.'[9]

On a steamy Spring evening in Manhattan's West Village, Barbara Rick is speaking at a seminar for up-and-coming documentary filmmakers. As usual, she is disarmingly frank, and it soon becomes clear just how deep her commitment goes. This woman who once shared ownership of an airplane now works a second job to keep her film company afloat. She has had to learn the ancient mendicant art of begging for funds. She has struggled to release her anxious grip and 'trust the Spirit'. She speaks of her filmmaking as a 'vocation – not in any messianic sense, but in the sense that this is what I deeply believe I am called to do in the world, and if I can make space for the Spirit then the vision and the means will be given'. In a brief exchange when strategies for fundraising are being earnestly debated, Rick says plainly, 'The people I ask for money are not my true 'source'. They are simply a generous expression of it'.

Rick goes on to talk about the duty she feels to be 'responsible, frugal and practical' with the funds she is given. She speaks of 'surrender and trust', of 'putting in the effort and leaving the outcomes to God', of 'following your call' – and suddenly I am struck by the similarity between her words and the admonitions given to spiritual seekers in any number of traditions. The conclusion becomes clear: for Barbara Rick, filmmaking is not just grounded in a spiritual vision, it is itself a spiritual practice. For all the challenges and the uncertainty, she clearly feels a new sense of freedom and purpose that brings creativity and vision into her life.

The more I listen to her, the more I understand how Rick was drawn to the story of Jeannine Gramick. Sister Jeannine could easily have been one of Rick's convent schoolteachers. For many years she was, in her own words, 'a good little nun', wearing the habit and following the rule. Then in 1971 a young man named Dominic told

---

9 Quoted on the company's website: www.outofthebluefilms.com

her he was gay. As a good nun she was accepting and compassionate – and then he challenged her: 'What is the Catholic Church doing for my gay brothers and sisters? And what are you doing, Sister? You better do something!' Gramick says she looked at this whole class of people who were neglected, silenced and oppressed in the name of Christ, and knew her life was about to change. In Rick's film, Gramick says that today, after some thirty years of ministry to gay Catholics, she still feels Dominic at her side, supporting and encouraging her.

It is this profound sense of the dignity of each person that has compelled Gramick to persevere in her ministry. Where others see issues, she sees persons, and so she will face down the Vatican's condemnations by begging Cardinal Ratzinger, for example, to 'meet the wonderful lesbian and gay Catholics I have known', and she will refuse to condemn those who condemn her, encouraging gay Catholics to have compassion for Church leaders since, 'we always have to meet each person where they are'. A moment in Rick's film captures this perfectly. As Gramick walks through St Peter's Square, bringing her troublesome little book as a gift for the man who silenced her, she says, 'We have to forge ahead. We have to keep taking steps that are liberating for others'.[10] This is true whether those 'others' are gay Catholics or red-robed cardinals.

In May 1999, when Jeannine Gramick was ordered to remain silent about her own experience of the Vatican investigation, she reached a turning point. 'Here I was being told I couldn't speak about my own life, about what I had gone through. That's not right. You can't deny a person the right to speak about their own life.' It was at this point that she took her faith and her future in her hands and said, 'I choose not to collaborate in my own oppression'.

This simple statement echoed around the Catholic world. I remember reading it here in Australia and cheering for this nun. As a gay man and a Catholic, I sensed that this woman, after years of ministry to others, had finally been brought face to face with the deepest oppression of all: the oppression that we ourselves collaborate with, the oppression that has taken root in our own hearts. Gay people call this 'internalised homophobia', but it is common to all people who

---

10 Quoted in the film *In Good Conscience.*

have endured entrenched, sanctified abuse, denigration and hatred. At some point we learn to take the oppression into our own hearts and to act out of it, accepting it as the truth about ourselves and as the voice of God. There is nothing worse that can be done to a person's spirit, and nothing harder to undo. It is soul murder, and it bears deadly fruit.

This fruit can be as varied as the anguish of a young man who believes his only options are suicide or celibacy since he thinks he may be gay; or a young woman who hunches forward to hide her developing breasts. This poisonous fruit ripens at the point when we no longer need any religious authority to condemn us as 'unworthy', and we start doing it to ourselves. At so many levels, and with so many rationalisations, we learn to collaborate in our own oppression.

On this foundation rest all the protocols of duplicity, the abuses of power, the structures of patronage and hypocrisy that so disease the Church. People who believe, at depth, that they are 'unworthy' are easily intimidated by those wielding 'sacred power', and they readily learn how to survive in a system that rewards silence and pious complicity. How else can we explain the fact that in an age when there are more educated, articulate Catholics than ever before it is still so rare to hear any priest, theologian, bishop or lay person say the words Sister Jeannine said in 2000?

Barbara Rick says these words struck her to the core when she read them in the *New York Times*, and she knew immediately that this woman's courageous stance had to be put before the world. Four years of intense involvement with her subject have only deepened her respect. In Sister Jeannine she sees a woman who shows every woman, and every Catholic, that you can, and sometimes you must, stand up to abusive systems and refuse to collaborate. As we talk, Rick is anxious to ensure that I realise that the Vatican office to which Gramick delivered her book was the headquarters of the Inquisition. Its name has changed through the centuries, but here was housed the system that oversaw the torture of heretics, the condemnation of Galileo, and the burning of countless women who had been condemned as witches.

As she filmed Sister Jeannine walking up to that Vatican door, I wonder, did Rick see this nun as standing up for her, facing down the religious system that so repressed her as a young woman and that still treats her as inferior? When I put this to her, Rick responds with a passionate 'Yes!' She goes on to express her outrage at Archbishop

Sean O'Malley of Boston, who recently refused to wash the feet of women at the Church's traditional Holy Thursday liturgy. As an artist Rick understands the power of symbol, and as a woman she feels the pain of such toxic discrimination.

So this film, while it continues Rick's practice of exploring issues of justice, also emerges from that personal place where she has known the pain of oppression and had to find the path to freedom. There is something potentially transformative, I believe, about touching this place in oneself. It can move us from 'doing good for others' to realising that we are also the abused 'other', that we too have a right to liberation and that only when we claim our dignity can we truly stand in solidarity with other oppressed people. This is the moment when the political becomes personal. If we can integrate this experience we are freed to risk in surprising and radical ways.

I see this happening in Sister Jeannine herself. Throughout this film we see three deepening levels of liberation within her. Firstly, she says she is 'building bridges' between gay and lesbian Catholics and the Church hierarchy. Her role is to bring the two sides together in dialogue, without judging either side or declaring her own position. Admirable as this is, it remains a ministry to 'others'.

Secondly, we see her talking with groups of gay Catholics. Here it is clear that she is taking sides, she is passionately involved, she is committed to empowering gay Catholics to listen to their consciences in ways that liberate them.

It is this level of Gramick's ministry that most disturbed the Vatican. Unable to prove, however, that she had ever actually contradicted Catholic teaching, Church officials demanded that she reveal her innermost, private thoughts about gay love. She refused, and this was used to bolster the accusation that her ministry was 'ambiguous', 'confusing' and 'harmful' to the 'faithful'[11]. On this basis she was permanently banned from all pastoral ministry to gay people. Significantly, she accepted this ban, but continued to talk critically about her own experience of the Vatican investigation and to discuss issues related to homosexuality.

---

11 Ibid., The reference is to the 'Notification' concerning the ministry of Sister Jeannine Gramick and Father Robert Nugent, issued by the Vatican's Congregation for the Doctrine of the Faith in May 1999, authored by Cardinal Joseph Ratzinger.

The third level of liberation comes when Sister Jeannine is ordered, under her vow of obedience, to remain permanently silent about the investigation itself, about 'my own life, about what I had been through' – as she puts it. Here, the oppression that she had always opposed in the lives of others touched her in her own deepest place. Risking expulsion from her religious order, she responded by doing what she had encouraged others to do – she refused to collaborate in her own oppression. The political had become deeply, painfully personal.

My belief is that this moment will prove transformative for Sister Jeannine. For the time being she has side-stepped the looming crisis by transferring to another order of nuns, the Loretto Sisters, whose superiors are willing to support her in standing up to the Vatican. However, with the current controversy over same-sex marriage stirring Catholic bishops into something rather like a frenzy, it is hard to believe Church authorities will leave her alone for long. They will not have missed the fact she has begun speaking again, both in the United States and in Italy, where the new translation of her book is drawing widespread support. This speaking could look either courageous or foolhardy, but I suspect there is a growing freedom within Sister Jeannine that no Vatican edict will stop.

Throughout her life Gramick has steadfastly maintained two protocols. Firstly, she has never revealed her own sexual orientation, arguing that this silence keeps the focus on her ministry of 'bridge-building'. Several times in this film, however, she talks openly of her deepening unease about keeping her orientation private, especially since she has been so forthright in calling others to come out and claim their right to live with dignity. Listening to her, it is hard to resist the feeling that she is approaching a new edge of openness.

The second protocol is, perhaps, even more crucial since it concerns official Church teaching: Gramick has never openly stated what she personally believes about sexual expression in gay relationships. However, with the issue of same-sex marriage heating up, it is inevitable that she will be challenged on this. Over dinner I put this to her and she replies, 'I support the statement made by the National Coalition of American Nuns in 1996, that if heterosexual unions are recognised by the state, a lack of similar recognition of same-sex unions is an unambiguous discrimination based on sexual orientation. Such discrimination is politically and morally wrong'.[12]

Struck by this, I say to her, 'Does this mean you believe sexual expression in gay relationships can be good and even holy'.

She replies, 'As I say, I support the 1996 statement by the National Coalition of American Nuns'. Not to be outdone, I repeat, 'Yes, but do you believe sex within loving gay relationships can be good and holy?' She pauses then says, 'Yes'. A little stunned, I continue, 'You do realise what you are saying?' She smiles and says, 'Yes'. I sit back in my chair, take a breath and look across the table at Barbara Rick, who is also quietly smiling.

In this brief moment, in a noisy Manhattan restaurant, the liberation in love promised by Christ suddenly seems palpable. I look at these two very different women who have been brought together by their love of justice and their journeys of integration, and who even now are taking new risks as they embrace freedom for themselves and for others.

Is there a deeper purpose moving within humanity, I wonder, that inspires our small actions for justice, our brief moments of courage, our fragile hopes of freedom, and that gently, almost unobtrusively sweeps them up into a greater, grander story of liberation? Do we begin by caring for the oppressed other, only to discover that there is no 'other', and that liberation must take root in our own lives if we are ever to truly stand for justice? What is the hidden energy that draws us into freedom, leading us through the gateway of our own hearts and releasing us to risk everything for a vision of life that only love can give?

I look at Sister Jeannine, this woman who has spent her life challenging sanctified oppression on behalf of others. I think of how she is claiming her own freedom and saying 'Yes' at deeper levels. I raise my glass to her, and wonder who it is that works within us, often in spite of us, to draw us into a new life we hardly dared imagine. I take a sip from my glass and wonder if, even now, I am tasting the new wine of the Kingdom of God.

This essay, written in mid-2004, was published in Reflections, *the journal of Yale Divinity School, New Haven, CT, USA, in May 2006.*

---

12 Statement on same-sex marriage, National Coalition of American Nuns, 1996.

Catholic and gay

the wounded blessing

A talk given at the National 'Campfire' Gathering of Australian Reforming Catholics in Sydney, October 2004. Around this time the world-wide Anglican Communion was engaged in intense and public controversy concerning the episcopal ordination of Rev Gene Robinson, an openly gay man in a committed relationship with another man. This brought to a state of crisis the Church's ongoing discussions and arguments concerning same-sex unions and also the ordination of sexually active gay and lesbian candidates for ministry.

Well, they say this is a 'Campfire' rather than a 'Conference', and so I want to talk to you as if we were at a campfire – which is to say somewhat informally, and from my heart rather than my head.

To say that the 'gay issue' is contentious within the churches right now is to state the obvious – and yet the various churches are handling it very differently. As a Catholic, I was thinking just the other day that the Anglicans are having our fights for us at the moment – and they are fighting openly, painfully and publicly. () Some Catholics see this as yet another reason why Rome is somehow superior to Canterbury, but in fact we are going through precisely the same struggles as the Anglicans. The difference between our churches on this issue is not the struggle itself nor the anguish it evokes, but the fact that some, like the Anglicans, have an open, consultative structure while we have a much more authoritarian – some might even say a more draconian – structure which forces a lid on all the simmering discussion, discontent and disagreement, and gives an appearance of 'unity'. Let's face it, in the Catholic Church people are punished swiftly and efficiently for even suggesting that we should be having the discussions that the Anglicans are so publicly engaged in. In some ways we tend to stand back and watch the Anglican Church fight it out and watch it being almost torn apart – and we wait to see the outcome. What we are seeing, however, is our own struggle made public. The Anglican Church may be in the process of being torn apart publicly over the 'gay issue', but we need to face the fact that the Catholic Church is being torn apart too – but silently and in the midst of enforced uniformity and toxic, systemic denial. There will be no way forward unless we recognise this and allow the struggles to be faced honestly and with as much mutual patience and respect as we can possibly muster.

The 'unity' which is so prized by so many Catholic hierarchs is, all too often, just a communal acceptance of the demand for silence – a demand strengthened by looming threats. Consider the two priests who have been banned from speaking at this conference for example. Even as we anguish over this ban, we are watching the Anglican community arguing publicly about whether it will survive as a unified Church. I noticed the other day that Dr Muriel Porter, who is a well-known Anglican scholar, was commenting about this. She said that in some sense the 'Anglican Church has already split' (these are her words) and she was questioning whether or not it is worth going through this tortuous process of trying to tape together something that looks like structural unity – and all for the sake of what?

It made me think a lot about unity – the kind of unity that the Catholic hierarchy and some Catholic people want to parade, and also the different kind of unity that Anglicans or the Uniting Church seek to preserve (the Uniting Church is also being torn apart on this issue). Whatever our particular ecclesial community may be, we have to ask: What kind of 'unity' are we talking about? What is at stake in preserving 'unity'? Who is liable to be sacrificed for the sake of this 'unity'? What is unity if it involves enforced silence, threats and sanctions? What is unity if it involves offending against justice, against love? Unity must be accountable to justice and love, as must that much trumpeted word, 'truth'. Unity and Truth only have any meaning at all in the context of justice and love. Any truth worthy of the name 'Christian' certainly only emerges in the context of justice and love. Unity is only authentic if it nurtures and is itself the fruit of justice and love.

All of this is just as true for us Catholics as it is for our sisters and brothers in the Anglican Church. We may watch what the Anglicans are going through with discomfort or with detachment, but the reality is that the whole Christian Church – Christianity itself – is engaged in a profound struggle around the 'gay issue' because today, in our era, this issue touches the deepest call of justice and love, it exposes and challenges ancient fears and taboos, it invites radically new understandings of human sexuality, it demands mature, informed approaches to scripture and tradition, and it calls for a whole new way of discerning and receiving the voice of the Spirit among the People of

God. The Church as we know it is on the brink of radical reform, and the 'gay issue' is the flashpoint. Any wonder people are jumpy!

In many ways the issues surrounding gay and lesbian people within the churches look and taste very much like the fights in the early Church about the place of the Gentiles. As you know, the critical, epoch-making struggle then was around the question of whether Gentiles who became Christians had to, in effect, becomes Jews and embrace all of the Mosaic laws, the regulations about food and about ritual purity, the regular customs and practices of Judaism. Most especially, of course, did Gentile men have to be circumcised? So, did you have to become a Jew and stop being a Gentile in order to become a Christian? This was the first and most important crisis that the early Church faced, and it nearly tore the community apart.

Resolution only began to be found in the community after two events. First, Peter had a vision – a Divine intervention, if you like, that revealed that Peter had no right to 'call any person profane'. More on this later. Second, Paul confronted Peter and forced a showdown. This, you might say, was a human intervention and it brought all the communal tension to the surface and made healing and resolution possible. Both events were completely out of the control of any bureaucratic department of the first-century 'Curia' – so to speak – in Jerusalem. It was only after this revelatory dream and this human confrontation that the core revelation of Christ could burst open and empower the followers of Jesus to fully embrace Gentiles and welcome them into the community of the Church. At that point the message of the Gospel could begin to break like dawn upon the world – but first the community had to go through this gritty, messy turf war about who is 'in' and who is 'out', about who should be allowed on this bit of turf and what were the regulations, purifications and rules that should apply to those who would be candidates for membership? What bits of flesh had to be cut off if someone wanted to be part of this community? They had to go through that fight first. It seems we human beings can't avoid that fight, that inevitable, grimy, all too familiar fight over what is clean, what is unclean, what belongs, and what doesn't belong, who is 'us' and who is 'them'. Eventually, if we are listening to the Spirit as thoughtfully as Peter and Paul were, it starts to dawn on us that there simply is no 'clean' and 'unclean', no 'us' made secure by some who must remain 'them'.

That is what is happening I think in the gay issue today in the Churches. The ripples of that disturbing, shocking revelation have been spreading out through the ages, breaking down barriers and conventions and bringing liberation and a new way of being human together. Today the ripples have started to reach the issues, so long repressed, concerning gay and lesbian people, concerning human sexuality that is not 'justified' or 'made clean' by marriage or children, concerning embodied pleasure that lies beyond ritual conventions and sanctified social controls. It begins to dawn on us that sex and sexuality might be good in themselves, that gay and lesbian people might just be part of the ordinary 'us' of humanity and that pleasure, the body, and sexual expression might be meant for our delight and for deepening our loving communion with one another. It is the ripple of revelation – the same revelation that led the Church into that first crisis in the first century around the issue of Jews and Gentiles. Now it is reaching this other boundary of the so-called 'sacred' – this time concerning the place of gay people in the Christian community. Once again, as always, some righteous people want to draw lines in the sand and cry that this is the last straw and that the sky is falling and Satan is at the gates, and everything they held sacred is going to fall apart. Well, in a sense they are right – those 'sacred' structures are going to fall apart. Then the revelation of God's love in Christ can burst forth again spreading freedom and liberation and joy that we had never dared to imagine, the glorious freedom of the children of God that Spirit had been preparing for us all along.

Not surprisingly, as we grow towards this freedom there will be struggles and anguish as those most invested in the 'sacred' structures and exclusions seek to hold them all together in the name of sacred truth and unity. As we struggle together, and as words like 'truth' and 'unity' are bandied around, we need to be asking questions. I suggest one core question we must be asking all the time and at every level is 'who is being sacrificed here – and in the name of what, and by whom?' Gay and lesbian people are always being told that of course the Church loves them and wants to welcome them, but, well, there is the issue of sacred 'truth' and unchangeable teachings; or of course we mustn't imperil Church 'unity' by moving too fast, and so on. We feel for your suffering but unfortunately you have to be sacrificed for the greater good. 'Unite your sufferings to the Lord's cross', they tell us.

Well, I want to say to my fellow Christians that Jesus died precisely so that no-one would ever have to be sacrificed ever again for the sake of anything 'holy'. Wasn't that the point of the 'Lord's cross'? Our Catholic 'truth' and our Christian 'unity' can never be about sacrificing, about finding someone who has to be 'other', someone who has to be outside the boundary so that we could have 'unity', so that we could maintain doctrines we think make us 'us'. Jesus allowed himself to become the cursed one, the one cast outside the camp, the one hanged on the tree, to say to us: 'If you want to look for the revelation of God this is where you have to look: among those cast outside your camp, among those excluded by your regulations of the 'holy', among the ones human righteousness judges as accursed, among those forced to occupy the place of shame. This is where the revelation of God's love takes flesh – in every age and in every community.' And yet here we are still back in our sacred enclaves playing little holy games, drawing lines and making some people sacred and pushing everyone else out, refusing to open our ears, let alone our hearts, to anything or anyone who challenges our notion of 'truth' or our precious 'unity'. And so we betray the whole point of the life and death and resurrection of Christ.

Let me be clear. This struggle to embrace the shocking revelation of God's love in Christ reaches new frontiers in every age - our age is nothing special here. Today, however, this struggle is focusing on the place of gay and lesbian people within the Church and in discussions around the nature of human sexuality. This is a blessing – a tough blessing, a wounded blessing – but by God, it is a blessing! It is also the ongoing revelation of incarnation.

The Mystery of the Incarnation is, perhaps, the core Christian revelation – and the one that the Church itself has never fully grasped. This revelation is not a set of propositions – never has been, never will be. It is a person. The theologians have traditionally talked about both the 'message' and the 'person' of Christ – but of course in Jesus you really cannot separate them. God reveals Godself in Christ – and this only has meaning in the interpersonal encounter with Christ and with other persons. Furthermore, the personal dimensions of that revelation in Christ, the depth and mystery of 'person', have profound implications for understanding the depths of any person and for the way we live together as persons in community. This is all part of the revelation in Christ. The dimensions of the Incarnation which can't be contained in propositions – indeed, the very core of that mystery – can only be accessed through communion with other persons. You are only going to be able to become open to the core reality of the Incarnation through profound, intimate communion with other persons. So you have got to put your propositions, your doctrines and teachings, aside for a while and engage with persons, engage with them with reverence and open-heartedness, in a spirit of justice and love, if you are ever to understand even a hint of what God is revealing in the mystery of Christ.

This encounter is going to radically reform all your propositions and doctrines and teachings because they are only ever a stammering attempt to name something which cannot be named, and they are always in need of reform in the light of justice and love. Once you start to mistake the stammering for the mystery that is being revealed in persons, you have moved away from the communion of the Christian revelation. You risk betraying the Gospel itself.

One distressing, graphic example of this was contained in the recent Vatican document on same-sex unions – the declaration concerning certain legislative proposals to give legal recognition to same-sex couples, issued by the Congregation for the Doctrine of the Faith, Vatican City, July, 2003. I don't know how many of you read it; you all should have read it! If it had been about Jewish people, for example, you would have read it and you would have been horrified and there would have been justified horror all round the world. But it was about gay people and so there wasn't. A lot of people wrung their hands in private, but where was the outrage? I talked to some people in positions of influence in the Church and asked them where their outrage was. They replied: 'Oh, I don't read that stuff!' This is known as a cop-out, and it is not a valid basis for moral discernment.

That Vatican statement is a classic example of the failure to engage with persons. Gay people are never addressed directly – we are objects to be talked about, not persons to be engaged with in a spirit of respect. There is no affirmation at all of our attempts to shape lives of love and integrity. The document is filled with judgement and condemnation. One thing the Vatican document didn't do was to state that gay people are evil. Virtually every other negative statement possible was made – that was the only step it didn't take. However, as one theologian pointed out, the document does provide a clear theoretical basis for quarantining gay people. It doesn't actually recommend that, but if a government wanted to take up that document and use it as a theological basis for setting up camps, the basis is there. I could point to it quite easily. It is very clear. This document was issued in the name of the worldwide Church. All politicians are supposed to obey it and all people are called to support and implement its demands – which involve the total and immediate repeal of any legislation that gives civil rights of any kind at all to same-sex couples.

There is something very profound and disturbing going on here. I haven't much time to go into it. My concern is not just about the need to be nice to a group of people in the Church who have been beaten up for a very long time, or about the need to recognise that maybe gay people have something worthwhile to say to the Church. This is all true, of course. However, there is something here that is much, much more core, more foundational than that. The issue here is certainly about sensuality, sexuality, pleasure, the body. It is about Incarnation. It is about how the Church engages or fails to engage with persons. It is about asking: Where do we find truth? How does truth emerge? What is truth accountable to? It is about asking: how do we engage with one another in ways that are loving and honest?

To give just one example of this issue of personal and communal honesty and integrity: we all know that for centuries gay men have been ordained as priests and consecrated as Popes and Cardinals and Bishops. The question isn't whether we should ordain gay people; the question is whether we should tell the truth, and honestly accept, acknowledge and celebrate the gifts of gay people within the Church. At a deeper level still, it is about stopping the sacrificing of gay people. I have to say this: we are in this bizarre situation where fifty, sixty, seventy per cent of the ruling class within the Catholic Church who maintain all of this are themselves closeted homosexual men. They have sacrificed a certain dimension of their personhood. To justify that sacrifice, to prove to themselves that they were right and righteous, they have to endlessly repeat that sacrifice by sacrificing other gay people again and again and again. They continually tell us that this is in the name of God and they can't do anything else because this is what is in Scripture. Nonsense! This is not what is in Scripture. This is not what Scripture is about. Anyone can pull out bits of Scripture for almost any purpose. In this case there are just six verses that are used to justify the condemnation of gay people (and at least five of these are highly problematic!). There are far more verses on lots of other issues that no-one, including the hierarchy, takes any notice of. More importantly, the core of Scripture is not at all about these rigid, non-negotiable, blanket condemnations.

I think we are in a very unique moment in the Church. If you look at what is happening in the Anglican Church, it seems the whole thing could fall to bits tomorrow. And that is the way it is for us Catholics as well – except that there is this iron fist ready to come down on anyone who speaks up. (Apparently I can't speak on Church property, for example).

I'd like to return to that image of the argument that divided the early Church. You might remember that scene in the Acts of the Apostles when Peter went to the house of Cornelius. (In this commentary I am following the work of British theologian Dr James Alison, whose writings are largely inspired by Rene Girard's ground-breaking thought on the nature of the sacred and human violence.) The day before he met that household he had a vision. Now Cornelius and his household were all pagans. They were not gentile Christians; they were un-evangelised, uncircumcised pagans. They hadn't even heard the word of Christ. Just before meeting them Peter had this vision of a great blanket being dropped down from heaven with all kinds of animals in it, animals both clean and unclean. In the vision Peter was told to kill and eat – sorry, this was not a very good vegetarian sort of command – but the point is that at first he refused to kill and eat any animals that were 'unclean' according to Jewish dietary laws. The voice in the vision said to him, 'What God has made clean you have no right to call profane' – so Peter killed and ate. Peter realised in that moment that none of these animals was unclean. We can't imagine the revolution this was for a Jewish mind of the first century. Anyway, not long after he came out of his trance, Peter was called to the house of all these unclean, un-baptised pagans, and when he arrived he told Cornelius that he was fine with visiting them because 'God has made it clear to me that I must not call any person profane or unclean'. Peter then began to talk to them all about the mystery of Christ.

Suddenly, as he was still speaking, the Holy Spirit came down upon the whole household, and all these pagans started speaking in tongues and proclaiming the wonders of God. Then Peter said, 'O, my God. I'll have to baptise them I suppose. What else can I do? They have obviously received the Holy Spirit as much as we have, without being baptised, without becoming Jews, without having bits of their flesh cut off. Just as they are, the Holy Spirit has filled them. We'd better baptise them'. And that was where the whole thing burst open – right then at that moment.

Now it seems to me – I am hardly the only one thinking this that something very similar is happening right now regarding the place of gay and lesbian people within the church and within society. The Holy Spirit is bursting out, bubbling up, pouring forth in the lives of gay and lesbian people – whether religious officials like it or not. Despite all the religious regulations, the theological issues, the rubrics or the sanctified condemnations, gay and lesbian people are being revealed as filled with love, goodness and the Spirit every bit as much as our straight sisters and brothers.

Some people are getting it – both within the church and within society. Actually, it is secular society that is increasingly saying to church officials: 'You can't sacrifice these people any longer. They are ordinary human beings just as much as we are, with the same dignity and worth. They should have the same rights; they should have the same freedoms; they should have the right to employment; they should have the right to have loving unions with legal protection and maybe even marriage.' Society is saying this. Society, even without recognising it, is being empowered by the Holy Spirit beyond the boundaries of the so-called clean and sacred and religious, and is furthering the work of the Gospel. And gay people are saying, 'Grace has shown me that my life reveals God's love every bit as much as your life does. Sure, I have my brokenness and my mess, but so do you. I am just a human being like you, filled with the Holy Spirit just like you, trying to live out the love of God in my relationships and my sex and my joy and my work and my prayer and my faith. Let's be companions for one another on the journey'. This is a wonderful, stunning, grace-filled moment in history!

However, sadly, in this case 'Peter' is not there yet. Peter hasn't quite got to the point where he can say: 'My sisters and brothers, you're obviously filled with the Holy Spirit just as much as we are! Welcome! Now come and teach us a bit because we have been caught in all these old sacred regulations and rigid structures. Let's celebrate and release the Holy Spirit together with even more power and vitality!' Peter isn't quite at that point. Peter is running around frantically trying to tell the vibrant, glowing, Spirit-filled gentiles to 'Keep silent! Stop speaking in tongues! Stop proclaiming the wonders of God without our permission or you will never preach in this town again!' Or words to that effect. That is what Peter is doing at the moment.

However, the Holy Spirit will not be contained or censured or dammed up. She blows with power and glows with glorious freedom wherever she wills – both within society and within the Church. In many ways, it is through secular society that the Spirit is offering to the Church this new gift of freedom, this deeper revelation of Divine Love made incarnate in the lives of gay and lesbian people. Again we learn the wonderful lesson that the revelation of Christ is not about Church or religion – it is about life in its fullness and about people learning to live as sisters and brothers in love and justice, and together bringing forth the Reign of God. If you want to see where the Spirit is working today, look at the places where this revelation is coming to birth – the revelation that nurtures honesty, justice and love. Opening to this revelation, in any and every age, will break us apart both as individuals and as communities, and amid the ruins of our old sacred securities the Word of God will burst into flame. This is how it always is – in the place of the wound we find the blessing!

Shortly before this gathering, Cardinal George Pell, Archbishop of Sydney, forbade the Sisters of St Joseph from hosting the conference on their property, and banned two diocesan priests from speaking at it. The gathering went ahead at a nearby secular venue, with the Sisters of St Joseph offering to cover the extra costs involved. The talk references works by Dr James Alison, including, *Faith beyond resentment: fragments catholic and gay*, Darton, Longman and Todd, London, 2001; and also *On being liked*, Darton, Longman and Todd, London, 2004.

The Feast of Purification

At the beginning of February the Church celebrates the Feast of the Purification of Mary, the mother of Jesus.

This ancient feast has become a charming enough affair these days – some blessed candles, a few prayers, perhaps a small procession in honour of Our Lady. However, many Christians, and especially Catholics raised on images of Mary as the 'gentle, chaste and spotless maid', might wonder what the Blessed Mother had to be purified of. The answer is simple: childbirth.

Ancient Jewish Law decreed that a woman would be 'unclean' for forty days after the birth of a son and for eighty days after the birth of a daughter. She would then have to bring two doves to the Temple. These would be sacrificed by the male priest in order to purify the mother. After this ceremony she could participate again in the cultural and religious life of the community, and would no longer spread 'uncleanness' to those who touched her. Mary, the mother of Jesus, had to go through this ritual 'purification' like any other mother in her culture.

To modern people both these rituals and the religious worldview that underpinned them may well feel alien and even abhorrent. It's hard not to see them as simply a ritualised denigration of women based upon ancient fears and taboos around blood, birth, sex and female procreative power. We are glad we live in more enlightened times. It is sobering, however, to realise that not only does the Church still celebrate the 'feast' of Mary's 'purification', but that plenty of contemporary Christian women have undergone the ritual of 'Churching' after childbirth.

As recently as the 1960s Church manuals recommended that as soon as possible after giving birth a mother should present herself outside the door of her local church. She would kneel holding a lighted candle and the male priest would come out and sprinkle her with holy water, bless her, then lead her into the church. She would kneel outside the sanctuary while he said a prayer: 'Save your handmaid, O Lord. Let the enemy not prevail against her. Let the son of iniquity not approach her ...' After being sprinkled with more holy water she would be given a final, solemn blessing.

The updated, 1965 version of the ceremony that I consulted for this article had a brief preface that included a rather revealing disclaimer: 'It should be noted that there is no mention of a purification of the mother ...' wrote the ecclesiastical editor. The fact that he felt compelled to tell the reader what is *not* included in the ceremony is significant. It offers a kind of back-handed reference to the real origins of the ceremony, as well as a rather lame attempt to counter the blatant symbolism of the ritual itself.

After several decades of feminism it is hard to imagine Christian women submitting to such a ritual today, yet the Church continues to celebrate the purification of Jesus' mother, or Candlemas, on February 2nd each year.

The timing of the feast is significant. The beginning of February was sacred in ancient European religions. For Celtic people this was the festival of Brigid, the great triple goddess of the hearth, of the smith and of healing. All over Europe people would light sacred bonfires and call on the goddess to sustain them and to bring forth the warmth and new life of Spring. Just as the Church replaced the pagan festival of the Winter Solstice with Christmas, so it repressed and replaced this ancient celebration of fire and feminine power. Over time, the sacred bonfires became church candles blessed by a male priest in memory of Mary being cleansed, as all women needed to be cleansed, of the mess of childbirth and the mire of femininity. For women, as the early church fathers noted, were the 'devil's gateway', and their dark, insatiable erotic energy could only be tamed through renunciation, prayer and submission to sacraments performed by celibate male priests. Such attitudes have survived into modern times in rituals like the churching of mothers, in attitudes towards contraception, in the condemnation of all forms of sexual pleasure outside of the procreative act within heterosexual marriage, in the exaltation of virginity and priestly celibacy, and in the resistance to women priests.

Given all this, it would be easy to suggest that the feast of the Purification should be eliminated from church life as soon as possible. However, as we so often find, the complex traditions surrounding this ancient feast contain resources for its subversion and, indeed, for the transformation of the Church itself.

A few years ago, I was part of a community that sought to re-imagine Christian life and ritual. Each February we would gather in a lovely old bluestone church in Richmond, Melbourne, and celebrate the Feast of the Purification – not of Mary or of women, but of the Church.

We prepared by re-arranging all the seats, getting rid of the straight lines and leaving only a large circular space. In the centre of our ritual circle we placed a large, clear bowl of water from the ocean – that ancient mother of life. With chants and prayers we gave thanks for the blessing of water and for all the forms of life that emerge from it and are sustained by it. We prayed that its salty vitality would purify and renew ourselves and our church, like tears cleansing a wound, like the waters of the womb. Taking large sprigs of green leaves we then moved in turn to the east, west, north and south walls of the church and playfully – but thoroughly – sprinkled them with sea water. We called on the divine feminine power of the Holy Spirit to come from the four directions and cleanse the church of the disease of misogyny, the fear of erotic energy, the addiction to power and control, the sin of homophobia and the rejection of earthy sensuality. Coming into the centre of the church, we then sprinkled one another, for all these religious infections have taken root, not just in structures and hierarchies, but in ourselves. Then, in solemn silence, we circled the table of the Eucharist, the pulpit and the Bible, sprinkling them and purifying them of all the fear, hatred, exclusion and cruelty perpetrated, and perpetuated, in the name of God.

We reformed our circle in the centre of the church, around another bowl – a metal cauldron holding methylated spirit, (which burns safely and without smoke or sparks). As we intoned an old Celtic 'ode to Brigid' – who is both Celtic goddess and an actual Irish saint – women carrying lighted candles came from the four directions. They gathered in the centre and lit the cauldron of spirit. A sudden flame shot up, burning with clear and startling brilliance. Chanting gently we circled the new fire, calling into our church new flames of feminine energy, a new passion for justice, new openness to erotic love and a new reverence for the earth itself. We lit tapers from the fire and passed them around as we finished our ritual by singing a modern hymn: 'Send down the fire of your justice! Send down the rains of your love! Come send down the Spirit, breathe life in your people and we shall be

People of God.' We then offered one another a tender, hearty hug and shared a feast of fruit and wine.

Our community found that this 'feast of purification' was a good way to begin February each year – in the midst of the sweaty sensuality of the Australian Summer. We found that it renewed our hope and enlivened our passion for the embodied, erotic transformation of our church. As we move into the twenty-first century, however, it sometimes feels as if our church is becoming even more dry and brittle, more addicted to patriarchy, more hostile to eros, more misogynistic, more homophobic. And yet, if the community of the church is to have a life-giving future in the century that lies ahead, we will need to embrace our sensuality and free the divine power of the feminine. We will need to find new forms, new rituals, new wisdom – and new images of God, the One who, as Julian of Norwich put it, 'lies forever on a maternity bed, giving birth'.

From the Ritual of Purification

God of Life, God of Love,
Giver of all joy,
Teach us to live with integrity and passion.
Teach us to love with tenderness and freedom.
Let us become prophets of hope
And servants of justice
That your people come to know life in all its abundance And open their souls to the mystery and diversity of your endlessly creative heart.

We ask this through Jesus, our brother, our lover and our lord, Amen.

This essay was published in the e-journal, Online Catholics in January 2005.

After Garrison

Dear Sacred Brothers,

As I write, a gorgeous silver moon is rising, wild and full, over the dark hills and the silent fields of a Trappist monastery in rural Massachusetts. I left Garrison on Sunday, enjoyed a ride and a chat with Charlie and Sheldon, then waited in the cold outside Worcester Railway Station till Brother Albert picked me up to take me to St Joseph's Abbey in Spencer for a few days. Albert, a chubby older man, was chatty, friendly, hilarious. He was also once a novice of a dear old departed friend of mine, Dan Kelliher, a gay monk who died a year or so ago at 78 years of age. Dan has seemed close to me on this whole journey – and various contacts I made with him have led me to this gracious stone abbey where some seventy men live out their lives in prayer, work and silence.

Last night I sat at the back of the soaring stone church, listening in the dark as scores of deep male voices chanted soft, warm prayers to the Blessed Mother. The rich, masculine, haunting tones rose and fell in the night, as the lamp flickered before the image of Mary, Sacred Mother, Divine Feminine. I thought of you, my brothers, and of our chanting in the night. As the monks bowed in their soft white robes, I thought of your sweaty bodies and your smiles, of your touch and your kiss, of bodies blessing bodies, hearts close, eyes bright. As the Abbott sprinkled us with holy water I thought of your tears, of the womb water of those hot tubs, of the river where we stood and prayed peace and transformation on the young men who were training for war, just across the water at West Point. As I caught a glimpse of young candidates among the old white-haired monks, I thought of the young men we blessed in our circle, young men who, I pray, will delight in the erotic beauty of their youth, not deny it.

We are different, these monks and I. I do not wish to be one of them. But I give thanks for their welcome, for their care, for the way they hold a place of silence and gentle warmth on the fringes of the Church. I also give thanks that they remind me, in their bodies and their lives, that it is not crazy to live out your life in devotion to the Spirit, to leave everything for one thing, to seek and search and yearn and trust in the night, year after tedious year, as the hidden eyes of your soul gradually, ever so gradually, become accustomed to the darkness of God.

I want to say to you, my sacred, erotic, sweaty, hugging, dancing, strong, wild, tender brothers, that those wonderful, blessed, frustrating, entrancing, initiating three days at Garrison can be a sweet memory, or they can become a gateway. You know this. I know this. We also know that the world needs new kinds of monks, new kinds of spiritual seekers, new images of holiness, new ways to wonder about the Mystery, new images of that which cannot be imaged. The monks here are old, most of their candidates will leave, their cemetery will fill soon enough.

In so many ways, I loved our three days at Garrison. I loved being with you, watching your beauty, hungering for you and letting you go free, touching and arguing and laughing and weeping. I loved being with you. Yet I want brothers who will walk beside me on the long, long, life-long journey into God, on the road into the desert of the Divine, on the path into silence, emptiness, humility and simplicity - as well as the path of erotic, ecstatic delight. There are men here, in this monastery, who would almost be such brothers, if I would only deny my sexuality, silence my body, repress my glorious gayness and promise never to touch anyone again. I will not do it.

And so I turn to you. Are we in this for a lifetime? Could we be on this road for a lifetime? Are there men of spirit here who will give their lives to this journey into Mystery? Who will be life-long brothers and lovers on the road into God, on that path where all that we are – body, soul, sweat, mind, heart, balls, brilliance – is realised, in emptiness and in ecstasy as the Beloved?

I have no doubt that there are such men among us already – such men were there at Garrison. I also have no doubt that many other men, at Garrison and around the world, young and not so young, want to be part of such a band of brothers. Well, brothers, the monasteries are emptying, the space is being vacated. Is God clearing the way for us?

A few years ago, my old gay friend Dan took me around the new extensions on the Trappist monastery at Snowmass, Colorado. Dan was just a few months away from death. He told me the community had shrunk to about fourteen men – in this beautiful, enormous building. 'I don't know who it's supposed to be for. The Holy Spirit is certainly emptying the place of us. It will have to be for some other groups.'

If you think I mean a physical building you are half-right. The other half is the place where our work awaits.

Thank you, thank you, thank you, for the gift of our time at Garrison – I will always be grateful, blessed and blessing, because of our time together. But what I really want to know is – can we walk, together, through the Gateway? How would we do it? What would be on the other side? What would it ask of us? Where would it lead us? What would we have to leave behind and what would we have to embrace? I don't know. I do know that I am in this for a lifetime. God is not a hobby. You know this. I know this. I also know I need to be careful what I ask for in the presence of that God.

Most of what I have written here is not what I expected to write. Blame the moon. Or blame the seventy sleeping monks who will rise, again, as they do every day, at 3.15 am, to chant their psalms through the darkness, side by side.

I am tired of being alone on the path. You say I am not alone. I accept that, I receive that – and so I ask you: how can we walk the path together, for three days and for a lifetime?

Well, as little Gretel said to Fraulein Maria, 'The sun has gone to bed, and so must I' (I am a gayman, after all, lads!). Please accept these ruminations, which I share with deep affection and respect.

Michael Kelly

This letter was written while I was a guest in the retreat centre at St Joseph's Abbey, Spencer, Massachusetts, in May 2004. A few days before, I had taken part in the 'Gay Spirit Summit' at Garrison Institute in New York State. This gathering brought together 135 gay men from around the world who have been leaders in the area of gay spirituality.

Greetings from New York

Manhattan, September 2017

A letter originally published in *Bent Street: Australian LGBTIQA+ Art, Writing & Ideas*, 1 – 2017 (Clouds of Magellan Press, 2017). Included for the first time in this updated edition of *Seduced by Grace*.

Dear Family and Friends,

I am writing to you on a sunny autumn afternoon in New York State, and sending you love and warm greetings.

It is now a bit more than three months since I set off from Tullamarine airport for Manhattan, and it seems high time that I wrote and let you know that I am thinking of you, as well as sharing with you some of my experiences. Please excuse this group email – I am not a fan of the genre, but at least it allows me to reach out and say hello to you.

It has been a very rich time on many levels – but not without its challenges and demands. Still, every time I was tempted to complain about the intensely hot and humid summer in Manhattan, I reminded myself that missing Melbourne's winter was not a bad trade-off – some nights in July, for example, could be 26C with 80% humidity!

The month-long Research Colloquium, which I participated in in July, was a great experience, and one moment stands out. As part of the program, we each took at least an hour to share something of the overall project we are involved in, and then invite discussion, questioning and ideas. When we had gone all around the circle – which was about half way through the month – I sat back and let myself be amazed by the many diverse ways in which these twelve people were working for transformation in our world.

That week I had the chance to have a discussion, in some depth, with Dr Christian Scharen, one of the key people who organised the Colloquium, and I asked him how these specific individuals were selected from the fifty or so who applied. He said that a key factor was that the scholars had to be more than just academics – they had to be people who were actively engaged, in some radical way, in bringing about change.

So, we had Francisco, a fiery young Lutheran leader who is studying a once all-white Lutheran congregation in New York that had transitioned peacefully and organically to being mainly a black community – and this would become part of his challenge to the whole Lutheran church in the USA. We had Amber, a dynamic young academic from St Louis, who is trans and a person of colour, and who is writing a book-length 'Letter to my Gender-fluid child'. We had Mark, a professor from Tennessee who is seeking to re-invigorate the Protestant left in the USA, and revitalise its commitment to social justice. We had Ann, a university lecturer and poet from York in the UK, who is seeking to develop a 'wild, Gaia-like sensibility as a way of rethinking our current world problems' in social, political, personal and environmental areas, and who is passionate about 'staying with the trouble' as a strategy of hope. We had Kate, a theologian from Cincinnati who does radical work with prisoners who are transitioning back into the community, and who is passionate about developing theological and prophetic approaches to 'the new racial caste system that is mass incarceration and which decimates families and communities materially and emotionally'. We had Zaynab, a Muslim woman of colour who is studying the roots of the exclusion/regulation of women in traditional Muslim and Jewish ritual spaces, and seeking to find new ways to reform ancient practices. We had Ursula, a Lutheran pastor and theologian from Germany, who is studying and writing about the church's attempts, and failures, in dealing with Luther's anti-semitic writings, and seeking to explore new frontiers in Jewish-Lutheran relations. We had Lek, a young Buddhist monk from Thailand, who was formerly a lawyer and an environmental activist, and who is now committed to developing a radical new approach to social justice within the whole Theravadan Buddhist tradition. We had Aimee from New York, who is studying how governments, local councils and real estate developers have used racially based policies to change whole neighbourhoods, to distort patterns of home ownership, and to accumulate wealth by systematically disenfranchising black communities. We had Sharon, from York in the UK, who is studying the emergence of women priests in the Anglican church in the UK, and exploring the ways they have become co-opted by the power structure, or, by contrast, have become resistors and reformers. And then of course, there was this fellow from Australia …

As I looked around that circle, I was moved to tears by the many different stories, by the differing passions and pathways, and by the common commitment to do what we could, in our own corner of this troubled world, to nurture more hope, more light, more justice, more compassion – and new kinds of vision. As I write these words, I am also deeply aware of you, dear friends, and the many different ways each of us tries to nurture a future that is more hopeful, more loving and more just.

When the Colloquium ended I was invited to spend August at a small retreat centre about ninety minutes north of Manhattan – it is run by a gay couple who are old friends of mine from my time in California in the early 1990s. It was lovely to spend some time in the country after the buzz of the city, and to settle into a gentler pace …

Throughout September I was back in the city, apartment-sitting for some friends, and catching up with some new contacts and colleagues. One the gifts of New York is that it brings all kinds of people together. One of the new friends I have made this time around, for example, has been Fr Bryan Massingale, who is a professor of moral theology at Fordham University – a Jesuit college in the city. He is the foremost theologian specialising in issues of racism and the Catholic Church. Getting to know him has been a highlight of my time here, and his interest in my own writing has been a real gift and a great affirmation. Knowing him has also made events like those in Charlottesville feel much closer and more urgent. Bryan was deeply disturbed and angered not only by the marches, the torches, and the racist and anti-semitic chants – he was, in some ways, even more distressed by the lukewarm responses from so many Catholic bishops. This is a dangerous and uncertain time in the US, and it is an honour to know someone like Bryan.

On Friday night last I took the train from Grand Central Station – on an unseasonably warm night, and headed back to the retreat centre – where autumn is finally beginning to colour the leaves. It's good to be back in the quiet – and I need to get to some serious writing if I am ever to deliver on my book deal with Routledge! My time in the city was great, though, with many meetings with friends, lots of meals, and a range of theatrical experiences – from the sublime to the (almost) ridiculous. As you can imagine, I have to manage my health and my energy very carefully when I am travelling and staying in one apartment after another, and New York City is both irresistible and exhausting.

I keep up-to-date fairly well with news from home – and it seems lots of people are working hard and with great passion to bring about marriage equality. It is especially great to see Fr Frank Brennan, the two major Jesuit schools, and countless Christians from all denominations speaking up for LGBT people, and for our relationships. Just a few years back, when I was deeply involved in the Rainbow Sash Movement, voices and views like these would have been unimaginable. Hopefully Martin Luther King was right, and the arc of history does bend towards justice …

Being here in the US, though, as this time is unsettling and disturbing. More than once a New Yorker has expressed real concern about the possibility of the city becoming a target in a North Korean conflict – and everyone who is sane continues to be horrified by the dangerous antics of Donald Trump, who is really exposing the deep darkness that has always been there in the soul of America. As Fr Massingale puts it, 'Trump is an exaggeration – but he is not an aberration'. This is undoubtedly the most unsettled and disturbing time I have ever experienced in the US – and I have coming here for extended periods since 1989.

For all that, however, there is so much about this country, and especially about New York, that is extraordinary and wonderful – for example, I attended a recent open debate/discussion on LGBT issues and the Catholic Church at Fordham University here in New York. A well-known Jesuit, Fr James Martin, has written a book about 'building bridges' between the LGBTI community and the hierarchy of the church – basing it on the teachings about sensitivity, compassion and respect. It's important work, but it does skirt the deeper issues. He was challenged by the man who is Chair of the Theology Department at Fordham, who is openly gay and married to his partner. This is the kind of event that New York offers …

I must admit that it is reassuring to have a ready passage back to Australia, even with all of our own craziness and darkness. Speaking of which, my current plan is to head across to the west coast, probably San Francisco, in early December, and then fly back home, arriving on December 14. I am sure I will be very ready to be home.

For now, though, I will enjoy the changing of the leaves and the brilliant autumn colours and the cool crisp days – just as I hope you are enjoying the coming of springtime. Please know that, despite the distances, you are in my thoughts and prayers each day, and I look forward very much to our next coffee, meal or glass of wine – preferably somewhere by the beach!

Appendix

The Rainbow Sash Movement

One evening early in 1997 a young friend of mine, Nick Holloway, rang to ask me a question: were gay Catholics who were public about their sexuality welcome to receive Holy Communion at Mass? That simple question, and the discussion and discernment it generated, would profoundly affect my life and shape both my thinking and my writing for years to come.

Nick's attempt to find a clear, honest answer to his question led to the development of the 'Rainbow Sash' as a symbol of gay visibility and dignity within the Catholic Church. My accompaniment of him throughout this process eventually led me to play a key role in developing the organization that would become known as the Rainbow Sash Movement. Since 1998 I have been the movement's writer, spokesperson and co-convenor.

A number of the essays in this book emerged directly out of my work with the Rainbow Sash Movement, and many more were informed by the lessons I learnt from that experience. While the writing is my own, it is important to state that I also wrote and spoke in the name of many courageous, committed and loving Catholics, of all sexual orientations, who have worn the Rainbow Sash. In particular, I wish to acknowledge those who, at various stages, have guided and inspired the movement, especially Nick Holloway, Fr Julian Ahern, David Barker, David McKenna, Ivan Tchernegovski, Geoffrey Baird, Don Vogt, Jan Coleman, Jane Lofthouse, Nan and John McGregor. I also wish to acknowledge my mother, Marjorie, who, in her late-seventies, wore the Rainbow Sash in solidarity with gay Catholics, faced down an Archbishop as he refused her Holy Communion, and said to the national media back at Pentecost, 1998: 'If I can love my gay son, why can't the Church?'

The Rainbow Sash Movement has been active in the Australian Church for almost a decade, and its impact on consciousness around gay issues within the Catholic community has been significant. It has also changed many lives, my own included. In 2000 the movement was launched in the United States at the National Conference of Catholic Bishops in Washington D.C., and it continues to be active in the U.S.

as the Rainbow Sash Alliance (publisher's note – the given address - www.rainbowsashallianceusa.org – is no longer active).

In Australia the movement has gradually changed focus, becoming primarily a network of advocacy and support, however, the power of the symbol itself remains potent. There may well come a time to take it up once again, and call the Church to renewal and transformation in this profound and challenging manner.

For those with particular interest in the movement, I am including several pages from our website which set out our rationale, our history, and the deeper vision that continues to motivate our work for change. These papers were written in 2000. (Publisher's note – the website www.rainbowsash.com – is no longer active).

History and Vision

The Rainbow Sash Movement is an organisation of gay, lesbian, bisexual, transgender Catholics, with their families and friends, who are publicly calling the Catholic Church to conversion of heart around issues of human sexuality.

Members of the movement are committed to bringing the gifts, the witness and the challenge of gay, lesbian, bisexual and transgender people into the heart of the church. Through our public, prayerful, visible presence at the Eucharist and in the ongoing life of God's People, through our work for justice, through speaking the truth of our lives and our loving, we call the whole church to build with us a future of liberation, reconciliation and joy for all people.

Our core statement

In wearing the Rainbow Sash we proclaim that we are Gay, Lesbian, Bisexual, Transgender people who embrace and celebrate our sexuality as a Sacred Gift. In wearing the sash we call the church:

- to honour our wisdom and experience
- to enter into public dialogue with us
- to work with us for justice and understanding.

Together, let us seek a new appreciation of human sexuality in all of its diversity and beauty.

Our core action

The movement's core action, or ritual expression, involves the symbol of the Rainbow Sash. The sash is a strip of rainbow coloured fabric which members wear over our left shoulders when we attend the celebration of the Eucharist. Carrying this symbol, we publicly claim our place at Christ's table, sacramentally expressing the truth of our lives, and calling the church to embrace a new day of integrity and freedom.

A question asked

The movement has its roots in a question asked by a young Catholic gay man, Nicholas Holloway, in 1997: 'Are gay Catholics who publicly proclaim their sexuality truly welcome at holy communion?'

After writing to church authorities, Nick attended Mass wearing a rainbow-coloured sash as the symbol expressing his sexuality. In both Melbourne, Australia, and Westminster, London, he was refused Holy Communion by the local bishop (in London, Cardinal Basil Hume; in Melbourne, Archbishop George Pell. Cardinal John O'Connor of New York, in Melbourne at the time, publicly supported this refusal.) A gay priest who wore the rainbow sash with Nick was also refused communion.

A movement begins

On Pentecost Sunday 1998 a group of seventy people attended Mass in St Patrick's Cathedral, Melbourne, wearing the Rainbow Sash.

A core group of leaders had been preparing, over a six-month period of prayer and discussion, to take up the sash again and wear it as a symbol of pride, dignity and challenge.

After writing a formal 'Letter to Pope John Paul 11', and a 'Letter to the Church', the leaders of the group wrote to the local Archbishop and informed him of their intention to attend Mass wearing the sash.

They assured him that their presence would be prayerful, reverent and peaceful in word and action.

In order to establish the Rainbow Sash as a recognised symbol, and to provide to the movement with a public voice in a church that refuses to listen, the leaders of the group also informed the national and local media.

On Pentecost Sunday, after meeting for prayer and preparation before Mass, the group moved across to the Cathedral. Amongst them were parents, family members and friends who chose to stand in solidarity with these gay Catholics.

At Mass, as the Opening Hymn began, these seventy people, dispersed in small groups throughout the congregation, put brilliant rainbow coloured sashes over their left shoulders. They participated in the Mass in the usual way, with reverence and respect.

As the distribution of Communion began, the Rainbow Sash wearers stood up in their places in silence. Then, as their turn came, they joined the line to receive Holy Communion. Every one of the Rainbow Sash wearers was refused Communion, including mothers and fathers of gay children. People wearing small rainbow ribbons were also refused.

On returning to their places, the Rainbow Sash wearers continued standing in silent witness. As the Mass concluded the Archbishop read a statement rebuking them, and most of the congregation applauded.

Outside the Cathedral, the interest amongst national and international media was intense. One person interviewed was a seventy-six year old woman: 'I go to Mass twice a week and say the rosary every night, but today I was refused communion by my own bishop. If I can love my gay son, why can't the church?'

Members of the group distributed hundreds of copies of the 'Letter to the Church' at the gates of the Cathedral.

As the controversy developed over the next few weeks, all of Australia's Catholic archbishops told the media that they, too, would refuse Holy Communion to Rainbow Sash wearers. At the same time, the movement emerged as a strong, new voice of challenge within the Catholic Church.

A momentum grows

Over the past few years the Rainbow Sash Movement has grown and matured. Members have made a practice of organising a high profile action in the local Cathedral at least twice a year, and especially on Pentecost Sunday. The movement has developed its public role, using regular articles, letters, and media commentary to build awareness and call for change.

As part of our actions we have highlighted various issues in the church's treatment of gay people:

- the damaging effect on young people of the church's teaching and discrimination against gay, Lesbian, bisexual, transgender people. This has often led to youth suicides, depression, harassment, and homophobic violence
- the actions and strategies of so-called 'gay cure' groups like Courage and Exodus, now active in Australia, and welcomed by many Catholic bishops
- the church's ongoing demand that it receive exemption from all anti-discrimination legislation passed by Federal and State Parliaments, and its refusal to hire openly gay, lesbian, bisexual, transgender people.

The movement has also focused on alerting the gay community to the policies, power and influence of right-wing Catholic leaders. It has also encouraged gay, lesbian, bisexual, transgender people to stand up within all non-Catholic churches, and claim the right to their spiritual heritage.

In addition to high profile events at the Cathedral, individuals and small groups of members have chosen to perform the Rainbow Sash action at various times in parishes and at key events in the life of the diocese, always informing church leaders, and always with quiet strength and dignity.

In spite of being repeatedly refused Communion, they continue to come forward with faith and dignity.

A vision embraced

The Rainbow Sash Movement began as a question. It developed into a form of visibility, protest and challenge. Today it is deepening into an ongoing expression of sacramental witness and an embodied call for justice.

The Rainbow Sash is also a gift.

When members attend the Eucharist wearing the Rainbow Sash they become a living symbol of the grace and presence of gay, Lesbian, bisexual, transgender people in the heart of the church.

They expose the injustice and break through the fear that have long poisoned the church's approach to human sexuality. In wearing the Rainbow Sash, members change the actual story, the 'the event' of the Eucharist, becoming visible as gay members of God's People, claiming their place at the table, and so changing the church.

Wearing the Rainbow Sash is an act of celebration, a prophetic proclamation, and a ritual honouring of the gift of gay, lesbian, bisexual, transgender people, and, even more deeply, of the whole human mystery of erotic love.

Wearing the Rainbow Sash is a joy. We who wear it call the People of God to share in this joy, to open their minds and hearts to the diversity and delight of human living, and to become the community of celebration, liberation and justice that Christ intended!

Author's Acknowledgements

A collection such as this, spanning ten years and written on three continents, inevitably reflects not only the experiences and ideas of the author, but also the encouragement and wisdom of many companions on the road. Among those who have graced my life and enriched my writing are those listed here, and to them, and to many others unnamed, I gratefully and reverently bow.

This project would have been impossible without the dedication and vision of Gordon Thompson, of Clouds of Magellan books, and without the support of his partner, Petrina Barson. Their patience, enthusiasm and professionalism have been invaluable. My grateful thanks also to Helen Bell, who edited the final manuscript. I thank Justice Michael Kirby for his generous and thoughtful introduction, and for the inspiration he gives to so many gay people. I am grateful to David Marr, Dorothy McRae-McMahon and Fiona Capp for their friendship and their supportive comments.

I also wish to thank James Button of *The Age*, whose affirmation and editorial skill guided me at a crucial stage in my writing.

Among my friends in the United States, I especially want to thank Joseph Kramer, for his encouragement over so many years. I thank Bill Glenn, Bob Goss, John J. McNeill, Dan Kelliher, Chester Mainard, Kevin Tortorelli, Brendan Fay and Tom Moulton for being brothers in spirit, and David Nimmons, Nick Calamusa, Franklin Clarke, Eddie de Bonis and Vincent Maniscalco, Skip Chasey, Michael Weigand, Jim Nickoloff and Robert McCleary, for opening their homes and hearths to me. I thank my friends in the Body Electric movement, and in Dignity, New York, for sharing new visions of community with me, and Barbara Rick and Jeannine Gramick for sharing their commitment and courage.

I owe a particular word of gratitude to John Stasio and the men of Easton Mountain Retreat Center in New York State, who have inspired me and welcomed me as a brother.

In London, James Alison, Bernard Lynch and Billy Desmond have enriched my soul and deepened my hope, as has Brendan O'Rourke in Dublin.

In Australia, I wish to thank Edmond Nixon, Pat Power, Claude Mostowik, Marcus O'Donnell, Ted Kennedy, Rod Pattenden, Paul

Collins, Maria Pallotta-Chiarolli, Bill Phillips, George Braybon, Mary Howson and Ray Maxent, and especially Brigid Arthur and the Brigidine Sisters, for their support and advice. I offer deep appreciation to Bob Hinkley and Mark McIvor, Robert White and Peter Grace, Peter Hudson, and Alex and Tracey Almatrah for their loving friendship over many years. I thank the friends with whom I shared the Rainbow Sash, specifically Nick Holloway, David McKenna, Geoffrey Baird, Ivan Tchernegovski, Don Vogt, Jane Lofthouse, Jan Coleman, Nan and John McGregor, Julian Ahern and David Barker.

In acknowledging these people I do not, of course, suggest that they agree with all of my views or support all of my actions. Their friendship has been deeper than that.

I thank the members of my family, my parents Marjorie and Bernie, my sisters Maureen and Noelene, my brother Brian, my extended family of Kerry, Pat and Garry and my nieces and nephews, for their love, patience and understanding as I have walked my somewhat unusual journey. In so many ways, you inspire me.

Finally, I thank all those who have, in their different and surprising ways, guided and held me as I learned how to open to love, both of soul and of body – and a special thanks to Francesco, of course.

Michael Bernard Kelly

www.ingramcontent.com/pod-product-compliance
Lightning Source LLC
Chambersburg PA
CBHW021140090426
42740CB00008B/863